THE
BOSTON RED SOX
FAN BOOK

THE
BOSTON RED SOX
FAN BOOK

Revised to Include the
2004 Championship Season!

David S. Neft,
Michael L. Neft,
Bob Carroll, and
Richard M. Cohen

St. Martin's Griffin ✖ New York

ISBN 0-312-34849-5
EAN 978-0312-34849-6

First Edition: April 2005

10 9 8 7 6 5 4 3 2 1

SPECIAL THANKS TO MICHAEL NORKIN FOR HIS CONTRIBUTIONS

Contents

1
TEAM HISTORY

Pilgrims' Progress, 1901–1909

Originally, they weren't the Red Sox, nor were they supposed to be in Boston.

The origins of the American League lie with Ban Johnson, the energetic president of what had been a smartly run baseball minor league named the Western League. When the National League closed four clubs at the end of the 1899 season, Johnson took the opportunity to change the league's name to American League and moved teams into vacated Cleveland and into Chicago to oppose the National League's Cubs.

While the A.L.'s Chicago White Sox didn't draw as well as the Cubs, they did make money. So before the 1901 season, Johnson proclaimed his A.L. a major league. The eight circuit teams would include Chicago, Cleveland, Detroit, Milwaukee and Buffalo from the previous season. New teams would be placed in Washington and Baltimore, both of which had formerly hosted National League clubs. Another newcomer would start up in Philadelphia, face to face with the N.L.'s Phillies. He hoped that by impinging on National League territory only in Chicago and Philadelphia, his American League could stay at peace with the older league.

Those hopes were quickly dashed. The National League immediately made it clear that it considered itself at war with Johnson and his "Americans" and would do its best to crush the upstarts. Once that intent was clear, Johnson decided to attack the National League at its base by moving the Buffalo team to Boston to compete with the N.L. club that had ruled the roost there since 1876.

Bankrolling the new Boston team was one Charles W. Somers. Almost as much as Johnson himself, Somers was responsible for the birth of the new league. A coal, lumber, and shipping millionaire, he was the American League's "angel," putting his money into the Cleveland, Chicago, and Philadelphia franchises as well as Boston. Such multiple ownership is no longer allowed by the league, but in those days it was common.

At first, the team went by several different names, none of them official. "Puritans," "Somersets" (in honor of the owner), "Plymouth Rocks," and the generic "Americans" were tried, but "Pilgrims" eventually got the nod. If nothing else, it was appropriate in view of the team's journey east from Buffalo.

The newborn Pilgrims found a place to erect a ballpark at the Huntington Avenue Grounds, which is today the site of Northeastern University's indoor-athletics building. In those days of wooden stands, the creation of a brand-new baseball park did not require nearly the time or money that it does today.

Nor did finding players to fill the new uniforms. With war between the leagues declared, the American Leaguers saw no impediment to signing scads of National League players, which they accomplished by offering the players more money. To make matters easier, the N.L. had painted itself into a corner by establishing a salary cap of $2,500 per season for its players. As long as there was no competition, the cap worked to the N.L.'s advantage. But as soon as players had somewhere else to go at higher pay, they went.

The Pilgrims were particularly fortunate in that the owners of the established Boston N.L. team—later called the Braves but at that time known as the Beaneaters—were unusually tightfisted even by the standards of the day. Boston fans themselves thought the Beaneaters were underpaid, and their loyalty was easily won when many of their heroes jumped to better contracts with the Pilgrims.

John "Buck" Freeman, a powerful-hitting outfielder-first baseman, and pitcher Ted Lewis were two Beaneaters who took a better paycheck to play for the Puritans in 1901. Freeman finished second in the league with 12 home runs and 114 RBI and third in batting average that year while Lewis won 16 games in helping the team to a second place finish.

The most important ex-Beaneater, however, was Jimmy Collins, regarded at the time as the best third baseman in the game. Collins was a consistent .300 hitter who hit with good power for that dead-ball era, but where he really excelled was on defense. Sure of glove and arm, he invented and perfected the technique of racing in, fielding bunts bare-handed, and firing the ball unerringly to the appropriate base. The way baseball was played in those days, with teams scrambling for a single run, Collins' ability to quash an opponent's bunting attack made him the cornerstone of his team's defense. He signed with the Pilgrims for $4,000, taking on the manager's duties as well as playing third base in every one of the team's games.

Even more important to the team's success was the signing of pitcher Denton "Cy" Young. The man for whom the modern outstanding pitcher award is named was unhappy pitching in the heat of St. Louis and jumped at the chance to earn more money in Boston's cooler climate. With Young leading the league with 33 wins and a 1.63 ERA, the first edition of the Pilgrims stayed in the 1901 pennant race to the end, finally finishing a creditable second, four games behind the 1900 champs, Chicago. The Beaneaters sank to fifth in the N.L., abandoned by many players and even more fans. From that first season, when the Pilgrims nearly doubled the Beaneaters' attendance, Boston was an "American League city." The "other" Boston team, which soon became the Braves, seldom approached their A.L. foes in attendance during the ensuing years, and after more than fifty years of lingering death, they moved to Milwaukee in 1953.

After slipping to third in 1902, the Pilgrims sprinted to the pennant in 1903, finishing 14½ games in front of second-place Philadelphia. Collins hit .304 and outfielder Patsy Dougherty led the team at .331 while leading the league in at-bats (590), hits (195) and runs scored (106). Moved to the outfield, Freeman led the league with 13 home runs and 104 RBI. The pitching was magnificent: Young, Long Tom Hughes, and Bill Dinneen gave Boston the league's first trio of 20-game winners.

In the interim, the National and American Leagues had patched up their quarrel and agreed to mutually exist without stealing players from each other. It was a compromise that amounted to total victory for the American League. Part of Ban Johnson's winning strategy had been to take on the N.L. in its own backyard. In 1902, he moved the Milwaukee team to St. Louis to contend with the Cardinals. After the season, he made his major move, shifting Baltimore to New York, where the Giants were ensconced. The National League, realizing that its Pittsburgh Pirates were next on Johnson's list, sued for peace.

Pittsburgh won its third straight N.L. pennant in 1903. Pirates owner Barney Dreyfuss thought it would be a good idea to renew the World Series that had been such a crowd-pleaser in the 1880s when the National League contended with the then-major American Association. He made his proposal to Henry J. Killilea, who'd taken over Pilgrims ownership from Somers. The challenge was accepted and the first modern World Series was on.

Unfortunately for Pittsburgh, by the time the teams took the field at the Huntington Grounds for Game One, the Pirates were down to one healthy pitcher. But for a while, that looked like enough. Control-artist Charles "Deacon" Phillippe beat Young, 7–3, in the opener, and came back to outduel Hughes, 4–2, in Game Three. Then, after a two-day travel break, he won over Dinneen, 5–4, at Pittsburgh. The Pirates led three games to one, but they still needed two more wins, the Series being set as best of nine. Young and Dinneen won the next two games to tie the Series. Phillippe returned in Game Seven, but this time Young had the better of him, 7–3. The teams returned to Boston. After another two-day break, Collins sent Dinneen to the mound, and Pittsburgh countered with Phillippe once more. When Dinneen pitched a four-hit shutout for his third win of the Series, Boston had a World Championship. The upstart American League had proved itself the equal of the National.

Killilea sold the team before the 1904 season to retired general Charles Henry Taylor, owner of the *Boston Globe*. The general turned the team over to his son, John I. Taylor, in hope that the new toy would wean the young playboy away from his pursuit of wine, women, and song.

Defending the world champion's crown proved difficult. Not even Young could match the numbers put up by Jack Chesbro of New York in 1904. "Happy Jack," one of the early spitballers, won a modern-day record 41 games. For most of the year, Chesbro and his unbeatable spitter kept New York ahead of Boston in the standings. But Collins' champs came on late.

The pennant was on the line on October 10, when the two contenders met for a doubleheader at New York's Hilltop Park. New York needed a sweep. Naturally, Chesbro started for New York in the first game. He was still pitching in the ninth inning with the game tied 2–2, a man on third, and two outs. At that moment, one of his spitters sailed high over his catcher's head. Chesbro's wild pitch

allowed the winning run for Boston, and branded the man who'd set
the all-time American League record for victories in a season as a
"goat."

There was no World Series in 1904. John T. Brush, owner of the
pennant-winning New York Giants, refused to let his team sully
itself in competition with the still-hated American League. Giants
manager John McGraw stoutly backed Brush's decision. At the root
of the Brush-McGraw brush-off was the strong showing New
York's American League team had made in 1904. For most of the
season, it looked like both pennants would fall to New York teams,
and it was the thought of legitimizing his city rival with a World
Series appearance that most offended Brush. By the time Boston
took the A.L. crown, Brush and McGraw were so often and so
vehemently on record as opposing a World Series that they couldn't
back down.

Boston couldn't claim another World Championship for 1904, but
it got a lot of mileage out of juxtaposing the names of Brush and
McGraw with such phrases as "dirty cowards." That was some consolation for the down days to come in the next few years.

The Pilgrims grew very old very fast. In 1905 they also became
known as the Puritans and dipped to fourth place. The next year, they
tumbled all the way to last. Manager Collins and owner Taylor rarely
saw eye-to-eye, and toward the end of the season, outfielder Chick
Stahl replaced Collins as manager.

It was a job Stahl hadn't sought, and as a close friend of Collins,
didn't want. But that hardly explains his actions during spring training in 1908. A doctor in one of the towns on the way north gave Stahl
a prescription for carbolic acid to be mixed with water and rubbed on
a stone bruise Chick had acquired in one of the spring games. Unaccountably, on March 28, Stahl drank a glass of the stuff and died
within minutes. Officially, it was called a suicide, although no one
could explain why the religious, happily married Stahl would end his
life.

In 1907, the Pilgrims' cross-town National League rival changed its
name from "Red Stockings" to "Doves" and switched the team color
from red to blue. John I. Taylor took the opportunity to rename his
team the "Red Sox," apparently hoping to divert fans' attention from
the last-place finish of 1906. Whether Pilgrims or Red Sox, the team
was destined for the bottom of the standings, despite Cy Young's 22

victories. Counting Stahl, Taylor employed five different managers in the process of finishing seventh in 1907.

Young enjoyed the final 20-win season of his long and illustrious career in helping the Red Sox up to fifth in 1908. In February of the next year, his contract was traded to Cleveland. In his eight seasons with Boston, Young won 192 games, a mark matched only by Roger Clemens in team history. Included among all those wins was the first perfect game tossed in the twentieth century on May 5, 1905.

Better days were on the horizon for the Red Sox, however. Their future was to be found in a number of youngsters who appeared in only a handful of games at season's end. These included an 18-year-old fireballing right-hander called "Smokey Joe" Wood, a smooth-fielding third baseman named Larry Gardner, a lantern-jawed catcher named Bill Carrigan whose pugnacious nickname was "Rough," and a ground-covering centerfielder from Texas, Tris Speaker. In 1909 when the Sox moved up to third, Carrigan, Speaker, and Wood became regulars, Gardner was ready to blossom, and strong-armed right fielder Harry Hooper arrived on the scene. These and a few other players would lead the Red Sox to their greatest heights during the next decade.

AS GOOD AS HIS WORD

Cy Young's favorite catcher was Lou Criger, a backstop with a weak bat but defensive skills that made up for his lack of batting prowess. When Ty Cobb came to the American League and began running wild on the bases, Criger was his nemesis. Lou's snap throws cut down the "Georgia Peach" with regularity.

Finally, Cobb had enough. One day he informed Criger that the next time he got on base, he intended to steal all the way around to home. Sure enough, Cobb reached first early in the game and immediately set sail for second. Despite his being forewarned, Criger's throw arrived too late.

As Cobb dusted himself off, he yelled in to the catcher, "And now, you old ice wagon, I'm on my way to third." Lou put all he had into his throw, but Ty slid into third base safely. "And now," Cobb announced, "I'm coming home!" And on the next pitch, he did. Safe, signaled the umpire. "I'll be damned," said Criger. And, from then on,

Cobb ran against Criger just as effectively as he ran on every other catcher in the league.

CY VS. RUBE

During his 22 major-league seasons, Young won an astonishing 511 games, but one of his most famous appearances ended in a loss in 1905. For the second game of a July 4 doubleheader, the 38-year-old Young took the mound against Philadelphia's great-but-eccentric lefty, "Rube" Waddell. Boston nicked Waddell for two runs in the first inning, and Philadelphia tied it with a home run in the sixth. After that, both hurlers held the opposition scoreless as the innings mounted. After nineteen frames, the score was still knotted.

In the 20th inning, an error helped the A's score twice, and Waddell held Boston in check in the bottom half to gain the win. Although he was touched for 18 hits (to Waddell's 15), Young negotiated his twenty innings without allowing a walk. "I don't walk anybody in twenty innings, and I still lose!" he exclaimed in amazement.

For Waddell, the victory involved a bonus. In later years when he was short on cash and credit, he was able to trade the baseball he "beat ol' Cy with" for a round of drinks. It's said that eventually no fewer than two dozen different Philadelphia bartenders owned the "authentic" ball.

"TESSIE"

During the 1903 World Series, Boston's "Royal Rooters" nearly drove Pittsburgh players and fans (and anyone else who wasn't a Royal Rooter) crazy by endlessly singing "Tessie," a popular song of the day. Here are the words, for anyone who happens to remember the tune:

> *Tessie, you make me feel so badly,*
> *Why don't you turn around,*
> *Tessie, you know I love you madly,*
> *Babe, my heart weighs about a pound;*

Don't blame me if I ever doubt you,
You know I wouldn't live without you,
Tessie, you are the only, only, only.

Diligent research has failed to uncover any connection between the lyrics and baseball, but apparently that didn't matter to loyal Boston fans.

The Best of Times, 1910–1918

The Red Sox spent 1910 and 1911 loitering in the middle of the American League pack. The cream of Ban Johnson's circuit was in Philadelphia, where Connie Mack's Athletics had too much pitching to be kept from pennants. The staff of Eddie Plank, Jack Coombs, Chief Bender, and Cy Morgan even set a league record with a 1.78 ERA in 1910. Mack always said that pitching was 80 percent of baseball, and certainly that was true during the deadball era when hits were hard to come by and home runs were even rarer.

But while they lingered with the also-rans, the Red Sox were not idle.

In 1910, Duffy Lewis joined Speaker and Hooper to form what some still consider the greatest outfield of all time. Speaker was by far the best hitter of the three, lashing out line drives with monotonous regularity, but Lewis usually checked in with a batting average around .300, and Hooper was a reliable leadoff man. On defense, they put all others to shame, chasing down fly balls that were sure hits in other outfields. Lewis was outstanding in left, and Hooper, with a cannon for an arm, was even better in right. Once again, though, it was Speaker in center who was nonpareil. "Spoke" played an extremely shallow center field which made him able to get to flares and bloops. Moreover, he was often able to race in, scoop up an apparent base hit, and get a force-out at second base. As shallow as he set up, he was still able to get back for long flies that would have gone over the heads of other fielders playing at normal depth. Speaker still is usually ranked in the upper echelon of all the center fielders in the long history of baseball.

The infield boasted strong hitting at the corners once Larry Gardner settled in at third base. The .300-hitting first baseman was Jake Stahl. In 1912, he was named Red Sox manager.

Jake was a lucky manager. The team he took over in 1912 was on the brink of success, and, as an omen, it had a brand-new ballpark in which to show off its charms. Fenway Park opened that year and has provided a friendly home for the Red Sox ever since.

The greatest source of luck for Stahl was "Smokey Joe" Wood. At the ripe old age of twenty-two, Wood, who had been threatening greatness for four seasons, suddenly put all his considerable skills together and became the best pitcher in baseball. For several years that honor had been reserved for Walter Johnson of the otherwise-undistinguished Washington Senators. Johnson didn't falter at all in 1912, even setting a new American League record by rattling off 16 straight wins. Yet, as the season wore on, it was Wood who came to the fore. Fans argued endlessly over which right-hander had the more potent fastball. Johnson himself said, "There's no man alive can throw the ball harder than Smokey Joe Wood."

On September 6, Wood went for his fourteenth consecutive victory against Johnson and the Senators. An overflow crowd estimated to be around 30,000 packed into Fenway in anticipation of the duel. Johnson was magnificent, allowing only a single run on back-to-back, two-out doubles by Speaker and Lewis in the sixth inning. Wood was even better. He shut out Washington and eventually ran his streak to 16 games and a share of the record before finally being beaten by Detroit in late September.

Wood finished the season 34–5. No Red Sox hurler has ever won more in a season.

Wood's great season keyed the BoSox to 105 victories and a first-place finish. Their World Series opponents were John McGraw's Giants, the same crew that had refused to play the Red Sox in 1904.

Wood got the Red Sox off on the right foot with a 4–3 win in the opener. Game Two was called because of darkness after eleven innings, and the Giants won Game Three. But Wood came back to put Boston in front again with a 3–1 victory the next day. The Sox stretched their lead to three games to one in the fifth game as Hugh Bedient outdueled Giant ace Christy Mathewson with a three-hitter.

The Giants won a second game but had to face Wood the next day. For once, Smokey Joe got smoked, as New York pounded him for six first-inning runs and tied the Series at three games apiece.

It was Bedient vs. Mathewson in the final game, and the Giants led 1–0 until the Red Sox tied the score with a run in the bottom of the seventh. Wood relieved in the eighth and shut out the Giants for two innings, but Mathewson was equally impenetrable, and the game went into the tenth.

New York squeezed out a run in the top of the inning. Mathewson started the bottom of the inning by getting pinch-hitter Clyde Engle to lift an easy fly . . . which center fielder Fred Snodgrass dropped! Engle was perhaps the only one in Fenway Park who didn't gasp in amazement at the muff; he was too busy hustling to second base.

Harry Hooper smashed a liner that could have, should have tied the game, but Snodgrass made a great catch to save the run. Engle tagged and went to third. Mathewson, whose control was legendary, then walked Boston second baseman Steve Yerkes, the potential winning run.

Speaker was next up, but Boston fans groaned when he popped a routine foul fly down the first-base line. New York first baseman Fred Merkle had it all the way, but for some reason Mathewson kept yelling for his catcher Chief Meyers to take it. Merkle backed off, but Meyers couldn't make the play and the ball fell safely in foul territory.

One reprieve was enough for Speaker, who singled to score Engle with the tying run and send Yerkes to third. McGraw ordered Duffy Lewis intentionally passed, bringing up Larry Gardner. The BoSox third sacker needed to put the ball in the air, and that's just what he did. His long fly plated Yerkes and Boston had its second World Championship.

Jake Stahl's luck didn't continue into 1913. It ended when Wood came down with a sore arm. Although he could occasionally pitch effectively on guile alone, the fastball that had put terror in the hearts of A.L. batters was gone forever. Late in the season, Rough Carrigan replaced Stahl as manager and began rebuilding the pitching staff.

For one brief season—1914—Boston's "other" team actually outshone the Red Sox. Under manager George Stallings, the Braves made a "miracle" stretch run from last place to the National League pennant and then shocked the Philadelphia Athletics by taking the World Series in four straight games. It was a one-shot moment of glory, and the Braves immediately slid back into the doldrums.

Meanwhile, Carrigan tinkered with the Sox pitching staff. In 1915, he was ready. For starters, he had right-handers Rube Foster and Ernie Shore, who won 20 and 19, respectively. Wood sore-armed his way to 14 victories and managed to lead the league in ERA. Dutch Leonard was a crackerjack lefty, but the *wunderkind* of the staff was a big twenty-year-old left-hander with a world of talent named George Ruth, nicknamed "Babe." His 18–5 record made him the league's win-loss percentage leader. Surprisingly, the kid could hit pretty well, too. In fact, his four home runs (in just 92 at-bats) were twice as many as anyone else on the team and just three behind the league leader.

After losing the 1914 World Series to the "Miracle Braves," Connie Mack had been forced by economics to break up his great team. Boston benefited by acquiring Jack Barry, a smooth gloveman, from what had been called the Athletics' "$10,000 Infield," and Herb Pennock, a young left-handed pitcher. Carrigan's Red Sox team had its strongest competition from the hard-hitting Tigers of Ty Cobb, but, as usual, pitching prevailed. Boston finished 2½ games ahead of Detroit.

The BoSox's World Series opponents were the Philadelphia Phillies, who had gotten there primarily on the arm of Grover Cleveland Alexander, who led the N.L. in wins, complete games, innings pitched, strikeouts and ERA. Alex was arguably one of the half-dozen greatest pitchers of all time, but in this series he was one great against a great staff. After Alexander won the opening game, Foster, Leonard, Shore, and Foster again won the next four. Another World Championship banner flew at Fenway, although the Series wasn't played there. The Red Sox had opted to play their home share of the Series at brand-new and bigger Braves Field.

When the Red Sox set out to defend their championship in 1916, something was missing, and it was Tris Speaker. Spoke had been paid royally the previous two years to keep him from jumping to the Federal League, an upstart aggregation that tried in 1914–1915 to become a third major league. When the Feds folded, Speaker saw no reason why he should make less money. Red Sox owner (and, by now, real-estate magnate) Joseph J. Lannin disagreed. One thing led to another, and Speaker was traded to Cleveland, where he went on to justify his salary by leading the American League in hitting in 1916.

Wood also had money squabbles and held out for the whole year, but the rest of the staff returned intact. Carl Mays, an underarm thrower who'd been in the bullpen most of 1915, blossomed into an 18-game winner in 1916.

The White Sox, who'd also benefited from Connie Mack's fire sale by acquiring the great second baseman Eddie Collins, chased the Red Sox down to the wire but fell two games short.

Surprise winners in the National League were the Brooklyn Dodgers, a feisty team but no match for the Red Sox. Again playing their home games at Braves Field, Boston blew them away in five games. The only loss came in Game Three at the hands of Jack Coombs, another one of Connie Mack's ex-A's. The gem of the Series was Game Two. Ruth hooked up with Brooklyn's Sherry Smith in a 14-inning duel won by Boston 2–1.

Lannin decided to go out on top by selling his World Champions before another season rolled around. The buyer was Harry Frazee, a New Yorker well known for producing Broadway shows of varied critical esteem. In one sense, he turned out to be the most significant owner in Red Sox history: not for who he signed but for who he sold.

After winning his second straight World Series, manager Rough Carrigan also retired from the scene, choosing to follow a career in banking. Carrigan had been a good catcher, but when he turned his mind to managing, he approached greatness, at least in the estimation of many of the men who played for him. Jack Barry took over and perhaps received more blame than he deserved for the BoSox second-place finish in 1917. The main knock against him was that he wasn't Carrigan. In truth, the White Sox were not to be outdone. Their pitching matched Boston's, and their hitting, with Collins, Shoeless Joe Jackson, and Happy Felsch, gave them a big edge.

Barry wasn't around to manage in 1918, but not because he was fired. Like many major-league players that year, Barry joined the armed forces to serve in World War I. The government issued a "work or fight" ultimatum, meaning that able-bodied American males could choose between working in a war-essential industry or carrying a gun. Baseball carried on as best it could, chopping the 1918 regular season off at September 1, to allow its employees to decide among patriotic careers.

Replacing Barry at the Red Sox helm was Ed Barrow, an experienced manager whose greatest claim to fame up to then was that he'd discovered Honus Wagner many years before. Barrow eventually earned entrance into the Baseball Hall of Fame, primarily for serving as New York Yankees president and guiding hand during the dynasty years of the 1920s and '30s. But something he did in Boston in 1918 helped get him to Cooperstown, too, although at first a lot of people thought he was crazy.

Barrow, in surveying his Red Sox, saw a hole in left field, which had been vacated by Duffy Lewis when he went off to the army. Needing a replacement and seeing what he had accomplished at the plate in limited at-bats, Barrow moved Ruth, twice a 20-game winner, from the pitcher's mound to the outfield.

As every fan knows, the position switch turned out to be one of the most unqualified successes in baseball history. Babe's booming bat would eventually change the way baseball was played, and Ruth himself would become an American icon. The bulk of Ruth's glory would be achieved in a city to the south of Boston (and under the aegis of Ed Barrow), but his league-high 11 home runs in 1918 helped the Red Sox win yet another pennant. The Babe still found time to win 13 games on the mound, but it was to be his final season as a double-digit winner.

The World Series of 1918, played in the first two weeks of September, matched the BoSox against the Chicago Cubs. Ruth got only five at-bats and didn't hit a home run, but he pitched a 1–0 shutout in the opener and won the fourth game 3–2, extending his consecutive scoreless World Series innings streak to 29⅔, a mark that stood until 1961. Carl Mays also won a pair of games, both by 2–1 scores, and that was all the Red Sox needed to hoist their fifth—and final—World Championship banner.

It was a wonderful time to be a Red Sox fan. In the American League's first eighteen years of existence, the Red Sox had taken one-third of the pennants. Even more impressive was their perfect performance in World Series competition—five-for-five. And with world peace restored, BoSox fans saw no reason why the success of their favorites should not continue unabated.

They should have asked Harry Frazee about that.

A "SHORE" THING

While Ruth excelled at both pitching and hitting, his self-control left a lot to be desired. On June 23, 1917, he opened a game against Washington by walking the leadoff man. This, he decided, was the fault of the umpire's poor eyesight, and he proceeded to say so loudly and profanely. The umpire in question suggested a shower might cool Ruth's temper. Actually, he ordered it by tossing the Babe from the game.

In came Ernie Shore, who had expected a day off. When Ernie was ready to pitch, the runner on first decided to steal second, but was thrown out. Shore then retired the next 26 batters without incident, and has been regarded ever since as having pitched a most unusual perfect game.

BEFORE THE BABE DID IT

Everyone knows Babe Ruth started as a pitcher and then became an outfielder, but how many remember Joe Wood did it first? Wood's switch wasn't dictated by his bat, however, but by his sore arm. After sitting out the 1916 season, he contacted his old Boston buddy Tris Speaker, who was now in Cleveland, about making a comeback. He pitched in five games for the Indians in 1917, but the arm was definitely gone.

But 1918 saw a lot of star players in the service or occupied in war work. Wood, who'd always been a pretty good hitter, made the Indians as an outfielder and hit .296 in 119 games. He went on to play four more years with the Tribe, including the World Championship season of 1920. His career batting average was a highly respectable .283.

The Worst of Times, 1919–1932

In 1925, Harry Frazee—by then the ex-owner of the Red Sox—had a monster Broadway hit in the musical *No, No, Nanette*. At one point, there were five road companies crisscrossing the country singing "Tip-Toe Through the Tulips" and raking in the dough. Had *Nanette* been written only a half-dozen years earlier, Red Sox fans might have been spared a ton of grief.

Unfortunately, during the time when Frazee owned the Sox, his productions on Broadway were generally big bombs. He was able to pay off his various actors, musicians, scene designers, stage hands, costumers, and so on by selling off in bits and pieces the one valuable commodity he held—namely, the Red Sox players. In doing so, he kept himself viable for his ultimate triumph with *No, No, Nanette*, but he also destroyed baseball at Fenway Park for more than a decade.

He didn't plan it that way, of course. In fact, in his pennant-winning season of 1918, he actually went out and got a valuable player, first baseman Stuffy McInnis, and his acquisition helped make the pennant possible.

However, before the 1919 season began, something prophetic happened. What with so many good players returning from the service, Frazee decided he had more than he needed to stay on top. It so happened that his Broadway office was only a few doors away from the office of Jacob Ruppert, the owner of the New York Yankees, an American League team that had never won a pennant and seldom come close. Jake had the money; Harry had the players. Before long, Duffy Lewis, Ernie Shore, and Dutch Leonard were in Yankee pinstripes in exchange for $15,000 and four minor leaguers. It wasn't the deal of the century. The Yankees got scant value. Lewis and Shore were nearing the end of their careers, and Leonard was quickly sent on to Detroit when he and Ruppert argued over his wages. Nor was Boston mortally wounded by losing the three. But in the theatrical terms of Frazee's world, the trade was "an ominous offstage rumble."

Frazee quickly found that though he had many good players returning, so did everyone else. The Red Sox floundered through the 1919 season and finally ended up sixth. The fans kept coming to Fenway nonetheless, if not to see victories, then to cheer home runs.

Babe Ruth's 11 homers of 1918 had been only a taste. In 1919, he blasted away at a record clip. First, he sailed by the American League record of 16 set by Socks Seybold in 1902. Then he surpassed the National League's record of 24 set by Gavvy Cravath in 1915. What could be next? It was noted by some antiquarian that Ned Williamson had popped 27 dingers in 1884 for Chicago during a season in which his team played at a ballpark that was 180 feet down the left field line. Playing on a real field, Ruth set a new record with 29 home runs.

Although Ruth brought lots of fans to Fenway Park, he couldn't bring enough to solve Frazee's continuous money crunch. And Ruppert's office and checkbook were so convenient. In mid-1919, right-hander Carl Mays, twice a 20-game winner, went to the Yanks for $40,000.

The backbreaker came the next winter. Desperate for cash, Frazee sold Ruth to New York. The official price was $125,000, but that was the smaller part. Ruppert lent Frazee $350,000 with Fenway Park as security. For the Yankees, *this* was the deal of the century. In his first year in pinstripes, the Babe smashed 54 homers, obliterating his previous record of 29. He raised the mark to 59 in 1921 and 60 in 1927. More importantly, he took the Yankees to seven pennants and four World Championships over the next 13 seasons. Of course, he had a lot of help—much of it out of Boston.

In the big picture, Ruth's going to New York was a good thing for baseball. It put the game's most charismatic star center stage so that he could help America forget that the Chicago White Sox had disgraced themselves and betrayed their fans by intentionally losing the 1919 World Series. To say, as some have, that he "saved" baseball is an exaggeration. Baseball wasn't quite yet on the critical list. What Ruth did was speed baseball's recovery and take it to new heights. And, of course, the response his homers received led owners to inject the baseball with rabbit in hope of spawning other Ruths, and that changed everything from a pitcher's game to a batter's. And *that* made for a far more entertaining spectacle than had been seen on diamonds before. So Bostonians could take solace in the thought that their sacrifice was for the greater good.

But on the whole, they would rather have sold Frazee to New York and kept the Babe.

When he got to New York, Ruth was installed in right field with the Yankees. That may have been why Boston's Harry Hooper wasn't traded to New York. The Yanks didn't need a second right fielder. Instead, Hooper was traded to Chicago. Everyone else of consequence was dealt to New York.

The roll call:

Catcher Wally Schang, a three-year Red Sox regular, arrived in New York in 1921, just in time to help the Yankees win three straight pennants. A .291 hitter in three seasons in Boston, he hit a similar .297 in five years in New York.

Everett Scott had been the regular Red Sox shortstop since his rookie season in 1914 when he was sent to New York in 1922. A brilliant defensive player who had the best fielding percentage among A.L. shortstops from 1914–23, he cemented the defense for the 1922 and '23 champs.

Third baseman Jumpin' Joe Dugan was another player more celebrated for his glove than his bat, but he gave the Yankees solid work with both for six seasons after coming over in the middle of the 1922 season after playing just 84 career games for Boston.

The Yankees received virtually a whole All-Star pitching staff from the Red Sox. Waite Hoyt, Sad Sam Jones, Bullet Joe Bush, Herb Pennock, George Pipgras and Carl Mays were all supplied by Frazee, and each of them became a Yankee 20-game winner!

These were not all cash-and-carry deals. In fact, the money Frazee got from Ruppert was rarely mentioned in print reports. Except for the Ruth sale, New York always threw a couple of players into the deal. And it is only fair to say that the Red Sox sometimes received legitimate major leaguers in these transactions, though never of the quality of those they gave up. The proof of the one-sided character of all this dealing lay in the American League standings, which saw the Yankees surge to the top while the Red Sox plunged to the bottom and remained there through 1933.

In July of 1923, a syndicate led by longtime baseball man J.A. Robert Quinn bought the Red Sox from Frazee. Quinn had been running the St. Louis Browns for owner Phil Ball and doing quite well. At that time, the Browns were more successful and more popular in St. Louis than the Cardinals. But Ban Johnson and several team owners who were sick of the shambles the Frazee-to-Ruppert pipeline was making of the league pushed Quinn to jump in and "save" the Red Sox. Unfortunately, by the time he arrived, there was precious little left to save.

With luck, Quinn might have been able to rebuild. But he had no luck. Or, more precisely, he had no money. First the chief financial backer of the syndicate died, and then along came the Great Depression. At one point, Quinn had to borrow on his life insurance to pay the team's bills. Without the wherewithal to buy top players and with almost no one left to dangle as trade bait, Quinn spent his years in Boston in the cellar. The Sox finished last in 1922, Frazee's final year. They stayed last in 1923, moved up one spot to seventh in 1924, and then fell back to last for six straight seasons. In 1931, the BoSox breathed sixth-place air, but set a team record with 111 losses in '32.

Managers came and went, but never had much to work with. Ed Barrow left after 1920 to become the Yankees' general manager. Hugh Duffy, a Boston favorite who set the all-time record for batting average back in 1894, presided in 1921 and '22 but couldn't teach anybody to hit as he had. Frank Chance, the "Peerless Leader" of four Cubs pennant-winners, escaped after one season. Lee Fohl, who'd managed for Quinn in St. Louis, lasted three years. Rough Carrigan was lured back for three seasons, but the magic was gone. Then, in quick succession, it was Heinie Wagner, Shano Collins, and Marty McManus. All but McManus left in last place. Marty was seventh when he drew his final check.

As bad as the BoSox were during the Quinn years, they nevertheless put some interesting players on the field from time to time.

Outfielder Smead Jolley, for example, was a .300 hitter but was so disastrous in the field that he couldn't stay in the majors. It was said his only defense against a fly ball was his cap. Another outfielder, Ike Boone, hit .333 and .330 in 1924 and '25 but was so painfully slow that he was sent back to the minors.

Pitcher Red Ruffing was another Hall of Famer who went to the Yankees, but unlike Ruth or Herb Pennock, Ruffing didn't look like much before he was dealt. From his debut in Boston in 1924 until he left the Red Sox early in the 1930 season, Ruffing was a disastrous 39–96, leading the league in losses in 1928 and '29. His ERA with Boston was 4.61, and it dropped below 4.00 only once—3.89 in 1928.

With the Yankees, Ruffing was a different pitcher. After posting 4+

ERAs in 1930 and '31, he didn't go over that mark until he left the Yankees to pitch nine games for the White Sox in 1947. He won 20 games with the Yankees four times, and finished his New York career 231–124 with a 3.47 ERA.

First baseman Dale Alexander, so big and clumsy in the field that he may have been a harbinger of future Red Soxer Dick Stuart, could hit a ton. He came over from Detroit early in the 1932 season and became the first man ever to lead the league in batting while playing for two teams. He was also the first Red Sox batting champ.

Outfielder Earl Webb had a short major-league career, but in 1931 he went "doubles crazy" and knocked out an all-time record 67 two-base hits, more than twice as many as he ever hit before or after.

Others worth noting included pitcher Howard Ehmke, who won 20 games for the last-place 1923 Sox; catcher Charlie Berry, an ex-football star who later became an umpire; reliable outfielders Ira Flagstead and Tom Oliver; and bespectacled Danny MacFayden, who pitched heroically for the Red Sox in their worst years and then went to the downtrodden Braves just as the BoSox were improving.

In truth, even at their worst, the Sox were probably never quite as horrendous as such legendary last-placers as the 1899 Cleveland Spiders or the 1952 Pittsburgh Pirates. There was nearly always someone on the team worth coming out to cheer for. Boston fans deserve credit for supporting their losing team at a subsistence level throughout the 1920s.

As the Depression deepened, the price of a Red Sox ticket became more of a burden than many loyal fans could bear. In 1932, attendance fell to 182,150—less than 2,400 a game—and easily the lowest figure in the team's history. The end had come for Bob Quinn.

LEFT(Y) IN THE LURCH

During the year that Frank Chance managed the Red Sox, he had in his employ a young pitcher named Frank "Lefty" O'Doul. The pitcher had a liking for nightlife and was often castigated and fined by Chance for missing curfews. One day the Peerless Leader stopped by the hotel barbershop where he observed Lefty enjoying a shave, haircut, manicure, shine—the works. What really raised the manager's hackles was the long, admiring look at himself Lefty took in the mirror before he left the shop.

As luck would have it, the Red Sox starting pitcher that afternoon against Cleveland was injured in the sixth inning and Chance had to call in a reliever. O'Doul was on tap and entered the game with a runner on third and two out. Unfortunately, he was both wild and hittable, a deadly combination. Instead of preventing the run from scoring, Lefty allowed that one and another and another. As hits and walks mounted, Chance was heard to mutter grimly, "I'm going to keep that looking-glass [bleep] in there, if he don't get them out all afternoon!"

By the time the inning ended, thirteen Indians had scored.

Perhaps the incident helped convince O'Doul that his talent lay in hitting baseballs rather than hurling them, as he eventually found stardom as an outfielder, twice leading the National League in batting.

I'D RATHER DO IT MYSELF!

There have only been eight unassisted triple plays in the majors during the twentieth century, and six of them were pulled off during the 1920s. Partly it may have been that the hit-and-run play was still as common as in the deadball days, while the livelier baseball made it far more dangerous. But obviously there was a certain amount of monkey-see monkey-do. The unaided triple-killing by Cleveland second baseman Bill Wambsganss in the 1920 World Series made him famous, and, after that, every infielder was looking for a chance to gain immortality.

Certainly that was the case on September 14, 1923, when Red Sox first baseman George Burns snared a drive off the bat of Cleveland's Frank Brower and tagged runner Rube Lutzke for the second out. Burns could have easily tossed to second base to put out baserunner Riggs Stephenson, but he saw that the Clevelander was just getting himself turned around near third. Both Stephenson and Burns sprinted madly for second base and slid in from opposite sides.

Burns, a split second quicker, got the out and gained his headline.

QUICK THINKING

One day in September 1923, Babe Ruth lifted a towering fly against the Red Sox. Boston outfielder Dick Reichle circled under it. The Babe kept running. Reichle kept circling. Suddenly, it was obvious that

Reichle had lost sight of the ball. By the time it landed unmolested, Ruth was nearly to third base, and he had no problem reaching home with an inside-the-park home run.

When Reichle came to the bench at inning's end, Manager Frank Chance deadpanned, "Pretty smart, Dick! It's late in the season, and I wouldn't get hit on the head either."

Buy Me a Champion, 1933–1946

To many baseball fans outside Boston, Tom Yawkey was just a rich man who tried to buy himself a pennant. It's certainly true that Yawkey spent liberally to bring star players to his Red Sox and then paid them well. But nearly every owner in his or her own way tries to "buy" a pennant for the team. Some, because of circumstance or personal preference, try to do it on the cheap. Others, again guided by circumstance or preference, are more liberal. Boston fans well remembered that Jake Ruppert bought pennants for his Yankees, because he bought them to a great extent from the Red Sox! And due to Harry Frazee's fire sales, followed by years of Bob Quinn's undercapitalized stewardship, Yawkey had little choice in his effort to rebuild the BoSox but to do it with his checkbook.

More than anything else, Yawkey was a baseball *fan*. But he was not a fanatic. He wanted to see good baseball played, and naturally enough he wanted to see his own team play well. He was unstinting in his efforts to build a team that all New England could take pride in. But win or lose, he loved the Red Sox. When they won, he was the last person to take credit. When they lost, he never regarded the losses as any sort of blot upon his personal honor. It was not his way to rant and rave and precipitously fire those who did not perform up to his hopes. Every team in baseball should be blessed with an owner like Yawkey.

Yawkey came by his love of baseball honestly. His uncle and later adoptive father, Bill Yawkey, had once been half owner of the Detroit Tigers, and legend has it that Bill's willingness to spend money on the ball club just about drove his frugal partner Frank Navin crazy.

The Yawkeys had extensive lumber and ore holdings, but Tom

Yawkey's love was baseball. He turned thirty on February 21, 1933, and came into the bulk of an eight-figure inheritance from his uncle, mother, and grandfather. Four days later, he bought the Red Sox. "I don't intend to mess with a loser," he told reporters.

Many rich men convince themselves that great wealth conveys great knowledge. The history of baseball is littered with the mistakes of egotistical owners who learned to their dismay that a big bank account is no substitute for baseball "smarts." Yawkey was too intelligent to fall into the trap of overestimating his own intelligence. His first move was to hire Eddie Collins as vice president and general manager. Collins, one of the greatest second basemen of all time, had been Yawkey's boyhood hero. That aside, he was also one of the brightest men in the game. At the time Yawkey offered him the job, he was serving as a coach for Connie Mack in Philadelphia and was Mack's heir-apparent. Collins went to Mack and told him of Yawkey's offer. "If you don't take the job," Connie said, "I'll fire you."

Yawkey's instructions to Collins: "I've got the money to spend, and I intend to spend it." Shortly thereafter, Collins secured the services of Rick Ferrell, perhaps the best catcher to wear a Red Sox uniform until Carlton Fisk. Ferrell was a consistent .300 hitter and a fine defensive backstop who was available only because the St. Louis Browns were in dire financial straits. The Yankees were fiscally sound, of course, but Collins talked them out of pitcher George Pipgras and infielder Billy Werber for about $100,000. Pipgras developed a sore arm, but Werber gave the BoSox four solid years at third base and led the league in stolen bases in 1934 and '35.

The Red Sox struggled up to seventh place in the first year of Yawkey's ownership, but better times were on the way.

So were better players.

During the remainder of the 1930s, the Red Sox imported a virtual roster of established major-league stars through the generous use of Yawkey's checkbook. Some didn't work out so well, but several loom large in Red Sox history.

The first huge purchase, for $125,000 and two players, brought Lefty Grove from Philadelphia on December 12, 1933, along with second baseman Max Bishop and lefty Rube Walberg. The Depression had hit Connie Mack hard, and he began dismantling the great team that had won three straight pennants from 1929–31. At the Boston training camp in the spring of 1934, Grove was felled by a sore arm. The next thing he knew, his great fastball was gone forever. Mack immediately offered to take Grove back and return the money, but Yawkey would have none of it, knowing that all parties had dealt in good faith. As it turned out, keeping Grove was a good move. Deprived of his high hard one, Lefty re-learned pitching, this time with cunning and control. He won 20 games in 1935, 17 in each of the next two years, and led the league in ERA four times.

Wes Ferrell, Rick's pitcher brother, had been a four-time 20-game winner for Cleveland, but a sore arm in 1933 seemed ready to end his career. Collins got him for a fifth of what he paid for Grove on the chance there was something left. In his first Boston season, he junkballed his way to 14 wins. In 1935, he won 25 and 20 the year after.

Between them, Grove and Ferrell led the league in temperament. Both were justly famous for their clubhouse tantrums whenever they lost a game. When manager-shortstop Joe Cronin booted a ball to make Grove a loser, he went into his office and locked the door as soon as the game ended. But the walls of his office didn't go to the ceiling. Grove stood on a bench by the partition, looked down into Cronin's office and screamed obscenities at the manager for half an hour. But no matter how towering Lefty's rage, by the next day, all was forgiven and he was friendly again.

Joe Cronin cost the Red Sox $225,000 in the fall of 1934. Only an ordinary defensive shortstop, Cronin was one of the best hitters ever to play that position. As player-manager for the Washington Senators, he'd won the 1933 pennant. Nevertheless, it wasn't only a great player and successful manager that Washington owner Clark Griffith sold to Boston. Cronin was also his son-in-law! It was the Depression and $225,000 was too much money for Girffith to pass up. Cronin remained an all-star shortstop throughout the 1930s, served as Red Sox manager from 1935–47, and then moved up to general manager. In 1959, he became American League president, and in 1974, A.L. chairman.

Home-run hitter Jimmie Foxx was one of the last of Connie Mack's stars to be sold off. Mack sent him to Boston in December of 1935 for $150,000 and two players. Foxx was one of the most powerful right-handed batters ever and probably the first to cut his sleeves short to intimidate pitchers with his bulging biceps. With the Athletics, Foxx had already won two MVP Awards. He won a third with the Red Sox in 1938 when he led the A.L. in batting and RBI. His 175 runs driven in remains the club record. Of his 50 home runs that season (second in the league to Hank Greenberg's 58), 35 were hit at Fenway Park. Nevertheless, teammate Doc Cramer always insisted the Fenway left-field wall hurt Foxx more than it helped because many of the slugger's best drives were still rising when they hit the high wall near the top.

Other useful players obtained by Eddie Collins during the period included outfielders Doc Cramer, Joe Vosmik, and Ben Chapman, all of whom had .300 seasons in Boston; pitchers Fritz Ostermueller, Bobo Newsom, and Joe Heving; and infielders Pinky Higgins and Jim Tabor.

Although no pennants were won—the Yankees always had too much pitching—the BoSox returned to the respectability of the first division and put on a good show for their fans. Attendance at Fenway Park rose steadily.

Ironically, the greatest gate attraction—and many would say the greatest player—ever to wear a Red Sox uniform was not one of the already-existing stars brought in by Collins at great expense but a player he discovered himself and got for next to nothing. In 1937, he took a trip to San Diego to look at infielder Bobby Doerr. He liked what he saw. Doerr joined the Sox in 1938 and went on to be the best they ever had at second base. But what really excited Collins was the batting swing of a skinny San Diego outfielder named Ted Williams. The kid's stats were only fair at the time, but Collins knew he was going to set records with that swing. In 1938, he put Williams in Minneapolis, where he tore up Triple-A. By 1939, Collins was ready to unleash him on the majors.

Arguments over the greatest hitter of all time usually narrow down to Ted Williams and Babe Ruth. Both were left-handed power hitters. Ruth's cumulative totals are better in home runs, 714 to 521, and RBI, and 2,211 to 1,839, but the Babe didn't lose five of his potentially most productive seasons to military service. And, for much of his career, Ruth played half his games in a ballpark that favors left-handed power hitters. Fenway Park, Williams's home field, favors right-handers. Williams's career batting average of .344 is only slightly better than Ruth's .342, but Ruth played the bulk of his career during a period of unusually high batting averages. An adjustment for time and place would probably mean a twenty-point difference in favor of Williams. Perhaps instead of number one and number two, Ruth and Williams should be considered one and one-A, respectively.

In 1941, Joe DiMaggio's 56-game hitting streak captured the public's imagination. As remarkable as the Yankee Clipper's achievement was, Williams was even better over the long haul of the season. He led the league in homers with 37, trailed DiMaggio in RBI by five with 120, and batted .406. He was the first hitter to hit over .400 since Bill Terry of the Giants did it in 1930 and the first American Leaguer to do it since 1923. It is still the last time anyone has hit over .400.

The Red Sox had a doubleheader scheduled for the final day of the season. Williams' average was .3996, technically .400. Manager Cronin suggested he sit out the games and protect his mark, but Williams would have none of that. He played—and went 6-for-8.

Many felt Williams deserved the MVP Award, but the voters opted for DiMaggio. In 1942, Williams came back to win the Triple Crown with 36 homers, 137 RBI, and a .356 batting average. The voters chose Yankee Joe Gordon as MVP.

The truth was that many of the sportswriters who voted for awards—including several from Boston—were not fond of Williams, whose greatest sin was a penchant for saying what he believed. When criticized, he tended to strike back. In short, many writers could never forgive him for acting like a young man in his twenties instead of a mature, middle-aged man. And, because of what he considered unfair criticism in his youth, Williams' loathing for some writers continued as he actually approached middle age.

Not even the most critical Boston writer could find fault with Williams' war record. While many ballplayers found sinecures playing exhibitions for the entertainment of other troops, Williams became a decorated Marine fighter pilot.

During the war years, most major-league teams marked time, filling their rosters with 4-Fs, overage veterans, and green youngsters waiting for their draft notices. In 1942, the Red Sox had finished second to the Yankees. Cronin had replaced himself at shortstop with Johnny Pesky, who hit .331. Dom DiMaggio, Joe's brother, was an exceptional center fielder and good hitter though lacking his brother's power. Right-hander Cecil "Tex" Hughson led the A.L. with a 22–6 record. Williams and Doerr were at their best.

Then during the next three years, the team finished seventh twice while BoSox fans waited for the return of the major leaguers. In 1946, they were back and Boston ran away from the rest of the league. They got off to a 32–9 start and coasted to the pennant by 12 games over Detroit. After all these years, Tom Yawkey finally had his flag.

Cronin had a terrific team. Doerr and Pesky were brilliant in the infield. Pesky batted .335; Doerr had 18 homers and 116 RBI. Veteran slugger Rudy York was brought in to play first base and had 117 RBI. Dom DiMaggio hit .316. Hughson won 20 games, and Dave "Boo" Ferriss, a sensational wartime discovery, won 25 against only six losses. Maurice "Mickey" Harris won 17 and Joe Dobson 13. Williams was named MVP at last—ironically, in a year when he won no part of the Triple Crown. He was, however, second in all three categories and first in runs scored with 142.

The Red Sox were favored in the World Series—they were, after all, 5-for-5 in previous World Championships. Their opponents were the St. Louis Cardinals, who also had a habit of winning the Fall Classic whenever they appeared. The Redbirds had come to the fore in St. Louis in the mid-1920s and since had won five Series. They also had Stan Musial, Enos Slaughter, Marty Marion, and a deep pitching staff headed by 21-game-winner Howie Pollet.

Hughson outpitched Pollet in the opener, but reliever Ernie Johnson got the win when Rudy York homered in the tenth inning. The next day, Cardinals lefty Harry Brecheen shut out the Red Sox 3–0 to even things up. Two days later at Boston, Boo Ferriss returned the favor by whitewashing the Cards 4–0. It was the fiftieth shutout in Series history.

Game Four was all St. Louis, as the Cards hammered out Hughson in two innings and went on to win 12–3. Once more, the Red Sox went in front, three games to two, when Joe Dobson threw a four-hitter in Game Five. He was touched for three unearned runs, but the BoSox scored six times on his behalf. The Series returned to St. Louis with Boston hoping to wrap it up, but Harry Brecheen scattered seven hits for his second Series victory, 4–1.

Game Seven was one of the most memorable of all time. The Red Sox jumped on Murry Dickson for a run in the first inning, but after that the little Cardinals right-hander was masterful, limiting the BoSox to one hit through the next six innings. Boo Ferriss, the Red Sox starter, was not at his best. He allowed the Cardinals a run in the second and two more in the fifth when Dobson relieved him. Dickson was responsible for the two fifth-inning runs, doubling in one and scoring the other on Red Schoendienst's single.

In the top of the eighth, Dickson weakened. Glen "Rip" Russell singled as a pinch hitter and George Metkovich pinch-hit a double to put runners at second and third with no outs. Cardinals Manager Eddie Dyer signaled to his bullpen and brought in Harry Brecheen. The crafty lefty struck out Wally Moses and got Johnny Pesky to line out while the runners held. With two away, Dom DiMaggio came through for Boston, smashing a double off the right-centerfield wall to tie the game. Leon Culberson replaced DiMaggio, who'd twisted his ankle in running to second, but Brecheen ended the inning by getting a pop foul out from Williams.

Bob Klinger, the Red Sox best reliever, came on to pitch the bottom of the eighth. Enos Slaughter greeted him with a single. Klinger settled in to retire the next two Cardinals. That brought up Harry "The Hat" Walker, the Cards' most effective hitter in the Series. When he lashed a drive to right-center, Slaughter was already on his way to second. Culberson, who had replaced the great defensive outfielder DiMaggio just half an inning before, was slow in handling the hit. Pesky took the relay and turned to see Slaughter racing through his coach's stop sign at third and on his way to the plate. He scored easily.

Boston opened the ninth with singles by York and Doerr, but then Brecheen put on the clamps. When pinch hitter Tom McBride grounded into a force play for the final out, the Red Sox had lost their first World Series.

Those more interested in assigning blame than saluting success fastened on Williams' .200 batting average on five singles (Musial hit .222), but the goat's horns were mostly assigned to Pesky, who supposedly hesitated before throwing home on Slaughter's mad dash in the seventh game. Many eyewitnesses denied that Pesky skipped a beat before making his relay, but that's the way it went out of the press box.

The Sox had dropped Tom Yawkey's first World Series, but with the crew of hitters and pitchers he and Eddie Collins had to call on, hopes were bright for many more Fall Classic appearances in the near future.

THE PERFECT DEFENSE

What kind of fear did the sight of muscular Jimmie Foxx striding to the plate engender in the hearts of pitchers? The Yankees' "Lefty" Gomez probably put it best. One day with Foxx at the plate, Gomez peered in at his catcher. And peered. And peered. Finally, shouts went up: "Throw the ball!" Quoth Lefty, "I don't want to."

No pitcher with half his marbles wanted to pitch to the man they called "The Beast." He didn't just hit homers; he demoralized pitchers with the length of his long blasts. Still, on June 16, 1938, the St. Louis Browns, not known for their pitching expertise, found a way to keep Foxx from getting the ball out of the infield.

They walked him six consecutive times.

A JABLONOWSKI BY ANY OTHER NAME

In 1932, Peter William Jablonowski pitched briefly for the Red Sox without much success—an 0–3 record. Soon Jablonowski was back in the minors, and while he was there he decided to change his name.

In 1936, the Washington Senators brought up a pitcher who won 14 games for them. The fellow's name was Pete Appleton. Same guy, but you couldn't tell it by the box score—or the results.

LET THE BOSS SHOW YOU HOW IT'S DONE

By 1943, Joe Cronin was mostly a bench manager. He'd slowed in the field but he still had a good bat. In the first game of a June double-header with the Athletics, the Red Sox were down 4–1 with two men on when Joe put himself in as a pinch hitter. He homered to tie the score, and Boston eventually won.

That felt so good that Joe pinch-hit again in the nightcap. Same result. Home run.

CALLING THEM AS HE SAW THEM

Jimmie Foxx always gave his all for Joe Cronin's Red Sox, even though sometimes he didn't see eye-to-eye with his manager's decisions. Foxx kept his own counsel until a reporter asked him, "How come Cronin isn't winning with so many of the same players that won championships for Connie Mack?"

"Well," said Foxx in his most tactful way, "one manager knew what he was doing and the other one doesn't."

Frustrations and a Dream, 1947–1967

The Red Sox were favored to repeat as pennant winners in 1947, but they were sideswiped by an incredible outbreak of aching arms. The three top starters from 1946—Tex Hughson, Dave Ferriss, and Mickey Harris—were all stricken in spring training. The hurlers who had posted a cumulative 62–28 record in 1946 slumped to 29–26. Tragically, none of them ever fully recovered.

It took a great year by Ted Williams, with ample help from Bobby Doerr, Johnny Pesky, Dom DiMaggio, and rookie Sam Mele, to bring the Sox in third behind the Yankees. Williams gained his second Triple Crown with a .343 batting average, 32 home runs, and 114 RBI. Yet, once more he was deprived of the Most Valuable Player Award in favor of Joe DiMaggio, whose figures were .315, 20, and 97. One Boston writer who'd had a nasty argument with Williams during the season did not list Ted among the top ten players in the league when he sent in his MVP ballot.

Joe Cronin retired as manager after the season and moved into the front office to replace the ailing Eddie Collins. To replace himself in the dugout, he lured the fabled "Marse Joe" McCarthy out of retirement. McCarthy had won eight pennants as Yankee skipper and was considered the best manager alive, although Jimmy Dykes, the long-time White Sox manager, looked at the wealth of Yankee talent and labled him a "push-button" manager.

Cronin set out to give McCarthy all the buttons he could ask for, bringing in veteran outfielder Stan Spence from Washington and pitchers Jack Kramer and Ellis Kinder from St. Louis. The shiniest new addition was slugging shortstop Vern Stephens, another ex-Brown with terrific right-handed power. Surprisingly, McCarthy handed the shortstop job to Stephens and shifted Pesky to third although Pesky was the better defensive player. The decision had more to do with egos than skills, as did many of the choices McCarthy was forced to make. The major question in 1948 spring training was whether the prickly McCarthy and the temperamental Williams would get along. As it turned out, that was never a problem: "Any manager who can't get along with a .400 hitter should have his head examined," McCarthy said. But, although McCarthy and Williams developed a warm friendship, other parts of the team did not jell so smoothly.

The 1948 Red Sox could hit with anyone. The team's 907 runs scored led the league, as did Williams' .369 batting average. Doerr, Stephens, and Williams all drove in over 100 runs. Yet the Red Sox got out of the blocks slowly and were only 14–23 by Memorial Day. In the outfield, Dom DiMaggio recorded 503 putouts, a record that stood until 1977.

The pitching was the weak spot. Jack Kramer led the league in winning percentage based on his 18–6 record, but his 4.35 ERA told how poorly he actually pitched. Eventually, Joe Dobson and rookie left-hander Mel Parnell came on to help Boston close with a rush. On the last day of the season, the BoSox tied Cleveland for first place. That set up a one-game playoff at Fenway Park the next day.

Cleveland started its sensational rookie left-hander, Gene Bearden, a 19-game winner to that point. McCarthy, unaccountably, went with 36-year-old Denny Galehouse, a journeyman with eight wins on the season. Led by two homers by playing-manager Lou Boudreau, who was having the best season of his career, Cleveland took the game and the pennant with an 8–3 win.

Ironically, Cleveland faced the Braves, making their last bid for Boston's fans, in the World Series. It was the closest Boston had ever come—or would come—to an "in-house" World Series.

When the Red Sox obtained Al Zarilla from St. Louis early in the 1949 season, the Red Sox had a true all-star lineup: Williams, Dom DiMaggio, and Zarilla from left to right in the outfield; .300-hitter Billy Goodman at first base completing an infield that had Doerr, Stephens, and Pesky; and peppery Birdie Tebbetts behind the plate. Yet again, Boston stumbled out of the gate and fell behind the Yankees early. On July 4, they trailed by 12 games.

The pitching staff had two aces. Mel Parnell was brilliant all year, winning 25 games, the most ever by a Red Sox lefty. Ellis Kinder, 34 years old and with an undistinguished career behind him, suddenly became a world-beater and won 23 games. But Joe Dobson was the only other pitcher who had appeared in at least ten games to have an ERA under 4.00. Down the stretch, as the Red Sox sought to overtake New York, McCarthy used Parnell and Kinder to start and relieve.

On the next-to-last weekend of the season, Boston swept three games from the Yankees and moved into first place by a game. They still held that lead going into the season's final weekend, which closed out with two games at Yankee Stadium. One win meant the pennant.

On Saturday, the Yankees came back from a 4–0 deficit to beat Parnell 5–4. On Sunday, New York led Kinder 1–0 in the eighth when McCarthy pinch-hit for his starter. In the bottom of the inning, he brought in the exhausted Mel Parnell. The Yankees scored four more runs, negating a three-run rally by the Sox in the top of the ninth. Once more Boston missed out on a pennant by a hairsbreadth and a questionable pitching decision.

Another MVP Award for Williams was small consolation. Although he had won the honor in two of the last five seasons he played, his supporters could argue with some justification that it should have been five-for-five.

During the 1950 All-Star Game, Williams broke his elbow crashing into Comiskey Park's left-field wall while making a catch. The injury limited him to 89 games, and some felt that was the difference when the Red Sox finished third in a four-team race with the Yankees, Indians, and Tigers. In truth, the Sox didn't miss Williams' bat. As a team, they hit .302 and scored 1,027 runs. Sensational first baseman Walt Dropo hit .322 with 34 homers to win Rookie of the Year honors. He and Stephens tied for the league RBI crown with 144. Every regular hit above .300 except Stephens (.295) and Doerr (.294), and they hit 30 and 27 home runs, respectively. Billy Goodman, who played all four infield positions and filled in for Williams in the outfield, was the surprise A.L. batting champ with a .354 mark.

In short, the Sox had all the hitting they could ask for. But the pitching was another story. Parnell and Kinder slumped and no one picked up the slack. The team ERA was an ugly 4.88. Before midseason, with the Sox at 32–30, McCarthy resigned. Steve O'Neill presided over the usual second-half surge.

As the 1950s wore on and the Red Sox great hitters aged, Boston slid to the middle of the pack. Dropo never repeated his rookie slugging and was traded to Detroit. Continuing back problems forced Doerr's retirement; he was replaced at second by Billy Goodman, who finally settled down to one position. Injuries and age took Stephens, Pesky, and DiMaggio. Williams missed nearly all of two seasons when he was recalled to active duty during the Korean War.

Yet Boston's woes nearly always could be traced to pitching deficiencies. Parnell had a few more good years, Kinder for a while became one of the top relief specialists in baseball, and youngsters Tom Brewer and Frank Sullivan pitched well at times. But the Sox never had a staff or even a rotation that could compare with those in Chicago or Cleveland, much less with the Yankees, who won eight of the ten 1950s A.L. pennants.

Throughout the decade, the Sox always had a cadre of hitting talent. Right-fielder Jackie Jensen was one of the best and most consistent RBI men in the league. Goodman was always a reliable hitter. Sammy White arrived to become one of the best catchers in club history. Williams returned from shooting down MIGs and hit as though he'd never been away.

One of the most exciting players on the team was center fielder Jimmy Piersall, whose career almost ended in his rookie year of 1952. The Red Sox tried to turn Piersall into a shortstop. That, together with family pressures, proved too much for him. He began exhibiting bizarre behavior on the field and eventually was sent to the minors. There, the problems continued. Eventually it was discovered that he had suffered a complete nervous breakdown. He had no memory of the preceding months or his odd conduct. Happily, he recovered, became a brilliant center fielder and sharp hitter, and was even able to write about his experience in the bestselling book *Fear Strikes Out*.

Harry Agganis' tale had a more tragic ending. "The Golden Greek" had been an All-American quarterback at Boston University and was one of the most popular athletes in New England. As a rookie first baseman with the Red Sox in 1954, he showed flashes of power that led many to predict he would become one of the American League's stars. Early in 1955, he was hitting .313 when he contracted pneumonia. Complications set in and Agganis died of a pulmonary embolism at age 25.

Infielder Elijah "Pumpsie" Green was a Red Sox rookie in 1959. Never an outstanding player, his batting average for five major league seasons was .246. Green's significance is that he was the first African-American player to wear a Red Sox uniform. Such African-American stars as Willie Mays, Hank Aaron, Ernie Banks, Larry Doby and Frank Robinson had been shaping pennant races for several years, and many felt the Red Sox delay in hiring African-Americans—12 seasons after Jackie Robinson arrived in Brooklyn—had a great deal to do with the poor showings of the team in the early 1960s.

Williams won his fifth and sixth batting titles in 1957–58. He could have had two more batting championships in the period, but qualification was based on at-bats at the time, putting Williams, who walked so often, at a disadvantage. Because of this, the standard was changed to plate appearances.

In 1959, Ted Williams hit .254. Although a neck injury was at the root of his hitting problem, many assumed the 41-year-old great had finally come to the end. Tom Yawkey was one of several who hinted that it was time for Ted to hang up his bat. But Williams refused to go out on a low note.

He returned for the 1960 season, determined to erase any memory of that dreadful .254. When Williams set his mind to something, it was as good as done. In his magnificent farewell, he batted .316—only four points below the league leader, Red Sox second baseman Pete Runnels—and slugged 29 home runs. His final homer came in his final at-bat against a pitcher born in 1939, Ted's rookie year. As the Fenway crowd roared its appreciation, Williams circled the bases head down and disappeared into the dugout. He still holds the club's career marks in home runs (521), walks (2,019), batting average (.344), on-base average (.482) and slugging percentage (.634).

Williams's successor in left field arrived in 1961. Because Yastrzemski was hard to spell and harder to pronounce, most fans called him "Yaz." No one could be "another" Williams, but Yaz carved his own niche and eventually joined his predecessor at Cooperstown. Yaz started less spectacularly than Williams, but in his third season, he won his first batting title. Another Red Sox batting leader was Runnels, a versatile player who played both first and second base. Pete won in 1960 and 1962.

A tremendous power hitter, Dick Stuart, held down first base for the Sox in 1963–64, hitting 75 homers and driving in 232 runs in those two years. Unfortunately, Stuart's abilities ended with his bat. His nickname, "Dr. Strangeglove," told it all. When it was determined that his defense was producing more runs for the opposition than his bat was for Boston, he was traded to the Phillies.

Tony Conigliaro, a hitter of nearly unlimited potential joined the Sox in 1964, breaking in with 24 home runs as a 19-year-old. When he turned twenty, he led the league with 32. Another outstanding player through the period was Frank Malzone, perhaps the finest Red Sox third baseman since the fabled days of Jimmie Collins.

Pitching, as usual, was the Red Sox weakness. Bill Monbouquette was the best starter of the period, winning 20 games for the seventh-place 1963 Sox.

One Red Sox hurler stood out as the best in the business during the period. Six-foot-six, 240-pound Dick Radatz was baseball's most imposing reliever. He was called "The Monster," and his fastball in his prime was truly monstrous. From 1962 through 1965, Radatz won 49 games in relief and saved over 100. Perhaps he was overused. By 1966, he'd lost a foot or two off his fastball and he had no other pitches to fall back on.

Despite the excellent work of Yaz, Conigliaro, Runnels, Malzone, Radatz, Monbouquette, and a few others, the first two-thirds of the 1960s were not great times at Fenway. The Red Sox tumbled into the second division. In 1967, when new manager Dick Williams took over, Boston had finished ninth in the expanded league two years in a row.

Williams was a former journeyman outfielder but with no relation to Ted by either blood or bat. He spent the spring concentrating on fundamentals and convincing the Red Sox players to believe in themselves. He hadn't taken the job to make friends, and, with his sharp tongue, he didn't make very many. Through the first half of the season, the results were not positive as other teams competed for the A.L. lead.

Then, coming out of the All-Star break, the Red Sox ran off a ten-game winning streak. Suddenly, the pennant race was a four-team race among the Red Sox, White Sox, Twins, and Tigers. Through July, August, and September, the four teams were seldom separated by more than three games in the standings.

For Boston, the biggest differences between the ninth-place team of the year before were Yaz, always a good hitter but now blossoming as a home-run threat, and pitcher Jim Lonborg, on his way to a Cy Young season. Yaz, easily the American League MVP, won the Triple Crown. Others, like first baseman George Scott, shortstop Rico Petrocelli, and outfielder Reggie Smith, contributed in the clutch even though their overall statistics were only ordinary. Sox fans called their pennant quest "The Impossible Dream," but as Boston stayed in the race, the "dream" began to seem plausible.

The team survived a frightening blow in August when Conigliaro was seriously hurt in a terrible beaning. His eyesight was affected, causing him to miss all of the following year. He made a partial comeback for a couple of seasons but then was forced to retire as his sight worsened.

As September neared its end, Chicago finally slipped out of the race. The Red Sox beat the Twins 6–4 on September 30, the day before the season closed, to pull into a tie with Minnesota for the lead with Detroit only a half game behind. The next day, they beat Minnesota again, 5–3, to knock out the Twins. That left Detroit with a double-header scheduled in California. The Tigers won the opener over the Angels and took a lead in the second game. But, with Red Sox fans on the edge of their chairs, the Angels rallied. Detroit dropped the nightcap, 8–5, and with it the tie for the pennant. "The Impossible Dream" had become a Red Sox reality.

The World Series against St. Louis proved a letdown, but only because Cardinals pitcher Bob Gibson was truly unbeatable. He won three games: 2–1, 6–0, and the finale, 7–2. Lonborg almost matched him, winning a one-hit shutout in Game Two and a three-hitter in Game Five, before weakening in Game Seven. Despite the loss, 1967 should be considered one of the most thrilling and satisfying ever for Boston fans.

BATTEN DOWN THE PITCHERS!

Oh how those Red Sox of the early 1950s could hit! In June of 1950, the St. Louis Browns arrived in Boston for a four-game series. The Browns had one of baseball's weakest pitching staffs so the Red Sox were expected to fatten their batting averages. Yet no one predicted the magnitude of the slaughter. In the opening game, the Red Sox scored 29 runs. The next day, they tailed off to 20. Perhaps exhausted from running the bases, Boston was content with scoring seven and then eight runs in the last two games, but that still brought the series total to 64.

However, for sheer cruelty to pitchers, the Sox socked Detroit for 17 runs in the seventh inning on June 18, 1953. Outfielder Gene Stephens had a record three hits and catcher Sammy White a record three runs scored.

RISING TO THE OCCASION

Ted Williams appeared in 18 All-Star Games and hit .304 against the best pitchers the National League could offer. His final All-Star at-bat was as a pinch hitter in 1960. He singled. Ted also walked eleven times to go with his 14 All-Star hits, giving him an on-base average of .438.

No doubt his most thrilling moment—and one of the greatest in All-Star history—came in 1941 when his two-out, three-run homer in the ninth gave the American League a stunning 7–5 win. However, most fans remember the 1946 game as his best. Williams had four hits, including two home runs. He batted in five of the A.L.'s 12 runs. But the *crème de la crème* came in his last at bat. The N.L.'s Rip Sewell was famous for his *eephus* pitch, a high lob that sometimes arched as high as 40 feet before coming down through the strike zone. With absolutely nothing on it, the *eephus* was considered "home-run proof." Sewell fed Ted an *eephus* and Williams fouled it off. The game was as good as won by then, of course, and it was funny to see baseball's mightiest hitter handcuffed by what looked like a sandlot pitch. Sewell threw another *eephus*. Williams took a little hop forward and blasted the ball into the stands. He laughed all the way around the bases.

THE SECRET'S IN THE WALLET

Tommy Henrich, the Yankees' "Old Reliable," always maintained that the reason New York won pennants and the Red Sox didn't was that Tom Yawkey paid his players too well. Yawkey was known for his generous payroll. Meanwhile, the Yankee players had to deal each year with George Weiss, the New York GM who never saw a penny he couldn't pinch. According to Henrich, the Red Sox played each year for a pennant; the Yankees played to make a decent living.

The Close-Call Years, 1968–1985

Nineteen sixty-eight was the "Year of the Pitcher," as the mounds-men dominated as they hadn't done since the deadball era fifty years before. In the National League, the Cardinals' Bob Gibson posted a 1.12 ERA. In the American League, the Tigers' Denny McLain won 31 games. Both pitchers earned MVP and Cy Young Awards for their leagues, but they were hardly alone in turning batters into helpless bystanders. National League hitters in total managed a paltry .243 batting average. That, however, was heavy hitting compared to the American League's miniscule .230. Only one qualifying A.L. batter topped .300 in the batting race—Boston's Carl Yastrzemski, with a glorious .301.

In Boston, the phrase "Year of the Pitcher" took on a different meaning. The high hopes for the season were dashed before it began when the Red Sox 1967 Cy Young winner, Jim Lonborg, tore up his knee in a winter skiing accident. From 22–9 in 1967 he fell to 6–10 in 1968 when he was finally able to return to the mound. And, for the rest of his career, he was never able to regain the form that he'd shown in the year of "The Impossible Dream."

Tony Conigliaro's hitting was missed, too. Ken Harrelson, who'd been acquired in late 1967, helped fill the void with 35 homers and a league-leading 109 RBI, but most Sox bats went into hibernation. Although Yaz led the league in batting, his home-run total dropped from 44 to 23. First baseman George Scott stopped hitting altogether. Boston finished fourth, a half game behind Cleveland but 17 behind pennant-winning Detroit.

The American League was split into Eastern and Western Divisions in 1969. The Red Sox finished third three times in a row. By 1972, the team had changed. Eddie Kasko was in his third season as manager.

Rico Petrocelli had moved from short to third to make room for veteran Luis Aparicio. Doug Griffin held down second, and Danny Cater, acquired from the Yankees for reliever Sparky Lyle, was at first base. The outfield had swift Tommy Harper, underrated Reggie Smith, and Yastrzemski. A most valuable newcomer was catcher Carlton Fisk, who hit .293 and was named Rookie of the Year. Pitchers Marty Pattin, Sonny Siebert, and John Curtis were average, but right-hander Luis Tiant was outstanding. Tiant had once been a 20-game winner with Cleveland, but arm miseries had forced him back to the minors, where the Red Sox found him. He went 15–6 with a 1.91 ERA to earn Comeback Player of the Year laurels.

A player strike at the beginning cost thirteen days of the 1972 season, and the owners ruled that the games would not be made up. This proved crucial when the Red Sox chased the Tigers down to the wire, for the Tigers played one more game than the Sox. Boston went to Detroit for the last series of the season, leading by half a game. The Tigers won the first two contests to clinch the Eastern Division title. A Red Sox victory in the third game still left them a half game behind—Detroit's "extra" game—and moaning about what might have been.

There was no catching Baltimore the next year, but in 1974 the Red Sox looked for a while like champions under new manager Darrell Johnson. The Boston farm system was one of the best in baseball. In 1974, it added outfielder Dwight Evans and shortstop Rick Burleson to the team. By late August, the Sox were in first place and pennant fever began to build. Then the Sox lost three straight in Minnesota, traveled to Baltimore to be shut out in three in a row, and dropped two more to Milwaukee back at Fenway. The eight-game losing streak knocked them out of the race.

After so much frustration, the Eastern championship in 1975 came almost easily. Boston took the division lead in late May and was never really contested. Two rookies led the way. Jim Rice took over in left field as Yastrzemski moved to first base. Before he was sidelined late in the season with a broken wrist, Rice hit a robust .309 with 22 home runs and 102 RBI. In most years, he would have been Rookie of the Year in a landslide, but 1975 also saw Fred Lynn arrive in center field for the Sox. As Super Rookie, Lynn batted .331 with 21 homers and 105 RBI while simultaneously earning a reputation as one of the A.L.'s best outfield defenders. After the season, he received not only the Rookie of the Year Award but also the MVP trophy. The pitching was also stronger and deeper than Red Sox fans had come to expect. Rick Wise paced the staff with 19 wins, Tiant won 18, and left-hander Bill Lee 17. Another lefty, Roger Moret, led the A.L. in winning percentage with a 14–3 mark.

Boston's opponent in the League Championship Series (LCS) was Oakland, winner of three straight pennants and favored to make short work of the Red Sox in capturing a fourth. The series opened in Boston, and Tiant thrilled the home crowd by tossing a three-hit, 7–1 victory. The next day, Reggie Cleveland was touched by the A's for three runs in five innings, but the Red Sox pulled even by scoring three of their own in the bottom of the fifth, with a two-run homer by Yaz the big blow. Moret and Dick Drago came in to hold the fort while Boston added three runs to its total to take a two-game lead. The series moved to Oakland, but the Red Sox were on a roll. They built a 5–1 lead before Rick Wise weakened for two runs in the eighth. However, Drago, the Sox's top reliever all season, was once more equal to the task, shutting down Oakland and making Boston an upset pennant winner.

One of the keys to the victory was Oakland's sloppy outfield play. Meanwhile, the Red Sox shone in that department, particularly Yastrzemski, who'd moved back to left because of Rice's injury.

If the Red Sox had faced a great team in the LCS, they found themselves up against an even greater one in the World Series. Cincinnati's "Big Red Machine" of Pete Rose, Johnny Bench, Tony Perez, Joe Morgan, George Foster, and Dave Concepcion bore comparison with such legendary clubs as the 1927 Yankees. Once more the Sox were decided underdogs.

Once again Tiant got Boston off on the right foot, as he shut out the Reds 5–0 on five hits in Game One. The next day, Lee also held the Reds in check through eight innings. He left in the ninth with a 2–1 lead and a runner on. Drago came in and got two out, but two hits and two Cincinnati runs followed before he got the third.

In Game Three, Cincinnati jumped off to a 5–1 lead before the Red Sox rallied. They tied it at five on Evans' two-run homer in the ninth. After Cincinnati's Cesar Geronimo opened the bottom of the tenth with a single, pinch hitter Ed Armbrister tried to sacrifice him to second. The ball landed just in front of the plate and Fisk leaped for it, colliding with Armbrister. When Fisk got to the ball, he threw wildly to second, allowing Geronimo to go to third and Armbruster to reach second. The Red Sox claimed interference but umpire Larry Barnett didn't see it that way. When the arguing ceased, Moret relieved Jim Willoughby, who'd been outstanding but unlucky. Rose was walked to load the bases. Moret struck out pinch hitter Merv Rettenmund for what would have been the second out had Arbruster been retired. As things stood, however, there was only one away and the Sox still had to keep their outfield drawn in. Morgan lifted a fly over Lynn's head for what might have been the third out, but instead the ball dropped for a hit while Geronimo trotted in from third with the winning run.

Undaunted, Boston sent Tiant out to even the Series in Game Four. It wasn't vintage El Tiante, but his nine-hit complete game was enough for a 5–4 win. The next day, however, Cincinnati forged back into the lead with a 6–3 victory as Tony Perez blasted a pair of homers.

That set the stage for the historic sixth game. After a day off for travel, Game Six was postponed another 72 hours by rain. That looked like a break for Boston because it meant Tiant was ready to pitch again. Lynn staked him to a lead with a 3-run homer in the bottom of the first. That lasted until the top of the fifth when the Reds solved Tiant for three runs of their own. In the seventh inning, Cincinnati added two more runs. Then Geronimo opened the eighth with a homer and Tiant was lifted.

Trailing 6–3, the Red Sox started the bottom of the eighth with a single by Lynn and a walk to Petrocelli. Rawley Eastwick relieved for the Reds and struck out Evans. Burleson lined to short for the second out. That left it up to pinch hitter Bernie Carbo, who'd homered as a pinch hitter in Game Three. This time he pounded one into the center-field bleachers to tie the game. Only one other man—Chuck Essegian of the Dodgers in 1959—had ever hit a pair of pinch-hit homers in a World Series.

The Red Sox loaded the bases with no outs in the bottom of the ninth, only to be retired without scoring. In the 11th inning, Morgan lined one for the right-field seats that had home run written all over it, but Evans made a great leaping catch and then threw in time to double up a runner off first. In the top of the twelfth, Cincinnati had two on and one out before Rick Wise, working in relief, retired Concepcion and Geronimo.

Pat Darcy, the Reds' seventh reliever of the game, had pitched two faultless innings when he opened the 12th against Carlton Fisk. The Red Sox catcher greeted him with a blast down the left-field line that was surely gone—but fair or foul? As he moved down the first-base line, Fisk waved his arms urging the ball fair. When his drive bounced off the foul pole, the Series was tied again.

After the thrills of Game Six, the seventh game was necessarily anti-climactic. In almost any other Series, it would have been memorable. Boston got off to a three-run lead behind Bill Lee, but the Reds got two back on Perez's homer in the sixth and tied the score in the the seventh. In the ninth, Ken Griffey walked for the Reds and reached third with two outs. Joe Morgan's looping single gave Cincinnati a 4–3 lead. Boston went down in order in their half of the ninth. As expected, "The Big Red Machine" reigned as World Champions, but the Red Sox had come oh-so-close in what many regarded as the greatest World Series ever.

After the thrills of '75, 1976 was one of the saddest years in Red Sox history. Holdouts by Fisk, Lynn, and Burleson got the team off to a grumpy start, and it puttered through an undistinguished season before finally edging Cleveland for third place. Johnson was let go after 85 games and replaced as manager by Don Zimmer.

In July, the Red Sox suffered a loss far greater than any they had ever encountered on the field when Tom Yawkey died. In his more than forty years of ownership he'd never seen his team win a World Series and had only enjoyed three pennants. But, if ultimate victory always escaped him, his years with the Sox were still a triumph. He'd brought them back from near extinction during the Depression, made them contenders, and kept them competitive in most seasons. A "fans' " owner, he always saw to it that the folks who bought the seats got their money's worth at Fenway Park.

But with Yawkey gone, the uncertainty at the top—ownership was split three ways—contributed to the frustrations of the next couple of years.

In one way, the 1977 Red Sox were like the Sox of 30 years before: lots of hitting, not much pitching. Boston batters slugged 213 home runs, led by 39 by Jim Rice. No fewer than eight Red Sox hit at least 14 dingers. However, the starting pitching was lackluster at best. Zimmer called in reliever Bill Campbell, acquired over the winter from Minnesota, a total of 69 times, often for several innings at a stretch. Campbell was marvelous, saving 31 games and leading the team in wins with 13, but his overuse probably contributed to his rapid decline in succeeding seasons. The Sox took over first place for a while in August but eventually lost out to the Yankees by 2½ games.

The pitching staff was revamped for 1978. Dennis Eckersley was acquired from Cleveland and went 20–8. Mike Torrez came from the Yankees and won 16. Campbell was struck down with a bad arm, but rookie Bob Stanley saved ten games and was a terrific 15–2. The hitting fell off a little, but no one could blame Jim Rice, who led the A.L. with 46 homers and 139 RBI on his way to an MVP season.

The Sox rolled to a 10-game lead in mid-July and were being compared with the greatest aggregations of Boston's past. A division title seemed assured, probably a pennant, and possibly the long-sought World Series win. Then the Sox began to lose and the Yankees, who'd been slumbering in fourth place, began to win. By September 7, when New York arrived at Fenway for a four-game set, the lead was down to four games. In a new version of the Boston Massacre, the Yankees slaughtered the Red Sox 15–3, 13–2, 7–0, and 7–4. By the following weekend when Boston invaded Yankee Stadium, New York was a game and a half in front. When the home team took the first two games of the series, the Red Sox looked dead in the water.

Boston won the third game to get back within hailing distance. Then in the final two weeks of the season, they rallied. On the last day, they tied the Yanks. Thirty years after losing the 1948 pennant in a one-game playoff, the Red Sox had a chance for revenge. The scene was even the same—Fenway Park.

Alas, it was not to be. The Red Sox staked Mike Torrez to a 2–0 lead through six innings. In the seventh, New York got two on with two out and light-hitting Bucky Dent at the plate. Dent lifted a routine fly into left field which Yaz appeared to have a play on. But suddenly the ball was in the screen above the Green Monster and the Yankees led 3–2. New York added two more runs for an apparently safe lead going into the ninth. The Sox rallied for a pair and had the tying run at third before Yankee reliever Goose Gossage retired Yaz for Boston's final out of the season.

The Red Sox closed the decade with a generic year—91 wins, third place. Lynn won the batting title. He and Rice each hit 39 homers and drove in 122 and 130 runs, respectively. Despite the glory of 1975, the 1970s would be remembered in Boston more for pennants lost than for the one pennant gained.

Near the end of the 1980 season, Don Zimmer was fired. In the three seasons he'd managed the Red Sox from start to finish, they'd won 97, 99, and 91 games and come close to two division titles. But "close," as the saying goes, only counts in horseshoes and hand grenades. The frustration of being good but not quite good enough was getting to Boston fans and management, some of whom believed that another manager might have been able to take the team to the playoffs. With five games left in 1980, the Sox stood at 82–73 and Zimmer was out of a job.

His successor was Ralph Houk, the man who'd won three pennants with the 1961–63 Yankees. But the team Houk inherited in Boston was less talented than those Yankees teams and even less talented than the Red Sox teams Zimmer had managed. Carlton Fisk became a free agent over the winter and signed with the White Sox. Fred Lynn and Rick Burleson were traded away before they, too, could become free agents. Butch Hobson was also traded and Carney Lansford replaced him at third base.

The 1981 season was like no other in that a player strike in the middle caused it to be split into first and second halves, with the winners of each segment playing off for the division crown. The Red Sox were unaffected, winning neither end of the season, but they did complete a winning year under Houk, going 59–49 overall. Lansford won the batting title with a .336 mark, and Dwight Evans tied for the home-run lead with 22.

Houk's Red Sox made some noise early in 1982, but they didn't have the starting pitching to stay the course. Third place was the best they could do.

The most significant Red Sox happening that year was the arrival of Wade Boggs. He didn't get into the starting lineup until late July when an injury sidelined Lansford. From then to the end of the season, he batted .361. Although Boggs didn't bat enough times to be eligible for the batting title, his overall mark of .349 was 17 points better than the actual winner, Kansas City's Willie Wilson. His hitting enabled the Sox to trade Lansford to Oakland for slugging outfielder Tony Armas.

Yastrzemski retired after the 1983 season. He'd worn a Red Sox uniform for 23 seasons. Yaz's career has often been compared with that of Ted Williams, the left fielder he'd replaced as a rookie in 1961. It was a comparison neither he nor more than a handful of players could ever stand up to. Although he'd won three batting titles, his .285 career batting average was far below Williams' .344. Williams also topped Yaz in homers, 521 to 452, despite playing in over a thousand fewer games. Yastrzemski's longevity gave him the club career lead in games, at bats, hits, runs, doubles, runs batted in, and total bases. Yaz's fans could argue that he played through a period of unusually low batting averages and that he was far superior to Williams defensively. If he ultimately fell short of Williams' accomplishments, Yastrzemski was certainly deserving of his election into the Hall of Fame in 1989.

Boston fans had little to cheer about for three seasons except individual accomplishments. The Red Sox were essentially a .500 club—a little under in 1983, a little over in '84, and right on the mark at 81–81 when John McNamara became the manager in 1985. Boggs won his first batting title in 1983 with a .361 mark and repeated in '85 at .368. His 240 hits were the most in the American League since 1928. Rice led the league in homers with 39 and tied for the RBI title with 126 in 1983. The next year, Tony Armas led the A.L. in both departments with 43 and 123; Rice was second in RBI with 122.

SUCCESS STORY

Haywood Sullivan is a throwback to an earlier era when ballplayers occasionally rose to become club owners. Two of the best-known examples were Charles Comiskey, who started as an 1880s first baseman and ended up owning the Chicago White Sox, and Clark Griffith, a star pitcher of the 1890s who went on to own the Washington Senators.

Sullivan was a baseball and football star at the University of Florida. He could have had a pro football career as a quarterback but chose instead to sign with the Red Sox as a catcher. A back injury limited him to 60 games with the Sox over four seasons before he was dealt to Kansas City in 1961. He managed in the minors for two years and then took over as skipper of the A's in 1965. The next year, at age thirty-five, he became Red Sox vice president in charge of player personnel. In 1978, when the club was purchased from the Yawkey estate, he became a partner, completing his rise from foot soldier to general.

Pitching and Heartache, 1986–2003

Going in, the 1986 season looked to be more of the same. The most noticeable change in the regular lineup was the addition of Don Baylor as the designated hitter. He'd come to the Red Sox for Mike Easler in a trade of DHs. Both were considered near the end of their careers. The pitching had potential. Bob Ojeda had been swapped to the New York Mets for a couple of relievers. Bruce Hurst, Dennis "Oil Can" Boyd, and Al Nipper were okay, and Bob Stanley was still available in the bullpen. Roger Clemens, the hard-throwing right-hander, had gotten his career off to a good start in 1984 and '85, only to have both seasons curtailed by injury. After arm surgery the previous August, he was a big question mark.

It took a while for Boston fans to get excited about their team, even though Dwight Evans began the season with by homering on the first major league pitch of the season. Even when Clemens proved he was all the way back with his major-league-record 20-strikeout game against Seattle in April, fans were not ready to jump on a BoSox bandwagon. In mid-May, Boston took a tenuous lead in the East. Nipper and Hurst were sidelined at times, but McNamara juggled his staff and the Sox stayed in front.

When it became clear that the Red Sox had a shot at winning the division, general manager Lou Gorman went and got some help, adding Spike Owen to take over at shortstop, Dave Henderson to platoon with slowing Tony Armas in center field, and aging Hall of Famer Tom Seaver to bolster the pitching staff. In the meantime, Baylor hit 31 homers and had 94 RBI in his first year with the club. Jim Rice, in his last big season, knocked in 120, and first baseman Bill Buckner drove in 102. Wade Boggs won another batting title with his .357 mark.

The man of the season, however, was Clemens, who went 24–4, including winning his first 14 decisions, and led the league with a 2.48 ERA. Fittingly, he won the Cy Young award and was named Most Valuable Player. He was also named MVP of the All-Star Game.

The League Championship Series pitted the Red Sox against the California Angels, seeking their first pennant. In a stunning reversal of form, Clemens was pounded, 8–1, in the opener at Fenway. Bruce Hurst evened the series with a 9–2 win in Game Two. The scene then shifted to California, where the Angels jumped on Boyd late for a 5–3 win. Clemens came back in Game Four and pitched shutout ball into the ninth, only to see the Angels rally for the three runs to tie. The game went into extra innings, with California winning in the 11th.

Had the LCS been in its original 3-of-5 format, the Sox would have been eliminated, but a best-of-7 format had gone into effect in 1985. That seemed academic the next day, when the Angels held a 5–4 lead with two outs in the top of the ninth and a 2–2 count on Dave Henderson. A Red Sox runner was on base, but the Angels had their ace reliever, Donnie Moore, on the mound. As Moore delivered, 64,000 Angels fans were on their feet and the Angels bench stood poised to erupt from the dugout. But Henderson deposited the pitch into the left-field seats to turn the game around.

California managed to tie the score in the bottom of the ninth, but Henderson's sacrifice fly in the 11th brought home the winning run. The stunned Angels and jubilant Red Sox returned to Boston where McNamara's band completed its comeback by winning Game Six, 10–6, and Game Seven, 8–1. A combination of veteran hitters, young pitchers, and a bit of luck had put the Red Sox back in the World Series for the first time since 1975.

Their opponents were the New York Mets, who'd won 108 regular-season games. As usual, Boston was the underdog. Bruce Hurst opened for the Red Sox at Shea Stadium against Ron Darling. Hurst held the Mets to four hits in eight innings, but Darling was even stingier, allowing three singles in seven frames. The Red Sox, however, pushed over a run in the seventh, and, when Calvin Schiraldi blanked New York in the ninth, Boston was up a game. The next day was billed as the pitching matchup of the year—Clemens vs. the Mets' Dwight "Doc" Gooden, who went 17–6 with a 2.84 ERA that year after going 24–4 with a 1.53 ERA in 1985. But neither lasted past the fifth inning, and the Red Sox prevailed, 9–3.

The Red Sox brought a 2–0 lead back to Boston, but proceeded to lose the next two games. In Game Five, Hurst was back on the mound for the Sox. He allowed ten hits, but managed to keep the Mets to three runs as the Sox scored four times in the first four innings against Gooden and held on for the win.

Game Six was, and always will be, one of baseball's most memorable games. Clemens went the first seven innings for Boston and was in line for a 3–2 win. But Schiraldi gave up a tying run in the eighth. In the top of the 10th, Dave Henderson smashed a homer off Rick Aguilera and Boston added a second run before they were retired.

Leading 5–3, only three outs separated Boston from its first Series win since 1918. Schiraldi retired the first two Mets of the inning. Then Gary Carter singled and Kevin Mitchell followed with another hit. Schiraldi zipped two strikes past Ray Knight—one strike away from victory—but he looped a single into center. Carter scored to make the score 5–4 and Mitchell raced to third.

Bob Stanley was brought in to face Mookie Wilson. He worked the count to 2–2, but then Wilson fouled off two in a row as the tension built. On his seventh delivery, Stanley threw a wild pitch on which Mitchell scored to tie the game and Knight advanced to second. Wilson fouled two more of Stanley's offerings. On the 10th pitch of his at bat, Mookie slapped an easy bounding ball to hobbled first baseman Bill Buckner. Somehow it went through Buckner's aching legs as Knight raced home with the winning run.

It was a crushing defeat. A rain postponement gave Boston an extra day before Game Seven, but it didn't help. The Sox scored three in the second inning on back-to-back homers by Dwight Evans and Rich Gedman and Boggs' RBI single. Hurst pitched five shutout innings, but then was rocked for three runs in the sixth. Schiraldi came in to pitch the seventh, and Knight greeted him with a homer for the go-ahead run. Before the inning ended, the Mets added two more runs to go up 6–3. Boston closed to 6–5 in the eighth, but New York matched them with two runs in the bottom of the inning. When the Sox went down one-two-three in the ninth, Boston had lost its fourth World Series since trading Babe Ruth to the Yankees.

Whether the "Curse of the Bambino" hovered over Fenway Park made little difference in 1987 as the Sox slumped to fifth place in the East. Boggs won another batting title with his .363 average and Clemens' 20–9 was good for his second consecutive Cy Young Award. Dwight Evans cracked 30 homers and drove in 123. Mike

Greenwell hit .328, but the Sox had too many holes in the lineup as Baylor, Rice, Buckner, and Gedman all slumped.

Nothing very exciting happened during the first half of 1988. At the All-Star Game break, with the team record at 43–42, McNamara was replaced as manager by coach Joe Morgan. When the Sox won 12 straight coming out of the break, they found themselves in the thick of the division race. Evans and Greenwell supplied RBI power, and Boggs, who won his fifth batting title at .366, led the league in runs scored with 123. Ellis Burks hit a solid .293 in center field. Clemens and Hurst had matching 18-win seasons, and big Lee Smith was a force out of the bullpen with 29 saves. The Sox slumped at the end of the season, losing seven of their last ten, but by then everyone else in the East was out of the race.

Three ex-Red Sox players helped Oakland win the opening game of the LCS. Dave Henderson drove in Carney Lansford for the go-ahead run off Bruce Hurst in the eighth inning, and then Dennis Eckersley came in to nail down the save. The next day, the Athletics edged Clemens, 4–3. The series moved to Oakland, and the Red Sox jumped out to a five-run lead in Game Three only to lose, 10–6. The A's wrapped up the pennant with a 4–1 win the next day.

Injuries waylaid the Red Sox in 1989. The lineup varied from game to game. Rice, Burks, and second baseman Marty Barrett missed extended periods and most of the other regulars were out from time to time. A muscle tear limited Clemens to 17 wins. Only a spurt at the end allowed the team to climb to an 83–79 record.

Ellis Burks led the Red Sox in homers in 1990 with only 21, the lowest total by a Sox leader since 1974. His modest 89 RBI also topped the club. Wade Boggs batted a career-low .302. But overall the team had a solid lineup that led the A.L. with a .272 average. Tony Pena came over from St. Louis to give the Sox quality catching. His influence was credited for the surprisingly strong showing of the pitching staff. By early September, Boston held a 6½ game lead, but then a shoulder injury sidelined Clemens.

As if to show how irreplaceable the Rocket Man was, the Sox promptly went into a slump and fell behind Toronto in the standings. However, the Blue Jays returned the favor, losing six of their last eight to practically give Boston the Eastern Division title.

The Oakland A's were widely regarded as unstoppable, and their performance in the LCS did nothing to change that opinion. They again defeated the Red Sox in four straight games. The most memorable moment of the Series came in Game Four with Clemens on the mound. In the second inning, he was unceremoniously ejected from the game for allegedly directing vulgar language toward the home plate umpire. With his ejection went any slight hopes the Red Sox may have harbored for a miracle comeback.

Boston was apparently out of the A.L. East race by August in 1991. Sox fans held a mock funeral to inter their hopes. But the team came back from the dead to make it close in September before finally finishing seven games behind Toronto. Clemens led the league in strikeouts with 241 and he pitched better than his 18–10 record would suggest, a fact recognized when he received his third Cy Young Award after the season. The news Joe Morgan got was less welcome as he was replaced as manager by former Sox third baseman Butch Hobson.

Perhaps Morgan was the luckier of the two, since he didn't have to endure the 1992 season—one of the darkest in Red Sox history. Promising first baseman Carlos Quintana missed the entire season due to injuries suffered in an auto accident. Ellis Burks and Mike Greenwell played only 115 games between them. As if losing three of their best hitters was not crippling enough, Wade Boggs suffered through a season-long slump that saw his batting average end at a career-worst .259. Slugger Jack Clark, who finished his career with 310 home runs, managed only five while hitting .210. The punchless Red Sox scored only 599 runs while finishing last in the A.L. East.

Wasted by the dismal offense was the great pitching of Roger Clemens, who nearly won another Cy Young by leading the league in ERA at 2.41, and some good work by lefthander Frank Viola. They and a few others gave Boston the league's second-best ERA.

Things got only marginally better in 1993, as Hobson led the Sox to an 80–82 record and a fifth-place finish. The good news for Boston was the emergence of Mo Vaughn, who hit .297 with 29 home runs and 101 RBI. Two of the previous year's youngsters also stepped into starting roles, shortstop John Valentin and third baseman Scott Cooper. Unfortunately, Cooper was replacing Wade Boggs, who left the team via free agency in the off-season. To make matters worse, Boggs left Boston to sign with the hated Yankees, and rebounded from his terrible '92 campaign by hitting .302.

Pitcher Aaron Sele showed great promise in his major league debut as well, going 7–2 with a 2.74 ERA in 18 starts. While Viola and

Danny Darwin combined with Sele to form a respectable rotation, Clemens injured his groin and was not the same pitcher as in years past. He went just 11–14 and had a 4.46 ERA, while the team as a whole was second in the league at 3.77.

Andre Dawson, imported from Chicago after hitting 22 home runs and driving in 90 for the Cubs in 1992, was a disappointment in Boston, hitting just 13 home runs. Still, he tied with Greenwell for the second-most homers on the team behind Vaughn. Boston's meager offense was perhaps best exemplified by catcher Tony Pena, who while never an offensive force, slumped to an unfathomable .181 batting average in 304 at-bats.

Boston moved up to fourth place in 1994, but saw its record fall to 54–61 in the strike-shortened season. While Boggs hit .342 with 11 home runs to lead the Yankees to a first-place finish, Boston ended the year 17 games behind New York. Clemens rebounded to post a 2.85 ERA with 168 strikeouts in 171 innings, Vaughn batted .310 with 26 home runs in just 111 games and Valentin hit .316 with 26 doubles and nine homers. But that was pretty much the extent of the positive contributions for the Red Sox. As a result, Hobson was fired at the end of the season and replaced by Kevin Kennedy.

The strike, which began at midnight on August 11, 1994, canceled the World Series for the first time since the Giants refused to play the A.L. champion Red Sox in 1904. The strike continued through the start of the '95 season, which was shortened to 144 games as a result.

With a cast similar to the '94 campaign and another groin injury for Roger Clemens, it might have seemed unlikely that the Red Sox would stand much of a chance of playing .500 ball. Instead, the Red Sox ran away with the East, going 86–58 and winning the division by seven games over the Yankees, who won the first A.L. Wild Card.

Vaughn was named MVP after hitting .300 with 39 homers and a league-leading 126 RBI. Valentin, solid in '94, had a career year, hitting 27 home runs, driving in 102 and even stealing 20 bases. Jose Canseco, one-half of Oakland's former "Bash Brothers" who defeated the Red Sox in the playoffs in 1988 and '90, hit .306 with 24 round-trippers.

Clemens, again hampered by injury, went just 10–5 with a 4.18 ERA in 23 starts, though he was 7–2 with a 2.88 ERA in August and September. The unexpected ace was Tim Wakefield, who had been signed to a Triple-A contract on April 27 after being released by the pitching-poor Pittsburgh Pirates. The knuckleballer went 16–8 with a 2.95 ERA. He was joined in the rotation by Erik Hanson, who won his first six games and finished the year 15–5. Mid-season acquisition Rick Aguilera saved 20 of 21 opportunities for the BoSox to lead a strong bullpen.

While the Red Sox ran away with the East, their first-round opponents were the Cleveland Indians, who finished the season 100–44. The Indians entered the playoffs with a vaunted offense that led the league in home runs, runs scored, RBI, stolen bases and batting average. While its pitchers were far less heralded, Cleveland also led the A.L. in ERA and saves, thanks to closer Jose Mesa's 46 saves and 1.13 ERA.

If the Red Sox seemed overmatched, they didn't show it in the series opener. The Red Sox led 2–0 through five innings on Valentin's two-run homer, before Cleveland scored three in sixth off Clemens to take the lead. The Red Sox tied the game in the top of the eighth on Luis Alicea's solo shot, and the game went to extra innings.

Tim Naehring homered to give the Red Sox a 4–3 lead in the top of the 11th, but Albert Belle countered off Aguilera to tie the game at 4. Two batters later, Aguilera hurt his left hamstring and had to leave the game. The Red Sox had lots of chances to take the lead, leaving runners in scoring position in five of the final six innings, before former Red Sox catcher Tony Pena hit a two-out homer off Zane Smith at 2:08 a.m.

After the crushing loss, the Red Sox went down quietly in the rest of the series, losing 4–0 and 8–2. The Red Sox hit .184 in the three-game sweep while compiling a 5.16 ERA. Mo Vaughn went 0-for-14 and Canseco 0-for-13 in the series.

Hopes were high for more Red Sox success in 1996, but it was not to be after Boston started the season 2–12. The Red Sox won 85 games, but finished third, seven games behind the Yankees. Offense, especially home runs, exploded throughout baseball in '96, and Boston was no exception. Vaughn dwarfed his MVP numbers of the year before by hitting .326 with 44 home runs and 143 RBI. Canseco hit 28 homers, new catcher Mike Stanley had 24, and part-time designated hitter Reggie Jefferson hit .347 with 19 dingers in only 386 at-bats.

But while the hitters excelled, the pitchers faltered. Clemens was healthy but went just 10–13 despite a 3.63 ERA and a league-leading 257 strikeouts. Wakefield, who had anchored the '95 staff, returned to his ineffective ways, posting a 5.14 ERA. Sadly, that was better than the mark posted by three of the other four starters who began 10 or more games: Tom Gordon (5.59 ERA), Aaron Sele (5.32 ERA) and Vaughn Eshelman (7.08 ERA). Even a seeming success on the mound with 31 saves, closer Heathcliff Slocumb caused more concern than he prevented, walking 55 hitters in 83 innings.

To make matters worse for Boston fans, they had to watch former Boston great Wade Boggs circle Yankee Stadium on the back of a police horse after the despised Yankees won their 23rd World Series—all of them after acquiring Babe Ruth from the BoSox.

Despite taking the team to the playoffs in 1995 and contending for a wild card spot until the final week of the '96 season, manager Kevin Kennedy was fired after the season. General manager Dan Duquette had blamed Kennedy for the bad start to the season, a perceived inability to handle young players and not presenting a united front with the rest of the front office. And Kennedy was just the first to go.

Mike Greenwell, who spent his entire 12-year career playing in front of the Green Monster for the Red Sox, called it quits after the season. He finished with a .303 batting average, 275 doubles, 130 home runs and just 364 strikeouts.

But the big blow was the departure of the Rocket, Roger Clemens. The man who tied Cy Young's club records for wins and shutouts and tied his own major league mark of 20 strikeouts in a game on September 18 against the Detroit Tigers, went to division rival Toronto as a free agent. It would turn out to be a crucial misstep for the Red Sox.

As they did the previous season, the Red Sox were led by two of the league's best hitters. One of them was once again Vaughn, who slumped slightly but was still impressive, hitting .315 with 35 home runs. Despite a defensive shift to third base, Valentin led the league with 47 doubles while hitting .306 and 18 home runs. The real star, however, was a rookie shortstop.

Nomar Garciaparra had come up during the '96 season, but hit just .241 in 24 games. But he came into his own in his rookie season, hitting in an A.L. rookie record 30 consecutive games while finishing the season with a .306 average, 44 doubles and 30 home runs and leading the league in at-bats (684), hits (209), and triples (11). Garciaparra was also a defensive whiz, earning the nickname "Spiderman" for his acrobatic plays in the field.

Once again, however, the pitching staff was a mess. Wakefield tied for a league-worst 15 losses while Sele, who once looked like the heir to Clemens's spot at the top of the rotation, compiled a 5.38 ERA. Where Wade Boggs had made the Red Sox look bad for not re-signing him by winning a World Series with the Yankees, it was now Clemens's turn to embarrass the Boston brass. Clemens won the A.L. Cy Young award for Toronto by leading the league in wins (21), strikeouts (292) and ERA (2.05) while tying teammate Pat Hentgen for the lead in complete games (nine), innings pitched (264), and shutouts (three).

The lone bright spot among the Red Sox staff was in the bullpen where starter Tom Gordon picked up 11 saves after being converted to closer following the trade of Heathcliff Slocumb to Seattle. That trade, however, was one of two deals that would reap huge benefits for the Sox in 1998 and beyond.

In exchange for Slocumb, who was 0–5 with a 5.79 ERA when he was dealt, the Red Sox acquired pitcher Derek Lowe and catching prospect Jason Varitek. While neither did anything noteworthy in '97, both would contribute to the future success of the Red Sox. The other deal was a trading-deadline swap that sent Mike Stanley to the Yankees for reliever Jim Mecir and pitching prospect Tony Armas Jr., the son of the former Red Sox center fielder.

While neither Armas or Mecir ever threw a pitch in the majors for Boston, the trade was significant because in the off-season, general manager Dan Duquette sent Armas and another pitching prospect, Carl Pavano, to the Montreal Expos for the reigning N.L. Cy Young award winner, Pedro Martinez.

Montreal, like Harry Frazee's Red Sox from 1918–23, was in dire financial straits in the mid-1990s despite having some of the game's best players. As a result, after the '94 season the Expos began to trade their established stars like John Wetteland, Larry Walker, Moises Alou, Wil Cordero, Mike Lansing, Marquis Grissom, Ken Hill, Mel Rojas, and Jeff Fassero. Some of them continued their great play outside of Montreal (Walker, Wetteland, Alou) while others faltered (Lansing, Rojas). Still, it was a tragic sight as player after player left Montreal, usually in exchange for minor-league prospects. The last, and likely the best, of the stars to leave in this exodus was Martinez.

The following season was one for prestigious feats in baseball—70 home runs for St. Louis's Mark McGwire and 66 for the Cubs' Sammy Sosa, 114 regular season wins for the Yankees and the end of Cal Ripken Jr.'s consecutive game streak at 2,632. But in Boston, 1998 meant a return to the playoffs.

While the Red Sox never had a shot at winning the Eastern Division, finishing 22 games behind New York, they did win 92 games and their first wild card. Vaughn returned to his old self, hitting .337 with 40 home runs while Garciaparra proved his great rookie season was no fluke by hitting .323 with 35 homers and 122 RBI. The rest of the offense was ordinary, but it was enough to finish third in the A.L. in runs scored.

Martinez was exceptional, going 19–7 with a 2.89 ERA and 251 strikeouts, but he lost out on the Cy Young award to Clemens, who won his second straight for third-place Toronto by going 20–6 and leading the league with a 2.65 ERA and 271 strikeouts. Tim Wakefield rebounded from two poor seasons to go 17–8 and Bret Saberhagen went 15–8. Tom Gordon, in his first full season as closer, set a major league record with 43 consecutive saves on his way to a club record 46.

Unfortunately for the Red Sox, they again faced Cleveland in the Division Series. While the Indians had many of the same players they did in '95, this team was not nearly as imposing as the previous incarnation. Still, Cleveland had advanced to the 1997 World Series and had made the playoffs every year since the '94 strike.

Behind Martinez in Game One, the Red Sox jumped out to a 3–0 lead after the top of the first and never looked back, taking the game 11–3. While Martinez pitched very well, Vaughn was the star of the game with two home runs and seven RBI. In fact, the only two BoSox to drive in runs were Vaughn and Garciaparra. The win was the Boston's first postseason victory since Game Five of the 1986 World Series.

Game Two also got off to a good start for Boston when the Red Sox jumped out to a 2–0 lead at Cleveland's Jacobs Field as both Indians manager Mike Hargrove and pitcher Doc Gooden were ejected. But Cleveland answered with one in the bottom of the first and five more in the bottom of the second to chase Wakefield and take a commanding 6–2 lead. The teams added a few more runs before Cleveland held on for a 9–5 win to even the series.

Once again the Red Sox scored first, pushing home a run in the bottom of the fourth of Game Three. Cleveland answered with four solo shots, once each in the fifth, sixth, seventh and ninth innings to take a 4–1 lead. The Red Sox started to rally behind a two-run home run by Garciaparra in the bottom of the ninth, but that was all the Red Sox could muster and they fell, 4–3.

As they did in every game of the series, Boston scored the first run in Game Four, on Garciaparra's third home run of the series in the fourth. Pete Schourek and Derek Lowe held the Indians scoreless, before Tom Gordon relieved in the eighth and surrendered a two-run double to David Justice. Mike Jackson closed out the game for the Tribe and the Red Sox had lost their fifth straight playoff series, dating back to the 1986 World Series.

Boston had just 12 hits in the last two games of the series, and while the top four hitters in the lineup batted .387 against Cleveland, the bottom five hit a meager .137.

The off-season was not kind to the Red Sox. Mo Vaughn, the slugger who had hit .304 with 230 home runs—the fifth highest total in club history—since coming up with the club in 1991, left to sign a six-year, $80 million contract with the Anaheim Angels. Matters got worse when Tom Gordon was lost for the season with an elbow injury early in the '99 season.

But somehow, with manager Jimy Williams juggling his starting lineup and rotation, the Red Sox led their division from May 18 through June 8, were in first or second from May 15 through July 24 and in second from August 13 through the end of the season, on their way to a 94-win season and the A.L. Wild Card, marking the first time since 1915–16 that the Red Sox had made the post-season in consecutive seasons.

In reality, this was a two-star team where everyone else played a supporting role. Martinez won his first American League Cy Young with an amazing 23–4 season. He dominated the league, winning the ERA crown with a 2.07 mark while the runner-up, David Cone of the Yankees, was at 3.44. He also struck out 313 batters, becoming the first A.L. pitcher to strike out that many since Nolan Ryan had 341 in 1977. And he did so while walking a mere 37 in 213 innings. Only one other Boston pitcher picked up 10 wins, and that was Bret Saberhagen who pitched well when he wasn't on the disabled list.

The rest of the rotation was a disaster compiled of journeymen like Mark Portugal (7–12, 5.51) and Pat Rapp (6–7, 4.12) and young-sters like Brian Rose (7–6, 4.87) and Jin Ho Cho (2–3, 5.72). Wake-field also made 17 starts before splitting closing duties with Derek Lowe, where each picked up 15 saves. Despite the lack of depth in the rotation, Boston still managed to lead the league with a 4.00 ERA.

With Vaughn gone, most of the offensive burden fell on Garcia-parra. He answered by hitting an A.L.-best .357 with 42 doubles and 27 home runs while striking out just 39 times. Five other players hit at least 15 homers for the BoSox and free agent acquisition Jose Offer-man was a great table-setter, batting .294 with 96 walks, 37 doubles and 11 triples out of the leadoff spot.

The Red Sox made the playoffs, only to find out they had to face their recent nemesis once again—the Cleveland Indians. Game One started out like many of the previous season's games, with a Nomar Garciaparra home run to give Boston a 1–0 lead. The Red Sox added a run in the top of the fourth before disaster struck. In the bottom of the inning, Red Sox ace hurler Pedro Martinez left the game with a pulled muscle in his upper back. A throwing error was followed by a two-run homer by Jim Thome to tie the game at 2-all in the sixth. The game remained knotted until the bottom of the ninth when Cleveland loaded the bases and Travis Fryman singled off Rich Garces for the Cleveland win.

While Boston scored first for the fifth straight time in the playoffs with a run in the top of the third of Game Two, Cleveland responded with six runs in the bottom of the inning and another five in the bottom of the fourth to put the game out of reach. The 10-run deficit in the 11–1 final is still the worst defeat in Red Sox post-season history.

Down two games to none, the series moved to Fenway. Pedro's older brother Ramon Martinez, who had made just four starts for the Red Sox after spending most of the season rehabbing his surgically repaired shoulder, got the start. To make the situation even worse, the Red Sox learned before the game that Nomar Garciaparra wouldn't be able to play because of a sore wrist.

Cleveland scored first this time, with a run in the top of the fourth, but Boston plated two in the fifth and Cleveland scored one in the sixth to tie the game at 2. Ramon Martinez left after 5⅔ innings, allowing just two runs and five hits to keep Boston in the game.

John Valentin, who had made a crucial error in Game One, homered in the sixth to give the Red Sox a 3–2 lead. Cleveland once again countered to tie the game at 3 in the top of the seventh. But in the turning point of the series, Boston rallied in the bottom of the inning with a two-run double by Valentin and a three-run homer by Brian Daubach to take a 9–3 lead. Derek Lowe pitched the final 2⅓ innings for the 9–3 win.

Garciaparra was back for Game Four, though for once, the Red Sox didn't really need him. The club set six post-season records, including most runs and most hits, in winning 23–7. The Red Sox scored two or more runs in every inning but the sixth (when they failed to score) including 18 runs in the first five innings. Valentin continued his torrid streak by hitting two home runs and driving in seven. His 11 total bases also set a Division Series record. Mike Stanley tied a record with five hits and Jason Varitek set one with five runs scored.

With the series tied at two games apiece, it all came down to Game Five in Cleveland; Bret Saberhagen against Charles Nagy. When they had met in Game Two, Saberhagen had allowed six runs in 2⅔ innings in Cleveland's 11–1 victory.

Boston got off to a better start this time, scoring first on Garciaparra's two-run homer in the top of the first. Cleveland pushed home three against Saberhagen in the bottom of the first, and then chased him from the game with two more in the bottom of the second. For the series, Boston's number two pitcher allowed 11 runs in 3⅔ innings.

Derek Lowe replaced Saberhagen and was the beneficiary of Boston's five-run third, highlighted by Troy O'Leary's pinch-hit grand slam. But Lowe surrendered an RBI-double to Manny Ramirez and Jim Thome's second two-run homer of the game in the bottom of the inning as Cleveland took an 8–7 lead. John Valentin's sacrifice fly in the top of the fourth knotted the game at 8.

But more important than what was going on in play was what was going on in the bullpen. As the Red Sox batted in the fourth, ace Pedro Martinez, sidelined since the fourth inning of Game One, was warming up. Martinez came in to relieve Lowe to start the bottom of the fourth, and for the next six innings, Cleveland couldn't manage a single hit off the game's best pitcher. While Martinez held Cleveland at bay, O'Leary hit a three-run homer to go with his earlier grand slam and Boston added another run in the ninth for a 12–8 victory and an improbable come-from-behind 3–2 series win.

With the win over Cleveland, who had beaten them in their past two playoff appearances, the Red Sox had exorcised one demon. But a bigger one lay ahead. The New York Yankees, winners of the 1996 and '98 World Series, had swept Texas to set up the first playoff meeting between these heated rivals.

To further heighten the stakes, Roger Clemens had been traded to the Yankees after two seasons in Toronto. Though he had a lackluster first year in pinstripes, the chance to beat the Yankees and their old ace at the same time was the opportunity of a lifetime for the Sox.

However, not just were the Sox the underdogs in the best-of-seven LCS, but because Martinez had pitched six innings on October 11, he wasn't available until the third game against New York. The well-rested Yankees, meanwhile, had three days off between their games to set their rotation. Thus, the Yankees were able to start Orlando Hernandez (17–9, 4.12) and David Cone (12–9, 3.44) in the first two games, while Boston had to counter with Kent Mercker (acquired late in the season from St. Louis) and Ramon Martinez. Boston's duo had made a combined total of nine starts for the Red Sox during the regular season.

Still, Boston jumped to a 2–0 lead in the first inning in Game One, and increased their lead to 3–0 an inning later. A two-run home run by Yankees third baseman Scott Brosius cut the lead to 3–2. The score remained the same until Derek Jeter's RBI-single off Derek Lowe tied the game in the bottom of the seventh.

The game stayed tied and went into extra innings. Jose Offerman started the 10th with a single. John Valentin grounded into a force play, though replays appeared to show that Yankees second baseman Chuck Knoblauch did not have control of the ball and Offerman should have been safe at second. A double-play grounder off the bat of Brian Daubach ended the inning.

And as quickly as the Boston rally had been snuffed out, the game was over when Bernie Williams hit the second pitch from Rod Beck over the center field wall for a walk-off homer and a 4–3 win.

Game Two was also a nail-biter. Tino Martinez's solo home run in the fourth gave the Yankees a short-lived 1–0 lead. Garciaparra's two-run homer in the top of the fifth gave the Red Sox a 2–1 cushion. The Yankees took the lead back in the bottom of the seventh with two runs. The Sox loaded the bases with one out in the eighth, but Butch Huskey struck out and Jose Offerman flied out to end the threat.

In their final at-bat the Red Sox got back-to-back two-out singles to put runners on first and third, but Yankees closer Mariano Rivera struck out Damon Buford to seal the 3–2 win.

Game Three in Boston was the game everyone had been waiting for: Two-time Cy Young award winner Pedro Martinez versus five-time winner and ex-Red Sox ace Roger Clemens. The anticipated pitching duel never materialized. Martinez did his part, holding the Yankees to two hits, two walks and no runs with 12 strikeouts over seven innings. But Clemens was awful, allowing five runs in two-plus innings. The Red Sox scored two runs in each of the first three innings, two more in the fifth, one in the sixth and four in the seventh for a 13–0 lead. The Yankees did manage a run in the eighth, but that was all, as Boston picked up its first playoff victory against New York. It also marked the worst post-season defeat in Yankees history.

Game Four was an ugly game for the Red Sox and their fans. Boston had a 2–1 lead going into the top of the fourth when the Yankees regained the lead, 3–2, with help from errors by Garciaparra and Saberhagen.

In the bottom of the eighth, Offerman singled with one out. Valentin grounded to Knoblauch at second base. Knoblauch tagged Offerman and threw to first for the inning-ending double play. However, replays showed that Knoblauch had missed the tag, and Boston should have had a runner at second with two outs. Instead the inning was over and the game moved to the top of the ninth.

Just like they did in Game One, the Yankees attacked after the questionable call went their way, scoring six runs, helped by two more Boston errors and a pinch-hit grand slam by Ricky Ledee.

Down 9–2, Garciaparra led off the ninth against Mariano Rivera and was called out on a close play at first. Manager Jimy Williams, upset over a number of calls throughout the series, came out to argue and was ejected. Some fans reacted to the ejection by throwing debris onto the field, and the game was suspended for several minutes. When the game resumed, the Red Sox put a couple runners on, but failed to score.

The Yankees started Game Five with Derek Jeter's two-run home run and added two more in the seventh. Jason Varitek homered in the eighth to end Orlando Hernandez' shutout bid, and Garciaparra chased Hernandez with a double. The Red Sox loaded the bases with one out, but Scott Hatteberg struck out and Trot Nixon popped up to end the inning. Jorge Posada hit a two-run homer off Tom Gordon in the ninth and Ramiro Mendoza retired Boston in order for a final 6–1 win. While that marked the end of Boston's season, the Yankees went on to win their third World Series in four years.

After getting very little production from center fielder Darren Lewis in 1999, the Red Sox made the first Everett-for-Everett trade in baseball history, sending shortstop prospect Adam to Houston for center fielder Carl. A great offensive player, Carl Everett was a dominant force for the Red Sox in 2000, batting .300 and leading the team with 34 home runs, 108 RBI and 11 stolen bases. However, Everett was also known for causing trouble, a reputation he further cemented in 2000. During the season, he had a clubhouse shouting match with a newspaper columnist, was suspended by the league for 10 games after bumping and "beaking" a home plate umpire with the bill of his cap, nearly came to blows with teammate Darren Lewis and got into a heated argument with manager Jimy Williams. In a feud that would continue into the following season, Everett was heard to say about Williams, "I never liked him anyway."

Despite the personality problems, Everett made the most of hitting just in front of or just behind the A.L.'s leading hitter, Nomar Garciaparra. The All-Star shortstop batted .372, becoming the first right-handed hitter in the American League to win consecutive batting titles since Joe DiMaggio in 1939–40. Garciaparra also finished in the top ten in eight other offensive categories.

While Everett and Garciaparra excelled, the rest of the offense sputtered. John Valentin blew out his knee and was lost for the season after just 35 at-bats. Jose Offerman slumped to .255 with only 14 doubles while outfielder Troy O'Leary went from 28 home runs in '99 to 13. First baseman Brian Daubach's batting average declined from .294 to .248 and catcher Jason Varitek saw his production decrease from .269 and 20 homers in 1999 to .248 with 10 home runs. General manager Dan Duquette tried to bring in help throughout the year, acquiring players like Dante Bichette, Mike Lansing, Rico Brogna, Sean Berry, Bernard Gilkey, Ed Sprague, and Midre Cummings, but none of them contributed much except further bloating Boston's already excessive payroll.

The Red Sox managed to win because along with Garciaparra and Everett, they still had Pedro Martinez and a good bullpen. Martinez captured his second straight Cy Young award with an 18–6 campaign, leading the league in ERA at 1.74. Once again, that mark dwarfed the ERA crown runner-up, a 3.70 mark for Roger Clemens. Martinez' other numbers were similarly awe-inspiring: a league-leading 284 strikeouts against 32 walks, only 128 hits allowed in 217 innings, seven complete games and four shutouts. No other A.L. pitcher had more than one.

The rest of the rotation, however, was a disaster. The always-fragile Bret Saberhagen missed the season after having shoulder surgery and promising youngster Juan Pena missed the year after an operation on his elbow in April. Ramon Martinez, who had given Boston hope with great appearances in the playoffs in 1999, had a respectable 10–8 record but an unsightly 6.13 ERA and also spent time on the disabled list with a knee injury. A couple of veteran left-handers, Pete Schourek (3–10, 5.11) and Jeff Fassero (8–8, 4.78) didn't fare too well. Neither did the hot-and-cold Tim Wakefield (6–10, 5.48). Young right-hander Brian Rose was dreadful (3–5, 6.11) before being dealt to Colorado in the deal to acquire Lansing and right-handed pitcher Rolando Arrojo, who was 5–2 with a 5.05 ERA in 13 late-season starts. Only Tomo Ohka showed any promise, compiling a 3.12 ERA in 13 games (12 starts) despite a 3–6 record.

Boston's salvation was its bullpen. While Tom Gordon was lost for the year with the same elbow injury that had sidelined him for most of 1999, Derek Lowe stepped into the closer's role and tied for the league lead with 42 saves. He was joined by a solid supporting cast, including Rich "El Guapo" Garces, former National League closer Rod Beck, left-hander Rheal Cormier and right-handed set-up men Hipolito Pichardo and Bryce Florie.

Boston managed to stay in the playoff hunt though for most of the year, even leading the A.L. East for the latter half of May and a few days in June. But a three-game sweep by New York from September 8–10 left them nine games back in the division. A late-season slump by the Yankees allowed Boston to close the gap, though the Red Sox were eventually eliminated from the wild card chase on Sept. 27 and the Eastern Division race on Sept. 29. And while the Red Sox watched the playoffs at home, the Yankees won their 26th World Championship.

The next 12 months were a roller-coaster ride for the Red Sox—high points separated by extreme lows that started to derail the team, all of which went on hiatus for six days in September when sports took a back seat to national tragedy.

The period started out on a high note when the Red Sox, desperate for a third big bat in their lineup to join Everett and Garciaparra, broke open the bank and signed one of the game's premier hitters, out-fielder Manny Ramirez, to an eight-year, $160 million contract. While his defense and base-running abilities left a lot to be desired, Ramirez was an outstanding offensive player. In the three years before joining the BoSox, the right-handed Ramirez had hit .324 with 127 home runs and an astounding 432 RBI in just 415 games in Cleveland.

While the Red Sox lost out on the top free agent pitchers available on the market, they did pick up a number of second-tier starters rather cheaply in Frank Castillo, Hideo Nomo and David Cone. The Sox hoped that those three, combined with the dominance of Pedro Martinez, would give Boston a strong enough rotation to match up with the rest of the league.

But those plans went awry before the season even began. All-star shortstop Nomar Garciaparra, who had first hurt his wrist when he was hit by a pitch by Baltimore's Al Reyes on Sept. 25, 1999, had the wrist swell up on him in spring training to the point where he couldn't throw a ball or swing a bat. While there was hope at first that rest would take care of the problem, it was not to be, and Garciaparra underwent surgery on opening day. He did not return to Boston's lineup until July 29.

Despite that devastating blow, the Red Sox, under manager Jimy Williams, played well in Nomar's absence, even without a quality shortstop to take his place. In fact, Boston took over first place in the East Division on May 31, and held the lead until July 3.

While Garciaparra was one of the trinity of great shortstops in the American League, Pedro Martinez had no equal. The winner of the A.L.'s last two Cy Young awards and perhaps the game's most domi-nant pitcher, Martinez went on the disabled list on June 26 with inflammation of his right rotator cuff. Martinez was again leading the race for another Cy Young award before his injury, going 7–2 with a 2.26 ERA and 150 strikeouts in 103⅔ innings.

While Martinez and Garciaparra were the biggest names to hit the disabled list in 2001, they were not the only ones. Some of the others who were out for at least a month were outfielder Carl Everett, catcher Jason Varitek, third basemen John Valentin and Chris Stynes and starting pitchers Bret Saberhagen, David Cone, and Frank Castillo.

Even with Garciaparra back for part of the time and a trading deadline deal for Montreal closer Ugueth Urbina, the Red Sox went 14–17 after the All-Star break and manager Jimy Williams was fired on August 16. Williams, despite leading Boston to consecutive playoff appearances and being named Manager of the Year in 1999, was not popular in Boston. He feuded openly with general manager Dan Duquette and center fielder Carl Everett. He juggled his batting order constantly, rarely using the same lineup twice, upsetting many of the veteran hitters. And he was not a media darling, often answering questions with the same two words: "Manager's decision."

Pitching coach Joe Kerrigan, with no managing experience on any level, was signed to a two-year deal to replace Williams after former Montreal skipper Felipe Alou turned down an offer to manage the BoSox. And once again, things started to look up for the Red Sox. The team won Kerrigan's first game as skipper, and went on a 6–3 run to move within three games of the East-leading Yankees on August 24. And more importantly, Pedro was coming back in just two days, making his first start in two months.

But it was not to be. The Red Sox lost in 18 innings the day before Pedro started, and then suffered a 5–4 defeat at Texas in his return. Martinez looked rusty, but nobody could know how bad things would get the rest of the way.

The loss to Texas was the start of a stretch in which Boston lost 13 of 14, including all six to the Yankees, dropping them 13 games behind New York and 13.5 behind Oakland in the wild card race, effectively ending any playoff aspirations for the team. The Red Sox finished the year 82–79, going a miserable 17–26 under Kerrigan.

While losing was bad, the turmoil in the clubhouse suggested more dangerous long-term ramifications.

One problem was with Martinez. Though he was brilliant, but not overpowering, in pitching six shutout innings against the Yankees in Boston on September 1, he was hurting. He came out of the game after throwing 87 pitches, leaving the Boston bullpen to turn the 1–0 lead into a 2–1 loss. After the game, Duquette questioned why Martinez came out of the game, which Pedro did not take kindly to.

Then after lasting only three innings against the Yankees in New York on September 7, Martinez suggested that he should be shut down for the rest of the season, to ensure his health for 2002. This came after Duquette was quoted as saying that the team was not going to do so and that "we're paying him a lot of money to pitch." The back-and-forth went on for a while, before it was announced that Martinez wouldn't pitch again unless the Red Sox re-entered the play-off race, a very unlikely scenario. Finally, Martinez caused some ripples when he flew home to the Dominican Republic with 17 games remaining in the season. Martinez was the only injured player allowed to return home. Others were with the team in Boston or at the team's training facility in Ft. Myers, Florida. While no Red Sox player criticized the decision, it certainly didn't help to further camaraderie on an already splintered team.

But that wasn't the end of the chaos in Boston. In the middle of the team's slide came a three-game sweep by the Yankees at Fenway, even though BoSox starters held New York to just 10 hits and no earned runs in 21⅓ innings. But minutes after the final game of the series, in which the team was one strike away from being on the wrong end of Mike Mussina's attempt at a perfect game, Duquette fired Kerrigan's unofficial replacement as pitching coach, John Cumberland, who had been with the organization since 1995.

The clubhouse exploded when informed of the move, the most critical comment coming from the team's offensive superstar, Nomar Garciaparra, who shouted to no one in particular "This is why no one wants to (expletive) play here."

The only thing that stopped the losing streak and the season from turning into an even bigger disaster was an actual disaster of historic proportions.

On September 11, four planes were hijacked and used as airborne bombs. Two, both of which had departed from Boston's Logan Airport, were crashed into the World Trade Center in New York. A third was crashed into the Pentagon in Washington, and the fourth, while aiming for a different target, crashed in rural Pennsylvania. As part of the Pentagon burned and the Twin Towers collapsed, baseball was insignificant. The season stopped while the nation mourned. As Kerrigan said: "The losses we had [before last week] really doesn't mean a hill of beans. It was really brought into perspective in a big way that it is just a game."

After six days off, baseball resumed, with the postponed games rescheduled for the end of the season. While most players focused on the national tragedy, Carl Everett focused on himself. Everett was fined for coming late to a team workout, at which point he erupted, cursing out manager Joe Kerrigan in front of the team. He was suspended for four games the next day, and ended up missing the rest of the season with knee problems.

The rest of the season for the Red Sox, however, was academic. Already out of the playoff race, the team played out the string, preparing for a winter of change.

Over the next few months, the entire hierarchy of the Boston Red Sox changed—the owners, the general manager, and the manager. The Yawkey Trust, which had been the majority owner of the team since 1987, sold the team, the stadium, and 80 percent ownership of NESN (New England Sports Network) to a group led by John Henry, Tom Werner, and Larry Lucchino for a reported $660 million and $40 million in assumed debt on December 20. Henry had been a limited partner of the Yankees and then the principal owner of the Florida Marlins from 1999 through 2001. Werner owned the San Diego Padres from 1990–94, selling the team to John Moores and Lucchino, who served as the team's CEO from 1995–2001.

The sale closed on February 27, 2002, and the next day, they replaced Dan Duquette with interim general manager Mike Port. While Duquette made some astute moves during his tenure, namely drafting Nomar Garciaparra and trading for Pedro Martinez, many of his other moves flopped and his handling of situations with Carl Everett, Jimy Williams, and John Cumberland was inept.

It took until only March 11 for the Red Sox to get a new manager as well, when Kerrigan was replaced by Grady Little. Though it didn't necessarily attract as much attention at the time, the biggest front office addition may have been the new assistant general manager, Theo Epstein, a Yale grad who had grown up in Brookline, just one mile away from Fenway Park.

The team that took the field in 2002 looked different, too. Helping the club to 93 wins, an improvement of 11 games from 2001, wasn't a new acquisition, it was moving Derek Lowe from the closer's role back to the starting rotation, where he went 21–8 with a 2.58 ERA and threw a no-hitter against Tampa Bay on April 27. Martinez joined Lowe in the 20-win club, going 20–4 with a 2.26 ERA and 239 strikeouts in just under 200 innings. Ugueth Urbina filled the closer's role admirably, saving 40 games.

A healthy Nomar Garciaparra contributed 56 doubles, 24 home runs, 120 RBI, and a .310 batting average. Manny Ramirez continued to be a force at the plate, hitting for a little less power (33 home runs in 2002 after 44 in 2001) but for a higher average (a league-leading .349 in 2002 compared with .306 in 2001). Johnny Damon was imported from Oakland to be the new center fielder and leadoff hitter, and he responded by scoring 118 runs and stealing 31 bases.

Boston got solid contributions from SP-RP Tim Wakefield (11–5, 2.81), SP-RP Casey Fossum (5–4, 3.46 in 106 ⅔ innings), SP John Burkett (13–8), RF Trot Nixon (24 home runs and 94 RBI), 3B Shea Hillenbrand (.293, 43 doubles, and 18 home runs), and 1B-DH Brian Daubach (20 home runs). However, the rest of the team didn't have much to add. In 36 games (23 of them starts) Frank Castillo went 6–15 with a 5.07 ERA. The popular reliever Rich Garces had a 7.59 ERA in 26 games before calling it quits. First baseman Tony Clark hit a meager .207 in 275 at-bats, and Rey Sanchez, starting at second base, had just 16 extra-base hits and 17 walks in 357 at-bats.

While the Red Sox stayed in the wild card race for a while, they eventually lost out to the Anaheim Angels, who went on to win the World Series over the San Francisco Giants.

The biggest loss for Boston wasn't on the field in 2002; it was the death of Ted Williams, the club's greatest hitter, on July 5. An embarrassing series of events took place after the Splendid Splinter's death as his son and daughter had Williams' body cryogenically frozen while their half-sister claimed Williams had wanted to be cremated. According to a Sports Illustrated report in 2003, Williams' head sat on a shelf in an Arizona cryogenics lab in a liquid nitrogen–filled, steel can while his body was in the same room, stored upright in a liquid nitrogen–filled, nine-foot-tall cylindrical steel tank. His son, John Henry Williams, died at the age of thirty-five in 2004 and was taken to the same facility to be cryogenically frozen alongside his father.

While the club conducted its search for a new general manager to replace the interim Port, it named well-known baseball statistician and author Bill James senior baseball operations advisor. Then, on November 25, the club promoted Epstein to general manager. At just twenty-eight years of age, Epstein was the youngest general manager in major-league history. He wasted no time in remaking the club in what was becoming known as the "Moneyball" image.

In 2003, author Michael Lewis published his book *Moneyball: The Art of Winning an Unfair Game*. The book looked at the Oakland A's and the logic their general manager, Billy Beane, used to construct his club. It consisted of an emphasis on statistics and past performance over athletic ability and untapped potential. Beane also highlighted that the key offensive statistic, in his estimation, was on-base percentage, followed by slugging average. Almost overnight, baseball was divided into "Moneyball" teams like the A's, the Toronto Blue Jays (where general manager J. P. Riccardi had once worked for Beane), and now, the Red Sox.

Out were players who didn't take walks or hit for extra bases, like Rey Sanchez and Tony Clark, who were let go. Brian Daubach, who hit 84 home runs in four seasons, was also allowed to walk. In their place Epstein signed second baseman Todd Walker, third baseman Bill Mueller, and designated hitter David Ortiz. All had the ability to take pitches and hit for extra bases, though none was as successful prior to joining the Red Sox as they would be in Boston. In a bizarre case, Epstein also added Kevin Millar, a blue-collar first baseman and outfielder, to the mix after he had already been released by the Florida Marlins and signed a contract to play in Japan.

Boston also pursued Cuban defector Jose Contreras, the starter who had pitched so well and struck out ten against the Baltimore Orioles in an exhibition game in Cuba in 1999. After the Red Sox lost Contreras to the Yankees (for four years and $32 million) team president Larry Lucchino blasted the Yankees, saying to *The New York Times*: "The evil empire extends its tentacles even into Latin America."

After losing out on Contreras, the pitching staff remained largely the same with one major change: closer Ugueth Urbina was allowed to leave, and was replaced by one of Bill James' ideas, a closer-by-committee approach. Under this theory, the ninth inning, when traditional closers were often used, was not always the highest leverage point in the game. Instead, James argued, the best reliever should be used for the most important outs, whether they occur in the sixth, seventh, eighth, or ninth inning. As a result, there was little need to overpay for saves; a team should instead fill its bullpen with quality relievers to go around. Ramiro Mendoza, a sinkerball pitcher imported from the Yankees via free agency, struggled with a 6.75 ERA in 33 games. Mike Timlin pitched well, and Alan Embree and Brandon Lyon were decent, but it was not enough.

On May 29, with Mueller hitting the ball well while playing third base, the Red Sox dealt fan favorite Shea Hillenbrand to Arizona for pitcher Byung-Hyun Kim, the Korean submariner who had blown successive World Series saves for the Arizona Diamondbacks at Yankee Stadium in 2001. Kim went on to save 18 games for Boston.

While the bullpen had its troubles, the starting pitching offered little relief. Martinez was his usual dominant self, with a league-leading 2.22 ERA, though he missed almost a month with a strained muscle in his side. The rest of the rotation was average, at best. Knuckleballer Tim Wakefield, pitching almost exclusively as a starter for the first time with Boston, went 11–7 with a 4.09 ERA. Derek Lowe, coming off such a strong 2002 campaign, won 17 games but had a 4.49 ERA. A sinkerball pitcher who relied on his defense, Lowe may have been hurt by the decline in Boston's infield defense on the right side, where above-average defenders Sanchez and Clark were replaced by below-average defenders Todd Walker and Kevin Millar, respectively.

Rounding out the rotation were John Burkett, who was disappointing again with a 5.15 ERA in 32 starts, and Casey Fossum, who could not match his prior year's success, going 6–5 with a 5.47 ERA in an injury-plagued year.

Despite the pitching problems, a strong offense carried the Red Sox, and on June 11 they were in first place, a half-game up on the New York Yankees. But as they dropped back into second place, Epstein went to work to shore up the team's pitching. Before the trading deadline he brought in three new relievers: Todd Jones via free agency, Scott Sauerbeck in a trade with Pittsburgh, and Scott Williamson in a deal with Cincinnati. On July 30, he also acquired ex-Boston starter Jeff Suppan from Pittsburgh.

Despite the effort, none of the new acquisitions pitched well for the Red Sox during the regular season and only Williamson had a positive impact in the postseason. Suppan went 3–4 with a 5.57 ERA in 11 starts and was left off the postseason roster. Jones had a 5.52 ERA, which was better than Williamson's 6.20 and Sauerbeck's 6.48.

Despite the poor pitching and second-place finish, six games behind the Yankees, Boston rode its MLB-leading offense to 95 wins and the wild card, clinching a spot with a 14–3 win over Baltimore on September 25 at Fenway Park. All told, the Red Sox led the majors in batting average (.289), runs (961), hits (1,667), doubles (371), extra-base hits (649, a new major-league record), total bases (2,832, a new major-league record), and most importantly to its new hierarchy, on-base percentage (.360) and slugging (.491, replacing the 1927 Yankees in the record book). They finished second in the majors with 238 home runs, as every starter had 12 or more home runs and six players had 25 or more. In addition, Bill Mueller won the A.L. batting crown with a .326 average and added 45 doubles.

Boston squared off against the original "Moneyball" team in the Division Series, facing the A.L. West champion Oakland Athletics. The Red Sox lost a heartbreaker in the opener. A solo shot by Todd Walker put Boston up 1–0 in the top of the first, but Martinez allowed three runs in the third to go down 3–1. The Sox rallied behind a solo shot from Jason Varitek and Walker's second home run of the game, this one a two-out, two-run shot in the seventh to give Boston a 4–3 lead. The bullpen failed once again, however, as Erubiel Durazo hit a game-tying single off Alan Embree with two outs in the bottom of the ninth. Boston squandered chances in the eleventh and twelfth innings, leaving two men on in each frame, before Oakland won the game with a surprise bases-loaded bunt single off Derek Lowe in the twelfth by Oakland catcher Ramon Hernandez.

The second game was less climactic, but the result was the same as Boston fell behind 2–0 in the series on Oakland's 5–1 win. Heading back east, the Red Sox were down 2–0 in the best-of-five series and the A's had already won games against Boston's best two starting pitchers.

Game Three was another extra-inning thriller, as the teams were knotted at one run apiece after regulation. The sloppy game (there were five errors between the two teams) ended when pinch-hitter Trot Nixon took a Rich Harden pitch into the center-field bleachers for a two-run, walk-off home run. Mike Timlin (3 innings) and Scott Williamson (1 inning and the win) had kept Boston in the game with four innings of perfect relief.

The Red Sox caught a break in Game Four when Oakland starter Tim Hudson left after one inning with a pulled muscle in his side. The game went back-and-forth until David Ortiz snapped an 0-for-16 skid, hitting a 3–2 pitch for a two-run, two-out double off Oakland closer Keith Foulke to give the Red Sox a 5–4 lead. The much-maligned Boston bullpen was brilliant for the second straight day, as Tim Wakefield and Williamson pitched 1-2-3 scoreless innings.

Game Five was back in Oakland, where Boston had lost the first two games of the series. It was also a match-up of Cy Young award winners: Pedro Martinez for Boston (1997 with Montreal, '99, and 2000) and Barry Zito for Oakland (2002). Oakland got on the board first on a Jose Guillen double in the fourth that made it 1–0. That score lasted until the sixth, when the Red Sox exploded for four runs. Jason Varitek led off the inning with a home run, and after a walk, foul out, and hit-by-pitch, Manny Ramirez blasted a three-run homer to make it 4–1. Oakland got a run back in the bottom of the inning and Martinez got out of the seventh with a 4–2 lead when Garcia-parra alertly threw Jermaine Dye out at second base after Damon and second baseman Damian Jackson had collided on Dye's short pop-up.

A leadoff double and single made the game 4–3 in the bottom of the eighth with none out, and Embree relieved Martinez and got the next two batters before Mike Timlin got the final out of the inning. Williamson came in to start the bottom of the ninth but walked the first two batters he faced, and Derek Lowe came in to replace him. A sacrifice moved runners to second and third, and then a strikeout and a walk loaded the bases with two out. But Lowe came through, strik-ing out pinch-hitter Terrence Long looking with a cut fastball on the inside corner to end the game and send the Red Sox to the ALCS against the New York Yankees.

Boston got off to a good start in the first game at Yankee Stadium, winning 5–2 behind Tim Wakefield and home runs from Ortiz, Walker, and Ramirez. The hero of the ALDS, Derek Lowe, didn't fare well in the second game, allowing six runs in 6⅔ innings as the Yan-kees evened the series with a 6–2 win.

Ramirez hit a two-run shot off Roger Clemens to give Boston a 2–0 lead in the first inning of Game Three, but Clemens retired thirteen of the next fourteen batters, while the Yankees built a 4–2 lead against Martinez. Boston scored once in the seventh, but Mariano Rivera was perfect over the last two innings to seal the game for New York.

Unfortunately, the story after the game had less to do with the score than the altercations that took place during the game. With runners on second and third, nobody out, one run already in, and left-handed hitter Karim Garcia at the plate, Martinez hit Garcia in the back. The players exchanged words, and on the next play, Garcia slid hard into second base attempting to break up a double play.

In the bottom of the inning, Roger Clemens threw a high fastball over the plate that Ramirez took exception to. Ramirez took a few steps towards Clemens, and the benches emptied. The 13-minute melee included 72-year-old Yankees bench coach and ex-Sox manager Don Zimmer running at Martinez, who grabbed Zimmer by the head and threw him to the ground.

Things got even weirder in the ninth inning when Yankees reliever Jeff Nelson and right fielder Garcia got into a fight with a Red Sox employee in the visitor's bullpen. Garcia was hurt in the altercation and had to be removed from the game.

After a rainout on Sunday, Boston evened the series at two behind another masterful game by Wakefield, who allowed just one run in seven innings. Walker put the Sox ahead 1–0 with his second home run of the series (and fifth of the postseason) and Williamson struck out the side in ninth, despite also allowing a solo homer to Ruben Sierra, to preserve the 3–2 win.

Lowe faltered again in the ALCS in Game Five, allowing three runs in the second inning, and the Yankees held on for a 4–2 win. Back in New York, the Red Sox once again evened the series in a slugfest, outlasting the Yankees 9–6 in a game that featured 28 hits, 4 home runs, and 11 pitchers between the two clubs. Nomar Garciaparra busted out of his series-long slump with four hits as the Sox battered Jose Contreras, the pitcher Boston coveted before the season, for three runs in the top of the seventh inning. Five Boston relievers held the Yankees to just one run over the final 5⅓ innings, including Williamson who was perfect in the ninth inning to earn his third ALCS save.

The final game of the series once again matched up the winners of the AL Cy Young Award every year from 1997–2001: Clemens in 1997, '98, and 2001, and Martinez in 1999 and 2000. Boston took a quick lead in this one, scoring three in the second and knocking Clemens out in the fourth with another run, making it 4–0. The Yankees picked up single runs in the fifth and seventh (when Martinez escaped further damage by fanning Alfonso Soriano with two out and two on) and the Red Sox made it 5–2 on Ortiz's solo shot in the eighth.

Derek Jeter doubled with one out in the eighth and Bernie Williams singled him home to make it 5–3. With lefty Alan Embree ready to go in the bullpen, left-handed hitter Hideki Matsui up for the Yankees, and Martinez already having thrown 115 pitches, it was expected that manager Grady Little's trip to the mound was to remove Martinez. But Little surprised everyone and left Martinez in, who then proceeded to surrender a ground-rule double to Matsui. Little stayed in the dugout as switch-hitting Jorge Posada blooped a double into center, scoring both runners and tying the game at 5. That was enough for Little, who finally removed Martinez.

Boston put a runner on in each of the ninth and tenth innings against Rivera, but couldn't score. Mike Timlin and Tim Wakefield matched Rivera, pitching a perfect ninth and tenth. Rivera went out for a third inning, retiring the Red Sox 1-2-3 in the eleventh. In the bottom of the inning, Wakefield, who had already won two games in the series, watched Aaron Boone hit the first pitch he faced into the left-field stands to send the Red Sox back to Boston instead of to the World Series.

Despite the loss, it was a successful season for the Red Sox. The team took on an identity as the season progressed, spurred primarily by Kevin Millar, who emerged as a leader in the clubhouse. About halfway through the season, a bizarre but endearing videotape of an 18-year-old Millar performing a rendition of "Born in the USA" by Bruce Springsteen emerged on the Fenway Park scoreboard. The performance quickly became known as "rally karaoke." Millar also introduced Boston fans to the phrase "Cowboy Up," which came to symbolize the team's never-say-die mentality. Mike Timlin made up T-shirts for the team saying "The time is now . . . so cowboy up," and the Fenway PA started playing the song "Cowboy Up" by Ryan Reynolds.

Reversing the Curse, 2004

Armed with a team-first mentality and clear organizational strategy, the Boston Red Sox began tweaking the team that had come so close in 2003. While manager Grady Little had led the team to within five outs of the World Series, he had made a crucial error in leaving Pedro Martinez in Game Seven. By that time it was public knowledge that Martinez faltered considerably after 100 pitches, and for a team that believed as heavily in statistics as the Red Sox, leaving Martinez in the game was a cardinal sin. Little paid for his error, and was replaced by Terry Francona for the 2004 season.

The Red Sox went hard after three players in the 2004 off-season, getting two and losing the other to the Yankees. On November 28, Boston acquired ace Curt Schilling from the Arizona Diamondbacks in exchange for a few young pitchers. Schilling was originally drafted by Boston, but traded to Baltimore with Brady Anderson for Mike Boddicker in 1988. In that time he had become one of the game's dominant pitchers, with 163 wins, a 3.33 ERA, and 2,542 strikeouts in 2,568 innings. Perhaps more importantly, Schilling had gone 1–0 with a 1.69 ERA over 21⅓ innings against the New York Yankees in the 2001 World Series which Arizona won four games to three. Overall, Schilling brought a postseason record of 5–1 with a 1.66 ERA with him to Boston.

Second on the shopping list was the closer the Sox had defeated in the 2003 A.L. Division Series, Keith Foulke. The perfect model of a "Moneyball" closer, in that Foulke could pitch multiple innings, he was a free agent and too expensive for the low-budget A's. Boston signed him on December 13 to a four-year, $24 million contract.

The last player Boston targeted was Texas shortstop and 2003 A.L. MVP Alex Rodriguez. Signed to the largest contract in sports, ten years and $252 million, the Rangers wanted to move the man known as A-Rod to give them greater payroll flexibility. Boston agreed to trade Manny Ramirez, himself the owner of a $160 million, eight-year contract, to Texas for A-Rod if Rodriguez would restructure part of his contract. At the same time, Boston was negotiating to trade Nomar Garciaparra, whose contract was due to expire after the 2004 season, with the most-reported destination to be Chicago for White Sox outfielder Magglio Ordonez.

Before the deal could be completed, however, the player's union voiced its displeasure with the contract restructuring, and A-Rod announced that he would only consent to the restructuring with the union's approval. When a new deal could not be reached, the trade fell through, leaving Boston with an unhappy Garciaparra.

Undaunted, the Rangers began discussion with the Yankees, and ended up dealing A-Rod and cash to New York in exchange for second baseman Alfonso Soriano and a minor leaguer. That began a war of words between Yankees owner George Steinbrenner and the Red Sox owners, one of whom had already nicknamed the Yankees the "evil empire" just one year prior. A few hours after the trade was announced, owner John Henry called for a salary cap in baseball. Steinbrenner responded: "We understand that John Henry must be embarrassed, frustrated and disappointed by his failure in this transaction. It is time to get on with life and forget the sour grapes."

In an e-mail to reporters, Henry responded: "There is really no other fair way to deal with a team that has gone so insanely far beyond the resources of all the other teams."

Steinbrenner answered: "Unlike the Yankees, he [Henry] chose not to go the extra distance for his fans in Boston."

The rest of the team was pretty much the same at the start of the 2004 season, with two exceptions. Todd Walker left as a free agent and was replaced by Mark Bellhorn, who had slugged .512 in 2002 before a disappointing 2003 season. And Bronson Arroyo, who had spent much of 2003 in the minors for Boston, was promoted and inserted into the starting rotation. One non-"Moneyball" player was also imported, infielder Pokey Reese, a defensive stalwart who was, to say the least, offensively-challenged.

The season started with Garciaparra and Trot Nixon on the disabled list, where they would stay until June 9 and 16, respectively, missing a combined 120 games to the DL. Despite the injuries, the Red Sox took three of four games from the Yankees at Fenway from

April 16–19 and then swept a three-game series at Yankee Stadium April 23–25. The last win gave them a 1½ game lead in the A.L. East, and they were tied for first at the end of May before a three-game losing streak dropped them to 3½ games behind New York.

Nearing the end of July, Boston was 9½ games back after a tough 8–7, Friday-night loss to the Yankees, in which a ninth-inning, RBI-double by A-Rod set the stage for a wild game the next day. On Saturday, the Sox were down 3–0 in the top of the third when starter Bronson Arroyo plunked Alex Rodriguez with a pitch. A-Rod jawed at Arroyo as he began a slow walk to first base, and Varitek got in between A-Rod and the mound. The situation escalated from there, as Varitek, still wearing his catcher's mask, pushed Rodriguez in the face.

Both dugouts and bullpens emptied, as they had in the playoffs the previous year. Several small fights took place, and Varitek, Trot Nixon, Rodriguez, and Kenny Lofton were all ejected. Sox manager Terry Francona was ejected in the fifth inning for arguing a call at second base.

The Sox rallied in the bottom of the inning, and had a 4–3 lead when the Yankees scored six in the top of the sixth, only to give four runs back to Boston in the bottom of the inning. It stood at 10–8 going into the bottom of the ninth when Bill Mueller hit a two-run homer off closer Mariano Rivera to give Boston an emotional 11–10 win.

The Sox won again the next day but were still 8½ games back at the July 31 trading deadline when they made a blockbuster deal, sending the hobbled and disgruntled icon but still fan favorite Nomar Garciaparra to the Chicago Cubs in a four-team deal that shored up Boston's infield defense by bringing shortstop Orlando Cabrera from Montreal (who homered in his first Sox at-bat) and first baseman Doug Mientkiewicz from Minnesota. After a 4–4 split after the trade, Boston went on a roll, winning 24 of their next 28 games, pulling them back to within two games of the first-place Yankees. A large part of the revival came from the improved defense, which allowed just 20 unearned runs in their final 60 games after having allowed 74 unearned runs through July 31.

Boston split their final six games with New York, though not without more controversy. On September 24, Pedro Martinez was winning 4–3 after throwing 101 pitches through seven innings. In a scene remarkably similar to the 2003 ALCS, Francona left Martinez in for the eighth inning, and he surrendered a solo shot to Hideki Matsui on his 104th pitch. Ruben Sierra later singled home the eventual winning run and chased Martinez after 117 pitches. After the 6–4 loss Martinez said: "What can I say—just tip my hat and call the Yankees my daddy. I can't find a way to beat them at this point . . . They're that good. They're that hot right now—at least against me. I wish they would disappear and not come back." Not surprisingly, the New York fans and press jumped on the comment, and Pedro was greeted with "Who's Your Daddy?" chants by the Yankee Stadium crowd for the remainder of the season and playoffs.

Two days later, the benches cleared one more time in a Yankees–Red Sox game, this time after Yankees starter Brad Halsey threw a pitch high and tight to Sox reserve outfielder Dave Roberts. Yankees manager Joe Torre and Halsey were ejected from the game and the players were kept apart. Despite their 11–3 win in that game, Boston would end the season two games in back of the Yankees, clinching the wild card on September 27 and finishing 98–63, a three-win improvement over 2003. It was the third-best record in the league (behind the Yankees and St. Louis Cardinals) and Boston had the best record in baseball after August 1 (42–18). It was also Boston's most wins since 1978 when they were 99–64.

The Sox were paced on offense by the dynamic duo of Ramirez (.308 average, 44 doubles, 130 RBI, and a league-leading 43 home runs and .613 slugging) and David Ortiz (.301 average, 47 doubles, 139 RBI, and 41 home runs). Ramirez and Ortiz became the first American League teammates since Babe Ruth and Lou Gehrig in 1931 to hit .300 with 40 homers and 100 RBI apiece, and the first Red Sox duo to hit 40 home runs each since Jim Rice and Tony Armas in 1984. Leadoff man Johnny Damon, who with his long Jesus-styled hair inspired the slogan "What Would Johnny Damon Do?" scored 123 runs and hit 20 home runs. In all, the Red Sox once again led the majors in runs scored (949), doubles (373, tying a major-league record), on-base percentage (.360), extra-base hits (620), and slugging (.472). Behind Bellhorn's team-record 177, the Red Sox also led the A.L. in batter's strikeouts.

On the mound, the one-two punch of Schilling and Martinez was among the league's best, despite a sub-par season for Martinez. Schilling led the majors in wins at 21–6 and had a 3.26 ERA and 203 strikeouts in 226⅔ innings. Martinez slumped to 16–9 with a 3.90 ERA, the highest of his career, though he still managed to strikeout 227 batters in 217 innings. Derek Lowe had his second straight disappointing season, posting a 5.42 ERA despite winning 14 games. Tim Wakefield went 12–10 with a 4.87 ERA and Bronson Arroyo was a pleasant surprise, going 10–9 with a 4.03 ERA. Keith Foulke was a huge addition to the bullpen, notching 32 saves with a miniscule 2.17 ERA. Timlin and Embree were once again valuable in their set-up roles, and when healthy, Scott Williamson posted a 1.26 ERA in 28 games. Beyond that was a collection of spare parts picked up during the season, including left-handed specialist Mike Myers (acquired August 6 from Seattle), Terry Adams (acquired July 24 from Toronto), and Curtis Leskanic (signed June 22). In all, the Red Sox were third in the American League with a 4.13 ERA and led the league with 12 shutouts and a .255 batting average allowed. They also tied for the fewest home runs allowed in the A.L., surrendering just 159.

With billboards sporting the slogan "Keep the Faith" popping up all over the city, Boston prepared to face Anaheim, the 2002 World Series winners, in the Division Series.

The team had also acquired a new moniker, thanks to outfielder Johnny Damon. Asked about being more business than "Cowboy" in a press conference before the first game of the ALDS, Damon referred to the Red Sox as "idiots," saying: "I mean, it's—you know, we are not the cowboys anymore, we are just the idiots this year, so we are going to go out and try to swing the bats, find the holes and, hopefully, good things happen." He continued, "We have that same attitude [as the 2001 Oakland A's], we feel like we can win every game, we feel like we have to have fun, and I think that's why this team is liked by so many people out there. You know, the kids watching us out there, you know, we got the long hair [Damon], we got the corn rows [Bronson Arroyo], we got just guys acting like idiots. And I think the fans out there like it."

Damon added, "Well, we know that we had some heartache last year. We felt like we had the best team out there. You know, and we were a bunch of cowboys out there last year, just enjoying every minute. Now we know we have something to prove. We don't want to be remembered as a team that, okay, we keep making it to the play-offs, but we keep having tough losses. I mean, we want to be known as a team that, you know, rewrites the history books."

The prophetic proclamation symbolized an important shift in attitude from previous Boston clubs that came up just short, and would eventually stand in stark contrast to the conservative image of their ALCS opponent. But first came the Anaheim Angels in the ALDS.

A seven-run fourth inning in the first game helped Boston to a 9–3 win and the Red Sox scored seven runs over the final four innings in Game Two for an 8–3 win, as they took the first two games on the road behind Schilling and Martinez.

Boston was cruising in the third game, up 6–1 before Anaheim rallied for five runs in the seventh, including a grand slam by Vladimir Guerrero. The game went to extra frames before Ortiz ended it with a two-run walk-off home run off lefty Jarrod Washburn. Derek Lowe, who was bounced from the postseason rotation, entered the game in the tenth inning and got the win, which sent Boston to the ALCS for consecutive years for the first time in team history.

And with that, baseball fans braced for a rematch of the 2003 ALCS—the Red Sox versus the Yankees with New York once again holding home field advantage.

During the regular season, Boston had taken 11 of 19 games from the Yankees, their first season series win since 1999. Of those 19 games, eight were decided in the final at-bat, with six of those being Boston wins. The Red Sox also held a 23–22 edge in regular and postseason games since the start of 2003. It also was a match-up of the two highest opening day payrolls in baseball: New York's $184 million and Boston's $127 million. While those were the top two, the gap between them ($57 million) was greater than the opening day payroll of thirteen other teams and about the same as the combined payroll of the Milwaukee Brewers and Tampa Bay Devil Rays.

The first game did not get off to a good start for Boston. Curt Schilling, who in his previous start against Anaheim had aggravated a torn ankle tendon that he most likely suffered in a September 21 start against Baltimore, lasted just three innings and 58 pitches, leaving the game down 6–0. New York tacked on two more in the sixth before Boston rallied for five runs in the seventh behind a two-run double from Kevin Millar, an RBI-single by Trot Nixon, and a two-run homer from Jason Varitek. In the next inning, against former Red Sox closer Tom Gordon, David Ortiz tripled off the top of the wall in center, plating two more runs and cutting the lead to 8–7. Before they could get any closer, Bernie Williams doubled home a couple of runs in the bottom of the eighth and Mariano Rivera closed out the game with a double-play grounder off the bat of Bill Mueller with two runners aboard.

Pedro Martinez wasn't sharp to start Game Two at Yankee Stadium, walking Derek Jeter, letting him steal second, and then nicking Alex

Rodriguez with a pitch to put runners on the corners. Gary Sheffield singled home Jeter with the first run before Martinez settled down, striking out the next two batters and getting the third to ground out.

The score stayed the same until John Olerud, filling in for an injured Jason Giambi who was left off the Yankees postseason roster, lined a two-run homer to the short porch in right field on Martinez's 106th pitch of the night. Meanwhile, Yankees starter Jon Lieber was on top of his game, allowing just two hits before a leadoff single from Trot Nixon in the eighth led to his removal after just 82 pitches. A double and a groundout scored one run, but Mariano Rivera came in and recorded the last four outs for his second save of the series. It marked the first time all season that Schilling and Martinez had taken a loss on consecutive days.

After a travel day and a rainout gave both teams two days off, the series resumed at Fenway Park. Boston excelled at home in 2004, producing the second-best home record in the majors at 55–26, behind only the Yankees. Boston's offense really exploded at home during the regular season, leading the majors in runs (517), batting average (.304), and on-base percentage (.378) while trailing only Colorado in slugging (.504 to .506).

In Game Three, both starters, Bronson Arroyo for the Red Sox and Kevin Brown for the Yankees, lasted just two innings, and both teams kept posting "crooked" numbers on the manual scoreboard in left field. In fact, neither team scored just one run in any frame, and the Yankees scored in six of their nine times at bat. At the end of the 19–8 drubbing the Yankees were one game from a sweep and a return trip to the World Series. Somewhat lost in the offensive fireworks was Tim Wakefield's decision to enter Game Three as a reliever. His 3⅓ innings were far from his best work, but by entering the game and voluntarily forgoing his scheduled Game Four start, the longtime Sox pitcher allowed the team's beleaguered bullpen to regroup for the uphill battle that awaited the team.

Things looked dark for Boston, as no team in major-league history had ever come back from a 3–0 deficit in a seven-game series. No team in MLB history had even forced a Game Seven after such a deficit, and just five of the previous twenty-five teams that fell behind 3–0 had avoided a sweep. In fact, in all of the North American major leagues, only twice before in 236 best-of-seven series (25 in MLB, 73 in the NBA, and 138 in the NHL) had a team managed such a comeback, and both times it was in the NHL: Toronto in the 1942 Stanley

Cup finals against Detroit and the New York Islanders against Pittsburgh in the second round of the playoffs in 1975.

In Game Four, an A-Rod home run off Derek Lowe, starting in place of the injured Schilling and resting Wakefield, gave New York a 2–0 lead in the third. Three walks and two singles led to three Boston runs in the fifth, but the Yankees responded with two runs in the sixth to reclaim the lead at 4–3. When Mariano Rivera came into the game in the eighth, the end appeared at hand for Boston. But even though Rivera had blown only three of his thirty-five postseason save opportunities prior to the game, this was not to be Rivera's night. Escaping the eighth after surrendering a leadoff single to Manny Ramirez, Rivera struggled in the ninth. Kevin Millar walked to lead off the inning and was pinch-run for by the speedy Dave Roberts. Everyone in the stadium knew that Roberts would attempt to steal second, which he did, just barely beating Derek Jeter's tag in what will likely go down as the most important steal in Sox history. Bill Mueller, who had hit the walk-off homer against Rivera in the brawl game on July 24, delivered an RBI-single to knot the game at 4. Boston managed to load the bases with two outs, but Rivera got Ortiz to pop out to second base to send the game into extra innings.

Both teams went quietly in the tenth, and Boston escaped a two-out bases loaded jam in the eleventh when Curtis Leskanic got Bernie Williams to fly out. A shallow bullpen came back to haunt the Yankees, as Paul Quantrill replaced Tom Gordon after he had pitched three scoreless innings. Ramirez opened the inning with a single, and then Ortiz, who missed his chance to win the game in the ninth, came through with a home run to right (his record second walk-off homer in the same postseason), giving the Red Sox a 6–4 victory in a game that lasted over five hours and didn't end until 1:22 A.M.

If that game seemed long, it had nothing on Game Five, which went 14 innings and lasted 5 hours, 49 minutes, the longest game by time in postseason history. Boston took a 2–0 lead in the second, but after Jeter's bases clearing double in the sixth off Pedro Martinez it was 4–2 New York. Mike Mussina, who had pitched so brilliantly in Game One left after Mark Bellhorn's opening double in the seventh, yet Tanyon Sturtze and Tom Gordon kept Boston off the board in that frame.

Gordon wasn't as successful in the eighth, allowing a leadoff homer to David Ortiz followed by a walk to Kevin Millar and single to Trot Nixon. Mariano Rivera came in and allowed a sacrifice fly to Jason

Varitek, which plated pinch-runner Dave Roberts with the tying run before getting out of the inning.

The Yankees almost took the lead in the ninth, but Fenway Park saved the Sox. Tony Clark's two-out double off Keith Foulke bounced over the short wall in right forcing Ruben Sierra to stop at third. If the ball had stayed in the field of play, Sierra would have scored easily. Miguel Cairo grounded out to end the threat, and Boston went quietly in the ninth after Johnny Damon's leadoff single was erased after he was caught stealing.

A succession of relievers followed for both teams, and the next real threat belonged to Boston in the eleventh. Mueller and Bellhorn led off the inning with consecutive singles, but Damon popped out on a sacrifice attempt and Esteban Loaiza came in to get Orlando Cabrera to ground into a double play.

New York had a chance in the thirteenth, mostly due to Jason Varitek's misadventures trying to catch Tim Wakefield's fluttering knuckleballs. During the regular season, Varitek gave way to backup Doug Mirabelli when it was Wakefield's turn to pitch, but with the season on the line, he stayed in the game. Sheffield struck out to begin the inning, but reached when the third strike escaped Varitek's grasp for a passed ball. Two more passed balls and an intentional walk put runners on second and third with two outs. Then with two strikes on Ruben Sierra, Wakefield threw another knuckler. To the surprise and delight of Boston fans, as Sierra swung through the pitch Varitek stabbed at the ball and managed to hang on, ending the Yankee threat.

After Bellhorn struck out to lead off the fourteenth, Esteban Loaiza walked Johnny Damon, who was just 2-for-24 in the series. A strike-out of Cabrera and walk to Ramirez put runners on first and second for the previous night's hero, David Ortiz. He delivered once again, dumping a soft single into center field on the game's 471st pitch to score Damon with the winning run. With that, the Red Sox sent the series back to Yankee Stadium, still down three games to two but having exhausted a depleted Yankees bullpen and twice surviving games in which they trailed with Mariano Rivera looking to close the game out for the Yankees.

In all, the three games at Fenway went 35 innings and lasted 15 hours and 11 minutes. There were 35 pitchers (19 for Boston) and 1,299 pitches thrown (663 by Boston). The last two wins also gave Boston a 7-0-1 record in postseason extra-inning affairs at home.

After his poor outing in the first game of the series and having his turn skipped in Game Four, there was plenty of speculation as to whether Curt Schilling was going to be able to take the mound for the Red Sox in Game Six. Wearing a specially designed boot, Schilling took the mound with a torn ankle tendon and three now-famous sutures put in place to stabilize the tendon. With blood dripping through his sock, he delivered a masterful performance, pitching a three-hit shutout until Bernie Williams homered with one out in the seventh. By that time the Red Sox were up 4–1, thanks in large part to a series of reversed calls by the umpires.

Already up 1–0 with two runners on in the fourth, Mark Bellhorn hit a ball over the left-field wall that was originally ruled a ground-rule double by umpire Jim Joyce, driving home one run. After conferring, the other five umpires agreed that the ball had actually cleared the fence and corrected the call to a three-run home run.

Another bizarre play took place in the eighth. Bronson Arroyo had replaced Schilling to start the inning and allowed a run on Jeter's RBI-single with one out. The next batter, A-Rod, squibbed the ball down the first-base line. As Arroyo picked up the ball and proceeded to try to tag Rodriguez right in front of the base, Rodriguez swung his hand, knocking the ball from Arroyo as Jeter scored all the way from first. After Francona came out to argue, the umpires ruled Rodriguez out for interference and sent Jeter back to first. Fans threw trash onto the field as Yankees skipper Joe Torre came out to argue the reversal, delaying the game for ten minutes. When it resumed, Gary Sheffield popped out to end the inning. The game was briefly delayed in the top of the ninth as well, after Orlando Cabrera was ruled safe at first on an attempted double play.

Keith Foulke made things interesting in the ninth, walking two batters, but struck out Tony Clark to end the game and send the series to a deciding seventh game for the second straight year. The Red Sox sent a resurgent Derek Lowe to the mound on two days' rest while the Yankees countered with Kevin Brown, who had been shelled by the Sox in Game Three.

After such a climactic series, the Red Sox took the suspense out of the clinching game quickly on David Ortiz's two-run home run in the first and Johnny Damon's grand slam in the second. The Yankees picked up one run in the third, but Damon hit his second home run of the game in the fourth, a two-run shot, to make it 8–1.

There was a little tension in the seventh when Francona replaced

Lowe with Pedro Martinez, who after being greeted by a reprise chorus of "Who's your daddy?" allowed back-to-back doubles to start the inning. After a groundout, an RBI-single made it 8–3 with a runner on first and just one out. But Martinez settled down, retiring John Olerud and Miguel Cairo to end the inning.

The Yankees managed a couple of runners in the ninth, but by that time the Red Sox had tacked on another two runs on Bellhorn's solo shot in the eighth and Cabrera's sacrifice fly in the ninth. Alan Embree retired Ruben Sierra for the final out in the 10–3 win to seal the comeback and Boston's eleventh American League pennant.

It was no hyperbole when owner John Henry said after the game that it was "the greatest comeback in baseball history." The Yankees kept the stadium open for the Red Sox players, and they celebrated their victory with hundreds of Sox fans who made their way to the seats above the visitor's dugout. Trot Nixon even ran out to the center-field bleachers to talk to some friends and shook hands with fans down the right-field line. David Ortiz, with a .387 average, 3 home runs, 11 RBIs, and two game-winning, walk-off hits was named MVP of the series.

Of course, to fully reverse "The Curse of the Bambino" the Red Sox still had one more obstacle, the St. Louis Cardinals and the World Series. Only two players on the Red Sox World Series roster had rings: Mike Timlin had two (Toronto in 1992 and 1993) and Curt Schilling had one (Arizona in 2001). Only two others had even reached the Fall Classic before: Alan Embree with Cleveland in 1995 and Manny Ramirez with Cleveland in 1995 and 1997.

The Red Sox had previously faced the Cardinals twice in the World Series, losing in seven games in both 1946 and 1967. St. Louis also took two of three regular season interleague games between the two teams at Fenway from June 10–12, 2003. However, in an interesting twist of fate, Boston clubs in the other three professional leagues all broke championship droughts against teams from St. Louis: the Celtics beat the St. Louis Hawks for their first title in 1957; the Bruins beat the St. Louis Blues in the 1969–70 Stanley Cup finals, winning their first title since 1940–41; and the New England Patriots beat the St. Louis Rams in the Super Bowl for their first championship in the 2001 season.

The first game, at Fenway Park, started with a familiar postseason sight—a David Ortiz home run, marking the 28th time a player homered in his first World Series at-bat. This one was a three-run shot, that along with Bill Mueller's run-scoring single gave Boston a 4–0 first inning lead. A sacrifice fly in the second and a home run by Larry Walker in the top of the third cut the lead to 4–2 before Boston rallied for another three runs against St. Louis starter Woody Williams. In a testament to how hittable Williams was, of the 70 pitches he threw in 2⅓ innings, Boston hitters only swung and missed twice.

Still, the Cardinals would not go quietly. They knocked out Boston starter Tim Wakefield in the fourth after their own three-run rally that included both a Boston error (the first of four on the day for the Sox) and passed ball. Bronson Arroyo came in to prevent any further damage and pitched a perfect fifth as well before running into trouble in the sixth. After retiring the first two batters of the inning, So Taguchi reached on an infield single and advanced to second on a throwing error by Arroyo. Edgar Renteria and Walker followed with consecutive doubles to knot the game at 7.

It stayed that way until the bottom of the seventh when Boston tagged St. Louis reliever Kiko Calero for a couple of runs. Bellhorn and Cabrera walked, with a groundout in between, and Manny Ramirez followed with an RBI-single. Left-handed specialist Ray King came in to face Ortiz, who responded by lacing a ball that took a hard hop and hit St. Louis second baseman Tony Womack in the collarbone. The result was a single, scoring Cabrera from third and giving Boston a 9–7 lead.

That lead was also short-lived, as a pair of Manny Ramirez errors in left helped St. Louis tie the game at 9. Boston responded in their half of the inning, when with Varitek on first after a Renteria error, Bellhorn took an inside fastball down the right field line. As Cardinals pitcher Julian Tavarez tried to wave the ball foul and players scurried out of the Boston dugout to watch, the ball clanged off the Pesky Pole for a two-run home run. Foulke, who had retired the last two batters in the eighth inning, closed the door in the ninth to preserve the 11–9 victory.

Curt Schilling took his torn ankle tendon to the mound for the Red Sox in Game Two and pitched brilliantly. He allowed just four hits, one walk, and one unearned run in six innings and left only after Boston had the game well in hand with a 6–1 lead. He also survived three errors (tying a single-game Series record) by third baseman Bill Mueller, the second of which led to the unearned run in the fourth. All told, Boston committed a World Series record eight errors in the first two games.

St. Louis starter Matt Morris was not nearly as sharp as Schilling. The Red Sox pushed home two runs in the first on Varitek's triple to deep center after consecutive two-out walks to Ramirez and Ortiz. St. Louis picked up an unearned run in the fourth before Boston doubled its output in the bottom of the inning on a hit-by-pitch and back-to-back doubles by Mueller and Bellhorn. The Red Sox made it 6–1 on a two-RBI single by Orlando Cabrera off reliever Cal Eldred and St. Louis scored the final run of the game on a sacrifice fly in the eighth off Mike Timlin. The win made Terry Francona the winningest post-season manager in Red Sox history with nine victories in just his first season on the job. Bill Carrigan went 8–2 en route to two World Series wins in 1915 and 1916.

The series shifted to St. Louis for the third game, a match-up of Martinez and Jeff Suppan, whom the Red Sox had left off their post-season roster in 2003. As with the first two games, Boston scored in the first inning, this time on a Ramirez solo shot. Not atypically, Martinez struggled in his first inning as well. After retiring the leadoff hitter on a groundout, he walked Larry Walker, allowed an infield single to Albert Pujols, and then walked Scott Rolen to load the bases. Jim Edmonds followed and lofted a ball to left fielder Ramirez—the same Ramirez who had committed two errors in the same inning in the first game. This time Manny came through, catching the ball and throwing out Walker at home to complete the double play.

St. Louis had another rally in the third, after the pitcher Suppan beat out an infield single and Renteria doubled over a falling Trot Nixon in right to put runners on second and third with none out. Larry Walker followed with a chopper to second, and Bellhorn, seemingly willing to concede the run, threw leisurely to first to record the out. However, following a miscommunication with the third base coach, Suppan, who had tentatively left third and stopped halfway down the line, now tried to retreat to third—where Renteria was already heading as he attempted to advance from second. First baseman Ortiz, normally the designated hitter but forced to play the field in the National League park, started moving towards Suppan, eventually throwing to third baseman Mueller who tagged Suppan out to end the Cardinal rally. The double by Renteria was the last hit Martinez allowed in the game—he finished the game with seven shutout innings, allowing three hits and two walks while striking out six. He left after throwing 98 pitches.

Meanwhile, Boston had added another run on a Mueller double

and a Nixon RBI-single in the fourth and chased Suppan with two more in the fifth, thanks to a double and three singles. Larry Walker hit his second home run of the series in the ninth off Foulke to spoil the shutout, but Boston was now up 3–0 in the best-of-seven series.

The Red Sox kept up their streak, scoring in the first inning of Game Four, as they had in the previous three games (as well as in the last game of the ALCS). This time it was on a leadoff home run by Johnny Damon on just the fourth pitch of the game. St. Louis starter Jason Marquis ran into more trouble in the third. With one out and runners and second and third after a Ramirez single and Ortiz double, Varitek smashed a grounder to Pujols at first, who threw home and caught Ramirez trying to score. A semi-intentional walk to Mueller loaded the bases with two out for Trot Nixon. Marquis nibbled at the strike zone but fell behind in the count 3–0. Nixon crushed the next pitch off the wall in right-center field, clearing the bases.

That was all the offense Derek Lowe needed. Lowe bested Martinez's outing from the previous night, allowing just three hits and one walk over seven shutout innings. At one point, between the first and fifth innings, he retired 13 straight. Arroyo and Embree worked the eighth and Foulke came in to pitch the bottom of the ninth with a 3–0 lead. Unlike the Yankees, there would be no choke for the Red Sox this year. At 11:40 P.M. EDT on October 27, 2004, Keith Foulke corralled Edgar Renteria's chopper and flipped the ball to first baseman Doug Mientkiewicz, who had entered the game in the seventh for his defense, for the final out of the 2004 World Series.

On the radio, the final call by Joe Castiglione went like this: "Swing and a ground ball, stabbed by Foulke. He has it. He underhands to first. And the Boston Red Sox are the World Champions. For the first time in eighty-six years, the Red Sox have won baseball's world championship. Can you believe it?"

Thirty-one thousand, four hundred and fifty-nine days after winning their last World Series, the Boston Red Sox were World Champions once more! It had been 86 years of heartbreaks, failures, and near misses, of Johnny Pesky, Bucky Dent, and Bill Buckner, of lifelong Red Sox players like Ted Williams and Carl Yastrzemski who never got to win a World Series. And for 86 years, it had been the "Curse of the Bambino." Now, after the greatest comeback in baseball history against the team the Babe was traded to and a four-game World Series sweep of the National League champions, the suffering was over. The Red Sox were the last team standing.

Curt Schilling summed it up perfectly after the game: "We're World Champions," Schilling said. "There's no living player who can say what we can say today: We're the World Champion Boston Red Sox."

Manny Ramirez was named World Series MVP after batting .412 with a home run and 4 RBI. David Ortiz tied a postseason record with 19 RBI, along with batting .400, walking 13 times, and slugging 5 home runs. With one homer in the ALDS and two more in the ALCS, Jason Varitek set a new club record with nine career postseason home runs. The Red Sox never trailed in the World Series and were tied just twice.

Newspapers across New England carried word on Boston's victory the following day. The *Boston Globe* front page read "YES!!!" while the *Boston Herald* went with "AMEN! Series Sweep Answers Sox Fans' Prayers." The *Telegram & Gazette* (Worcester, Mass.) headline was "Hallelujah!" and *The Sun* (Lowell, Mass.) had "Cursed to First!" In Rhode Island, *The Providence Journal* headline read "Champions of the World!" while in Nashua, New Hampshire, *The Telegraph*'s headline was simply: "Finally!" with 1918 in big, bold red type, followed by the years 1946, 1967, 1975, and 1986, all in black, crossed out with red X's, finally followed by 2004, in the same big, bold red font as 1918.

Of course, the New York tabloids had their own take on Boston's World Series win. The back page of the New York *Daily News* was "See you in 2090!" and The *New York Post*'s back page was simply " 'Bout Time." New York *Newsday* even ran a pale picture of Babe Ruth in the background of its front page, with the text reading "Ghost Busters! Red Sox reverse the Curse of the Bambino, win first World Series since 1918."

An estimated 3.2 million fans gathered in Boston for the team's victory parade on October 31. Signs throughout the crowd referenced the impact the Red Sox have on Boston and of how many lived a lifetime without a Red Sox championship. One sign along the route read "Our (late) parents and grandparents thank you."

POSTSCRIPT TO A CHAMPIONSHIP SEASON

While Boston celebrated, the front office went to work on assembling a team to win a second consecutive World Series in 2005. Complicating matters was the number of free agents on the Boston roster. Key players like Jason Varitek, Pedro Martinez, Derek Lowe, and Orlando

Cabrera were free to sign with any team, and their postseason experience only helped drive up their contract demands. Boston had managed to sign two potential free agents earlier in the year. Before the season began, the Red Sox signed Trot Nixon to a three-year, $19.5 million contract, and on May 21 the team inked David Ortiz to a deal well below his market worth, getting him for $11.75 million over two years with a $7.75 million option for 2007.

The team realistically knew it couldn't keep the entire nucleus together, and watched as the New York Mets signed Martinez to a $53 million, four-year deal on December 15. Boston's best offer was reportedly $40.5 million for three seasons. Martinez went an astounding 117–37 in seven seasons with Boston, the best winning percentage for any pitcher who won at least 100 games with one team.

Boston passed on re-signing Cabrera, instead opting to ink his World Series counterpart, Edgar Renteria, to a $40 million, four-year deal on December 17.

To fill out the rotation, Boston planned on letting Lowe walk and instead signed three pitchers to replace him and Martinez: Matt Clement of the Cubs to a $25.5 million, three-year deal; forty-one-year-old left-hander David Wells, twice an ex-Yankee, for two years at $8 million that could go up to $18 million depending on the number of starts he makes each year; and Wade Miller, coming off shoulder problems in Houston, to a $1.5 million, one-year deal that contains another $3 million in possible bonuses. They'll join Schilling, who is expected to be out until May after ankle surgery, Arroyo, and Wakefield.

Perhaps most importantly, the Red Sox signed Varitek on Christmas Eve to a deal worth $40 million over four years and named him the team's new captain at the same time. He becomes the first Boston captain since Jim Rice held the honor from 1985–89 and only the third since Mike Menosky was captain in 1923. (Yaz was the other.)

The biggest remaining question is whether World Series MVP Manny Ramirez will still be with the team in 2004. After almost trading him for A-Rod and then leaving him exposed on irrevocable waivers (where he went unclaimed) in 2003 it's possible that Boston will find someone to take his burdensome contract off their hands. While Ramirez remains one the game's most feared hitters, his lack of acumen on the bases or in the field and his large contract might make him expendable, allowing the Red Sox to spend the money they'd save elsewhere.

Otherwise, the core of the team is expected back in 2005, including Schilling, Keith Foulke, set-up men Mike Timlin and Alan Embree, Ortiz, Bill Mueller, Trot Nixon, Johnny Damon, and Varitek, the newly named captain.

A NEW TRADITION?

Appearing on TV after the end of the World Series, Kevin Millar revealed the Red Sox good luck tradition that they began before Game Six of the ALCS against the Yankees. "It was about thirty-five degrees out there at Yankee Stadium," Millar said. "I went around and got a thing of Jack Daniels and we all did shots of Jack Daniels about ten minutes before the game. And we won Game Six. So game Seven of course, we had to do shots of Jack Daniels. And we won Game Seven, so guess what? I'm glad we won in Game four (in the World Series) because these Crown Royal shots and Jack Daniels shots started to kill me. And that's how the Sox did it."

POSTSEASON COMPOSITE BOX SCORE

PLAYER	G	AB	R	H	2B	3B	HR	RBI	BB	SO	SB	AVG	OBP	SLG
Damon, Johnny	14	71	13	19	3	1	3	9	3	11	5	.268	.297	.465
Ramirez, Manny	14	60	8	21	3	0	2	11	9	11	0	.350	.423	.500
Cabrera, Orlando	14	59	9	17	4	0	0	11	8	8	1	.288	.377	.356
Mueller, Bill	14	56	10	18	3	0	0	3	7	2	0	.321	.406	.375
Ortiz, David	14	55	13	22	3	1	5	19	13	10	0	.400	.515	.764
Varitek, Jason	14	53	10	13	1	1	3	11	5	15	0	.245	.328	.472
Nixon, Trot	13	51	5	13	4	0	1	8	3	7	0	.255	.296	.392
Bellhorn, Mark	14	47	8	9	3	0	3	8	15	17	0	.191	.397	.447
Millar, Kevin	14	42	8	10	4	0	1	6	8	7	0	.238	.373	.405
Kapler, Gabe	8	10	2	2	0	0	0	0	0	1	0	.200	.200	.200
Mientkiewicz, Doug	11	9	0	4	1	0	0	1	0	1	0	.444	.444	.556
Mirabelli, Doug	2	4	1	1	0	0	0	0	0	1	0	.250	.250	.250
Reese, Pokey	10	2	1	0	0	0	0	0	0	1	0	.000	.000	.000
Martinez, Pedro	5	2	0	0	0	0	0	0	1	2	0	.000	.333	.000
Lowe, Derek	4	2	0	0	0	0	0	0	0	1	0	.000	.000	.000
Youkilis, Kevin	1	2	0	0	0	0	0	0	0	1	0	.000	.000	.000
Roberts, Dave	3	0	2	0	0	0	0	0	0	0	1	.000	.000	.000
BOSTON	14	525	90	149	29	3	18	87	72	96	7	.284	.374	.453
OPPONENTS	14	509	69	126	32	2	15	64	56	111	5	.248	.332	.407

PITCHER	W	L	ERA	G	GS	SV	IP	H	R	ER	HR	BB	SO
Martinez, Pedro	2	1	4.00	5	4	0	27	23	12	12	2	13	26
Schilling, Curt	3	1	3.57	4	4	0	22.2	23	11	9	3	5	13
Lowe, Derek	3	0	1.86	4	3	0	19.1	11	4	4	1	3	10
Foulke, Keith	1	0	0.64	11	0	3	14	7	1	1	1	8	19
Arroyo, Bronson	0	0	7.82	6	2	0	12.2	15	11	11	3	5	14
Timlin, Mike	0	0	6.17	11	0	0	11.2	15	8	8	1	7	7
Wakefield, Tim	1	0	9.82	4	1	0	11	12	12	12	2	8	8
Embree, Alan	0	0	2.45	11	0	0	7.1	10	3	2	0	2	6
Myers, Mike	0	0	10.13	5	0	0	2.2	5	3	3	1	2	5
Leskanic, Curtis	1	0	10.13	3	0	0	2.2	3	3	3	1	3	2
Mendoza, Ramiro	0	1	4.50	2	0	0	2	2	1	1	0	0	1
BOSTON	11	3	4.47	14	14	3	133	126	69	66	15	56	111
OPPONENTS	3	11	5.59	14	14	2	130	149	90	81	18	72	96

Fenway Park

In the 1980s, a National League pitcher remarked that he could stand on a mound in any one of the "cookie-cutter" stadiums and not know if he was in Philadelphia, Pittsburgh, or Cincinnati. A visit to one of those all-purpose stadiums with ersatz grass, analogous foul lines, and antiseptic ambience will leave any Red Sox fan homesick for Fenway Park. Fenway is unmistakably of baseball, by baseball, and, most definitely, for baseball.

For their first eleven seasons in the American League, the Red Sox played at the Huntington Avenue Grounds. But in 1912, Fenway was built. Sox owner John I. Taylor named it without any great show of originality: "It's in the Fenway section [of Boston], isn't it? Then call it Fenway Park."

Fenway was scheduled to open with the Red Sox against New York on April 18, 1912, but two days of rain pushed the initial game back two days. Those who worried about ill omens were mollified by Boston's 11-inning, 7–6 win against the team then known as the "Highlanders." Tris Speaker drove in the winning run against New York to send 27,000 Red Sox fans home happy. The event would have been front-page news in Boston had it not been bumped by the story of the sinking of the *Titanic*.

The Red Sox were able to initiate their new park into the World Series in that first year, as Boston beat the Giants in a classic. Two years later, Fenway hosted another World Series, but this one didn't involve the Red Sox. The 1914 Braves put on a "miracle" drive at the end of the season to win one of their two twentieth-century National League pennants. And, because Braves Field was still only a construction site, they played—and astonishingly beat—Connie Mack's Philadelphia Athletics for the World Championship. The Red Sox won pennants in 1915 and '16, but by then Braves Field, with its larger capacity, was open and the Boston games of both Series were played there.

That wasn't the last time the Red Sox deserted their home for Braves Field. Sunday baseball was approved in 1929, but for the first couple of years the Sox played their Sunday games at Braves Field because Fenway Park was near a church. Finally, on July 3, 1932, Fenway saw its first Sunday game—a 13–2 loss to the Yankees.

On May 8, 1926, a fire destroyed the bleachers along the left-field foul line. Team owner Bob Quinn was barely able to meet his payroll and had nothing left over for new seats. For the rest of the time he owned the Sox, infielders could dash behind the third-base grandstand to catch foul balls.

As soon as Tom Yawkey took over, he launched a rebuilding program. Another fire in left was a setback, but by 1934, Fenway was as good as new.

That year, a crowd of 46,766 showed up on August 12 to say good-bye to Babe Ruth, then in his last season with the Yankees. A week later, that record was broken by the 46,995 who came out for a doubleheader with the pennant-bound Tigers. The all-time Fenway Park record was set on September 22, 1935—47,627 for a Yankee doubleheader. The park will never see such crowds again unless there's a major reconstruction because fire laws passed during World War II prohibited such overcrowding.

Fenway Park's most famous feature is its left-field wall. Originally, it was just a humdrum, ten-foot-high wood fence, but a ten-foot-high incline, which acted much as today's warning tracks do, extended all the way across left field at the fence. Duffy Lewis quickly became the master of playing the incline, and it became known as "Duffy's Cliff." Visiting outfielders unfamiliar with this particular piece of real estate had fits playing balls off the wall. The wall itself was raised to its present 37.17 feet in 1917. The lower part was concrete; the upper part was tin-covered wood.

That changed after the 1975 World Series, when Fred Lynn crashed into the concrete wall trying to make a catch, and then lay on the ground for minutes afterwards. So since 1976, the wall has been a hard plastic, with padding at the base.

When Yawkey revamped Fenway in 1934, he had "Duffy's Cliff" flattened. The 23-foot screen was placed on top in 1936, not to save baseballs, but to save windows on Lansdowne Street. Until 1947, fans could read ads about Gem Blades, Lifebouy Soap, and Vimms on the wall, but that year it was covered with a coat of green paint and became the "Green Monster."

In 1940, one year after left-handed pull-hitting Ted Williams made his debut, bullpens were constructed in right field, bringing the fence 23 feet closer to home plate. The new bullpens thus became known as "Williamsburg."

Skyview seats were installed in 1946, and the next year saw lights for night games placed in Fenway. The Red Sox first home night game was a 5–3 over the White Sox on June 13, 1947.

In Fenway, even the foul pole has its own name—Pesky's Pole. According to Johnny Pesky, it was dubbed as such by Sox pitcher Mel Parnell in the 1950s after Pesky hit a home run just beyond the right-field foul pole to give Parnell the win in the game. It was one of only six home runs Pesky hit in his career at Fenway.

The Red Sox dropped plans to move out of Fenway when the new ownership group came in, and instead focused on ways to improve the existing park. In 2002, the team converted standing room into 400 seats without changing capacity. In 2003, the Red Sox created a new experience for their fans, adding 174 seats atop the fabled Green Monster in left field. The new seats were an instant hit, and *Boston* magazine dubbed them the best seats in Boston.

2
PUZZLES

ACROSS

1. The Monster who pitched in front of The Green Monster
5. Leonard, Ruth, Grove, Parnell, Hurst all threw——
10. A "bender" that is sometimes the chief
11. 1,451 RBI
12. Won 25 in 1949
13. Triple Crown in 1967
16. Three-time RBI champ of the 1950s
17. Batting champ of 1950
20. 23-game winner in 1949
21. All-time doubles champion
22. Jimmie, Shano, or Eddie
24. Rocket
26. 34–5 in 1912
29. Rookie of the Year in 1950
31. One Joe hurt us in 1975; another led in '88
33. Everett or Boomer
34. This one was splendid
35. Vern Stephens

DOWN

1. Batting champ in 1960 and '62
2. Won three Series games in 1903 (variant spelling)
3. Three times better than a single
4. Sox first home-run champ
6. "The Beast"
7. "The Hawk"
8. No. 1 at second base
9. Lewis or Hugh
10. Managed 1915–1916 champions
12a. Rookie of the Year and MVP in 1975
14. Holder of Red Sox record for rookie hits
15. Play or header
18. Won number 300 in 1941
19. Author of *Fear Strikes Out*
21. Ted or Dick (or Dib in 1935)
22. Clark Griffith's son-in-law
23. You'll find it at home (but don't try to eat off it)
25. In French, *wrong-zone*; but he was right at third
27. "The Little Professor"
28. Wade or cranberry
30. Waved it fair in Game 6
32. Lewis, Speaker, and——

RED SOX HEROES

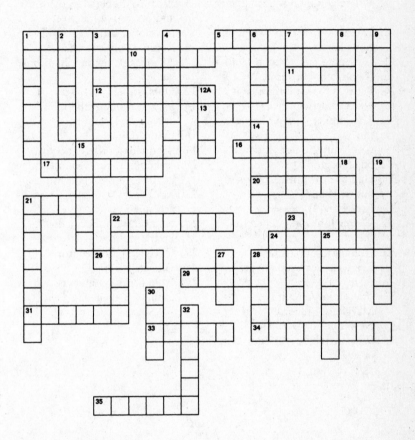

ACROSS	DOWN

ACROSS

1. Double play or a win over Minnesota
4. Foe in 1903
7. Where you'll find the manager and subs
8. The best place to be when on gameday
11. He scored from first in 1946
13. A half game better in 1972
14. Better to be on it than be it
15. Nee Orioles
18. The Yankee Clipper batted this way
19. Not really enough; it takes one more
21. Had us down three games to one in 1986
23. Park I and II
26. Walter Johnson pitched for them
30. One-ninth of a game
31. Every runner wants to get there
32. The Junior Circuit
34. Maryland's favorite birds
35. New York or Damn
36. What Armbrister tried to do in 1975

DOWN

1. The 1991 World Champions
2. Won the playoff in 1948
3. Perfect color for a Monster
5. What to do between the top and bottom of the seventh
6. Sox not at Fenway
9. Robin Yount's team
10. Clemens struck out 20 in one game
12. Outs, strikes, or bases
14. How certain northern birds are after a loss
16. Outfield limit
17. A hose of a different color
20. From Philly to K.C. to Oakland
22. Yankee shortstop who ruined Sox in 1978
24. He makes up the lineup
25. Brett's team
27. Once were the Senators
28. Outside the lines
29. 1986 Series opponents
33. Innings or on a side

RED SOX VILLAINS

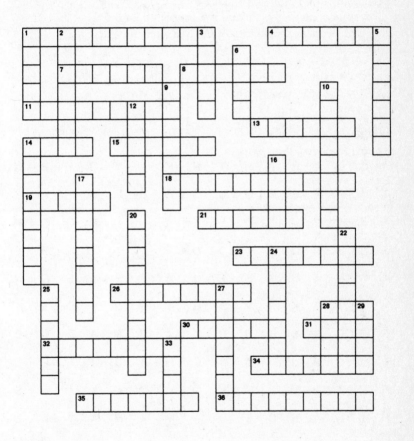

WHO'S IN CHARGE HERE?

Namesearch: Managers

In the NAMESEARCH maze below are the last names of 20 men who have managed the Red Sox at one time or another. All you have to do is circle them. Of course, to make it sporting, we spelled some backward, some diagonally, some down, some up, and only a few across. The first names or nicknames of the managers included are:

Joe	Darrell	Marse Joe	Ralph
Billy	Ed	Joe (again)	Don
Jimmy	Jake	Eddie	Butch
Lee	Lou	Pinky	John
Johnny	Hugh	Frank	Rough

M C C A R T H Y R H T Y G Z B N

O A R N S E C D G W B R U I A O

R K W U H L O S T A H L Z G R M

G E S N O O T D U R U T I K R E

A W N A U A B T J A F R T E O N

N J I B K R V S H M R C B O W T

R F G G E K H R O A R N W D U P

D R G F J O O L C N A G J L P E

U Z I M M E R V O C O L L I N S

H C H A N C E D R M K H A Y A K

R H R B S W N O S N H O J F O Y

T E A L H T N N C D P F I F M O

P F G O E I R K U A E R D U O B

A L C R N A M R E H U A S D E S

Red Sox Heroes Answers

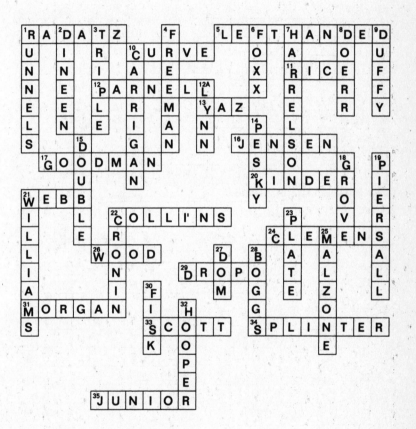

Red Sox Villains Answers

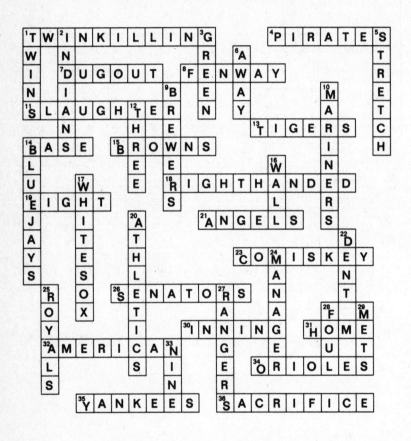

```
M C C A R T H Y R H T Y G Z B N
O A R N S E C D G W B R U I A O
R K W U H L O S T A H L Z G R M
G E S N O O T D U R U T I K R E
A W N A U A B T J A F R T E O N
N J I B K R V S H M R C B O W T
R F G G E K H R O A R N W D U P
D R G F J O O L C N A G J L P E
U Z I M M E R V O C O L L I N S
H C H A N C E D R M K H A Y A K
R H R B S W N O S N H O J F O Y
T E A L H T N N C D P F I F M O
P F G O E I R K U A E R D U O B
A L C R N A M R E H U A S D E S
```

3
TRIVIA QUESTIONS
AND ANSWERS

PILGRIMS' PROGRESS, 1901–1909

1. Before they were the Red Sox, the team was called the
   a. Beaneaters
   b. Celtics
   c. Red Caps
   d. Pilgrims

2. The team's first manager was
   a. Eddie Collins
   b. Jimmy Collins
   c. Tom Collins
   d. Phil Collins

3. The original owner of the Boston A.L. team was
   a. Tom Yawkey
   b. Arthur Soden
   c. Ban Johnson
   d. Charles Somers

4. Boston's A.L. team played its first home games at
   a. Huntington Avenue Grounds
   b. Braves Field
   c. Fenway Park
   d. South End Grounds

5. In their first season, the Bostons finished second to
   a. Philadelphia Athletics
   b. Chicago White Stockings
   c. Cleveland Indians
   d. St. Louis Browns

6. The first Boston player to lead the American League in home runs was
   a. Babe Ruth
   b. Jimmy Collins
   c. Buck Freeman
   d. Tris Speaker

7. The Pittsburgh pitcher who beat Boston three times in the first modern World Series was
   a. Deacon Phillippe
   b. Preacher Roe
   c. Parson Weems
   d. Pop Haines

8. Boston's pitching hero with three wins in the 1903 World Series was
   a. Cy Young
   b. Bill Dinneen
   c. Long Tom Hughes
   d. Jesse Tannehill

9. The song the Royal Rooters incessantly sang during the 1903 World Series was
   a. "Auld Lang Syne"
   b. "Slide, Kelly, Slide"
   c. "Sweetheart of Sigma Chi"
   d. "Tessie"

10. Whose wild pitch against Boston in 1904 cost New York the pennant?
    a. Sad Sam Jones
    b. Fat Freddy Fitzsimmons
    c. Happy Jack Chesbro
    d. Iron Man Joe McGinnity

11. Which team won the 1904 World Series?
    a. Boston
    b. New York Giants
    c. Chicago Cubs
    d. No one

12. The first pitcher to throw a perfect game in the twentieth century was
    a. Don Larsen
    b. Nolan Ryan
    c. Cy Young
    d. Rube Waddell

13. The team was named the Red Sox by
    a. Owner John I. Taylor
    b. Sportswriter Tim Murnane
    c. Mayor John F. Fitzgerald
    d. A.L. President Ban Johnson

14. What famous Philadelphia Athletics pitcher defeated Cy Young in a 20-inning game?
    a. Edide Plank
    b. Rube Waddell
    c. Chief Bender
    d. Jack Coombs

15. The Red Sox manager who died—an apparent suicide—during spring training in 1907 was
    a. Jake Stahl
    b. Chick Stahl
    c. George Stallings
    d. Chic Sales

THE BEST OF TIMES, 1910–1918

1. The only brothers to manage the same major-league team were the
   a. Alous
   b. Sewells
   c. Stahls
   d. Ferrells

2. The strong-armed Red Sox right fielder for this decade was
   a. Duffy Lewis
   b. Harry Hooper
   c. Tris Speaker
   d. Larry Gardner

3. The second Red Sox player to lead the American League in home runs was
   a. Babe Ruth
   b. Tris Speaker
   c. Braggo Roth
   d. Chick Stahl

4. How many consecutive games did Smokey Joe Wood win in 1912 to tie the record?
   a. 10
   b. 16
   c. 19
   d. 24

5. Who made an infamous muff of a fly ball in the 1912 World Series?
   a. Josh Devore
   b. Tris Speaker
   c. Fred Merkle
   d. Fred Snodgrass

6. The Red Sox hurler with the most wins in a season to date is
   a. Cy Young
   b. Dutch Leonard
   c. Smokey Joe Wood
   d. Ray Collins

7. What was Manager Rough Carrigan's position in the field?
   a. Catcher
   b. First base
   c. Third base
   d. Outfield

8. Who was the only pitcher to defeat the Red Sox in the 1915 World Series?
   a. Christy Mathewson
   b. Grover Alexander
   c. Herb Pennock
   d. Walter Johnson

9. What was the Red Sox home field in the 1915 and 1916 World Series?
   a. Fenway Park
   b. Braves Field
   c. Huntington Avenue Grounds
   d. Harvard Stadium

10. Where did Tris Speaker go when he was traded before the 1916 season?
    a. Detroit Tigers
    b. Boston Braves
    c. New York Yankees
    d. Cleveland Indians

11. Who was the winning pitcher in the 14-inning, 2–1 second game of the 1916 World Series?
    a. Babe Ruth
    b. Grover Alexander
    c. Christy Mathewson
    d. Sherry Smith

12. Who relieved Babe Ruth and went on to retire 26 batters in a row?
    a. Hugh Bedient
    b. Ernie Shore
    c. Carl Mays
    d. Rube Foster

13. What effect did the goverment's "work or fight" order have on the 1918 baseball season?
    a. None
    b. It was cancelled
    c. It ended on September 1
    d. Players held two jobs

14. The Red Sox's opponents in the 1918 World Series were the
    a. Brooklyn Dodgers
    b. Chicago Cubs
    c. New York Giants
    d. Philadelphia Phillies

15. Who made the decision to turn Babe Ruth into an outfielder?
    a. Rough Carrigan
    b. Harry Frazee
    c. Ed Barrow
    d. Jack Barry

THE WORST OF TIMES, 1919–1932

1. What was Harry Frazee's big Broadway hit?
    a. *No, No, Nanette*
    b. *Good News*
    c. *The Jazz Singer*
    d. *Where's Charley?*

2. Which of the following pitchers was *not* sent to the Yankees by the Red Sox?
    a. Herb Pennock
    b. Waite Hoyt
    c. Howard Ehmke
    d. Carl Mays

3. What was the security for the loan that was part of the deal that sent Babe Ruth to New York?
    a. Harry Frazee's estate
    b. Fenway Park
    c. Frazee's life insurance
    d. Rights to Frazee's next show

4. Whose all-time home-run record did Babe Ruth break in 1919?
   a. Frank Baker
   b. Ned Williamson
   c. King Kelly
   d. Roger Connor

5. The Red Sox longtime shortstop who became a Yankee in 1922 was
   a. Everett Scott
   b. Jack Barry
   c. Roger Peckinpaugh
   d. Stuffy McInnis

6. After he left the Red Sox, what team did Ed Barrow go to work for?
   a. Tigers
   b. Indians
   c. Yankees
   d. White Sox

7. Before managing the Red Sox, Frank Chance was the first baseman in an infield with what doubleplay combination?
   a. Honus Wagner and Dots Miller
   b. Fred Parent and Eddie Collins
   c. Joe Tinker and Johnny Evers
   d. Jack Barry and Hobe Ferris

8. What Red Sox pitcher won 20 games for a last-place team in 1923?
   a. Jack Quinn
   b. Howard Ehmke
   c. Herb Pennock
   d. Bullet Joe Bush

9. Before buying the Red Sox, Bob Quinn was a successful executive with the
   a. Chicago White Sox
   b. Philadelphia Phillies
   c. St. Louis Browns
   d. St. Louis Cardinals

10. The only Red Sox player ever to get an unassisted triple play was
    a. Ira Flagstead
    b. George Burns
    c. Rabbit Warstler
    d. Johnny Neun

11. Perhaps the worst fielder ever to play the outfield for the Red Sox was
    a. Tom Oliver
    b. Babe Ruth
    c. Harry Hooper
    d. Smead Jolley

12. What former Red Sox pennant-winning manager came back to try (unsuccessfully) again in 1927?
    a. Rough Carrigan   c. Jake Stahl
    b. Jimmy Collins   d. Ed Barrow

13. What future Hall of Fame pitcher lost 47 games for the Red Sox in 1928–1929?
    a. Danny MacFayden   c. Waite Hoyt
    b. Red Ruffing   d. Ed Morris

14. The Red Sox player who set the all-time record for doubles in a season was
    a. Phil Todt   c. Earl Webb
    b. Moon Harris   d. Buddy Myer

15. The first Red Sox player to lead the American League in hitting was
    a. Ted Williams   c. Tris Speaker
    b. Dale Alexander   d. Cedric Durst

BUY ME A CHAMPION, 1933–1946

1. What team had Tom Yawkey's uncle owned?
    a. St. Louis Browns   c. Philadelphia Phillies
    b. Boston Braves   d. Detroit Tigers

2. Who did Yawkey hire as his vice president and general manager?
    a. Eddie Collins   c. Tris Speaker
    b. Rough Carrigan   d. Ed Barrow

3. In one of the GM's first moves, what Hall of Fame catcher came from St. Louis?
    a. Wes Ferrell   c. Charlie Farrell
    b. Rick Ferrell   d. Duke Farrell

4. What Red Sox player led the A.L. in stolen bases in 1934–35?
    a. Tom Oliver   c. Doc Cramer
    b. Billy Werber   d. Max Bishop

5. Because of the Great Depression, what club owner sent two future Hall of Famers to the Red Sox in the 1930s?
   a. Clark Griffith
   b. Jake Ruppert
   c. Connie Mack
   d. Phil Ball

6. What Sox lefty led the A.L. in ERA four times in the late 1930s?
   a. Lefty Liefield
   b. Lefty O'Doul
   c. Lefty Grove
   d. Lefty Gomez

7. Joe Cronin was whose son-in-law?
   a. Tom Yawkey
   b. Connie Mack
   c. Eddie Collins
   d. Clark Griffith

8. The American League's MVP in 1938 with 175 RBI was
   a. Jimmie Foxx
   b. Joe Cronin
   c. Ted Williams
   d. Dale Alexander

9. Eddie Collins discovered Ted Williams on a trip to look at
   a. Johnny Pesky
   b. Bobby Doerr
   c. Pinky Higgins
   d. Dom DiMaggio

10. What was Ted Williams' batting average with one day left in the 1941 season?
    a. .406
    b. .399
    c. .3996
    d. .4001

11. Which pitcher joined Cy Young in 1941 as the only two pitchers to gain their 300th career win in a Red Sox uniform?
    a. Dick Newsome
    b. Tex Hughson
    c. Lefty Grove
    d. Lefty Gomez

12. Who was chosen over Williams as 1942 MVP?
    a. Joe DiMaggio
    b. Joe Gordon
    c. Joe Cronin
    d. Joe Kuhel

13. The leading A.L. pitcher in 1942, with a 22–6 mark, was
    a. Tex Hughson
    b. Tex Carleton
    c. Tex Ritter
    d. Tex Schramm

14. Whose tenth-inning homer won Game One of the 1946 Series?
    a. Ted Williams   c. Bobby Doerr
    b. George Metkovich   d. Rudy York

15. Whose hit drove home Enos Slaughter with the winning run in Game Seven?
    a. Harry Walker   c. Whitey Kurowski
    b. Stan Musial   d. Marty Marion

FRUSTRATIONS AND A DREAM, 1947–1967

1. Which of the following Red Sox pitchers did NOT come down with a sore arm in 1947?
    a. Tex Hughson   c. Boo Ferriss
    b. Joe Dobson   d. Mickey Harris

2. Vern Stephens was acquired by the Red Sox in a deal with the
    a. Cleveland Indians   c. St. Louis Browns
    b. Detroit Tigers   d. Washington Senators

3. Who was the starting pitcher for Boston in the 1948 playoff?
    a. Joe Dobson   c. Jack Kramer
    b. Denny Galehouse   d. Mel Parnell

4. What did Ted Williams do in the 1950 All-Star Game?
    a. Struck out 4 times   c. Hit 2 home runs
    b. Broke his elbow   d. Sprained his ankle

5. Who won the 1950 American League batting title?
    a. Ted Williams   c. Al Zarilla
    b. Johnny Pesky   d. Billy Goodman

6. What Red Sox outfielder suffered a widely publicized mental breakdown in 1952?
    a. Al Zarilla   c. Ted Williams
    b. Jimmy Piersall   d. Jackie Jensen

7. What Red Sox first baseman (and former All-American football star) died early in the 1955 season?
    a. Walt Dropo   c. Harry Agganis
    b. Jackie Jensen   d. Norm Zauchin

8. The first African-American player to wear a Red Sox uniform was
    a. Pumpsie Green   c. Billy Harrell
    b. Willie Tasby   d. Felix Mantilla

9. Since Ted Williams hit .406 in 1941, what major-league player has come the closest to hitting .400?
    a. Wade Boggs   c. George Brett
    b. Ted Williams   d. Tony Gwynn

10. In his final at bat, Ted Williams
    a. homered   c. struck out
    b. was intentionally walked   d. was hit by a pitch

11. Former Red Sox first baseman Dick Stuart was called
    a. The Boston Strangler   c. E-three
    b. Old Ironglove   d. Dr. Strangeglove

12. How old was Tony Conigliaro when he led the American League in home runs?
    a. 19   c. 36
    b. 20   d. 41

13. Reliever Dick Radatz was called
    a. Radical   c. The Green Monster
    b. The Ogre   d. The Monster

14. What Cardinals pitcher won three games in the 1967 World Series?
    a. Nelson Briles   c. Steve Carlton
    b. Bob Gibson   d. Ray Washburn

15. Name Boston's Cy Young Award winner of 1967.
    a. Jim Lonborg   c. Jose Santiago
    b. Gary Bell   d. John Wyatt

THE CLOSE-CALL YEARS, 1968–1985

1. What kind of accident derailed Jim Lonborg after his Cy Young season?
   - a. Train
   - b. Skiing
   - c. Auto
   - d. Mountain climbing

2. What was 1968 "The Year of"?
   - a. "Narrow Defeats"
   - b. "Chaos"
   - c. "The Pitcher"
   - d. "Managers"

3. The surprise A.L. RBI leader in 1968 was
   - a. Ken Harrelson
   - b. George Scott
   - c. Carl Yastrzemski
   - d. Reggie Smith

4. What Red Sox player won Rookie of the Year honors in 1972?
   - a. Carlton Fisk
   - b. Doug Griffin
   - c. Dwight Evans
   - d. Rick Burleson

5. Who was the Red Sox first full-time designated hitter?
   - a. Tommy Harper
   - b. Orlando Cepeda
   - c. Carl Yastrzemski
   - d. Dwight Evans

6. What Red Sox pitcher won Comeback Player of the Year in 1972?
   - a. Bill Lee
   - b. Marty Pattin
   - c. Sonny Siebert
   - d. Luis Tiant

7. When he won Rookie of the Year and MVP honors in 1975, Fred Lynn led the American League in
   - a. hits
   - b. runs
   - c. RBI
   - d. batting

8. The Red Sox pitching hero of the 1975 World Series, with two victories, was
   - a. Luis Tiant
   - b. Roger Moret
   - c. Rick Wise
   - d. Jim Willoughby

9. What Red Soxer became only the second player ever to hit two pinch-hit homers in a World Series?
   - a. Rick Miller
   - b. Jim Rice
   - c. Bernie Carbo
   - d. Cecil Cooper

10. Whose great catch of a Joe Morgan drive kept Red Sox hopes alive in Game Six of the 1975 World Series?
    - a. Carl Yastrzemski
    - b. Rick Miller
    - c. Fred Lynn
    - d. Dwight Evans

11. What Reds pitcher gave up Carlton Fisk's winning homer in Game Six?
    - a. Pat Darcy
    - b. Pedro Borbon
    - c. Will McEnaney
    - d. Rawley Eastwick

12. What Red Sox pitcher gave up Bucky Dent's playoff-game homer in 1978?
    - a. Mike Torrez
    - b. Bob Stanley
    - c. Dennis Eckersley
    - d. Luis Tiant

13. Who won the 1981 A.L. batting title?
    - a. Dwight Evans
    - b. Carl Yastrzemski
    - c. Jim Rice
    - d. Carney Lansford

14. How many batting titles did Yaz win in his career?
    - a. 3
    - b. 4
    - c. 5
    - d. 7

15. The Red Sox hitter who won both the home-run and RBI crowns in 1984 was
    - a. Jim Rice
    - b. Dwight Evans
    - c. Bill Buckner
    - d. Tony Armas

PITCHING AND HEARTACHE, 1986–2003

1. Roger Clemens's 20 strikeouts in a game in 1986 were against the
   - a. New York Yankees
   - b. Cleveland Indians
   - c. Texas Rangers
   - d. Seattle Mariners

2. With the Sox trailing 3 games to 1 in the 1986 LCS and trailing with two out in the ninth, whose homer kept them alive?
   a. Tony Armas
   b. Spike Owen
   c. Dave Henderson
   d. Bill Buckner

3. Name the Red Sox hurler with two wins in the 1986 World Series.
   a. Oil Can Boyd
   b. Bruce Hurst
   c. Roger Clemens
   d. Bob Stanley

4. Who hit the ball that trickled between Buckner's legs in Game Six?
   a. Ray Knight
   b. Mookie Wilson
   c. Gary Carter
   d. Darryl Strawberry

5. How many batting titles did Wade Boggs win?
   a. 3
   b. 4
   c. 5
   d. 7

6. In 1988, the Sox caught fire when who was named manager?
   a. John McNamara
   b. Joe Morgan
   c. Ralph Houk
   d. Dick Williams

7. How many playoff games did the Red Sox win from 1988 through 2001?
   a. None
   b. Seven
   c. Five
   d. Four

8. What happened to Roger Clemens in the second inning of Game Four of the 1990 LCS?
   a. He was ejected
   b. He gave up four homers
   c. He was injured
   d. He was hit by a batted ball

9. What did Boston fans hold to show how they felt about the Red Sox chances in August 1991?
   a. Coronation Ball
   b. Pool for clinching date
   c. Mock funeral
   d. Manager hanged in effigy

10. Which Red Sox pitcher goes by the nickname "El Guapo?"
    a. Rolando Arrojo
    b. Rich Garces
    c. Hipolido Pichardo
    d. Jim Corsi

11. Who became the fifth Red Sox player to win the Rookie of the Year award in 1997?
    a. Mo Vaughn
    b. Jason Varitek
    c. Nomar Garciaparra
    d. Aaron Sele

12. Members of the 1998 pitching staff had how many Cy Young awards between them at the start of the 2001 season?
    a. One
    b. Five
    c. Three
    d. Six

13. Who was the offensive star of Boston's playoff series win over Cleveland in 1999, batting .318 with three home runs and 12 RBI?
    a. John Valentin
    b. Jose Offerman
    c. Nomar Garciaparra
    d. Mike Stanley

14. The first Red Sox no-hitter since 1965 was pitched by
    a. Pedro Martinez
    b. Hideo Nomo
    c. Roger Clemens
    d. Danny Darwin

15. Which of the following players did *not* go on the disabled list in 2001?
    a. Jose Offerman
    b. Pedro Martinez
    c. Carl Everett
    d. Nomar Garciaparra

REVERSING THE CURSE, 2004

1. Who was never named captain of the Red Sox?
    a. Ted Williams
    b. Jim Rice
    c. Jason Varitek
    d. Carl Yastrzemski

2. Tim Wakefield has a chance to pass Roger Clemens and Cy Young in the Red Sox history book and become the all-time leader in which category in 2005?
    a. Wins
    b. Losses
    c. Walks
    d. Strikeouts

3. Jason Varitek now holds the career postseason mark for Red Sox home runs with nine. Whose record did he break?
   - a. Manny Ramirez
   - b. Nomar Garciaparra
   - c. John Valentin
   - d. Todd Walker

4. David Ortiz's 19 postseason RBI tied a record also held by Scott Spiezio for Anaheim in 2002 and this man:
   - a. Bernie Williams
   - b. Albert Belle
   - c. Derek Jeter
   - d. Sandy Alomar Jr.

5. David Ortiz hit postseason walk-off home runs in both 2003 and 2004. Which two other Red Sox players also accomplished the feat?
   - a. Carlton Fisk and Nomar Garciaparra
   - b. Nomar Garciaparra and Manny Ramirez
   - c. Trot Nixon and Manny Ramirez
   - d. Carlton Fisk and Trot Nixon

6. Which player's nickname is "Big Papi?"
   - a. David Ortiz
   - b. Manny Ramirez
   - c. Pokey Reese
   - d. Trot Nixon

7. Which Red Sox hitter tied a postseason record by hitting in 17 straight games?
   - a. Manny Ramirez
   - b. Bill Mueller
   - c. David Ortiz
   - d. Johnny Damon

8. With the New England Patriots Super Bowl win on Feb. 1, 2004, Boston became the third city to win the World Series and Super Bowl in the same calendar year. The first was New York (Mets and Jets in 1969). Which was the second?
   - a. San Francisco
   - b. Detroit
   - c. Pittsburgh
   - d. Baltimore

9. At the end of the 2004 season, which player had the highest lifetime slugging percentage for the Red Sox?
   - a. Manny Ramirez
   - b. Nomar Garciaparra
   - c. Jimmie Foxx
   - d. Ted Williams

10. With the mid-season trade of Nomar and Ellis Burks announcing his retirement at the end of the season, which current Red Sox player goes into 2005 with the most games played in a Boston uniform?

    a. Manny Ramirez   c. Trot Nixon

    b. Jason Varitek   d. Johnny Damon

11. Which player still active at the end of 2004 had pitched the most games in a Boston uniform?

    a. Tim Wakefield   c. Roger Clemens

    b. Derek Lowe   d. Pedro Martinez

12. Of the 25 players on the Red Sox 2004 World Series roster, how many were acquired by general manager Theo Epstein?

    a. 12   c. 18

    b. 15   d. 21

13. Kevin Youkilis was one of two players on the 2004 World Series roster for Boston who were originally drafted and signed by the organization. Who was the other?

    a. Tim Wakefield   c. Trot Nixon

    b. Gabe Kapler   d. Derek Lowe

14. Owner John Henry posted an announcement of the Curt Schilling trade on an Internet message board named SOSH. What does SOSH stand for?

    a. Sons of Sam Horn   c. Speaker Often Steals Home

    b. SO Says Henry   d. Speaking of Stanley's Home

15. What happened between 9:23 and 10:45 P.M. the night of the final game of the 2004 World Series?

    a. A mock Red Sox funeral   c. Trading was suspended on the Nisei

    b. A lunar eclipse   d. The Yankees signed three new players

MATCH THE PLAYER TO THE NUMBER

1. ____Wade Boggs   25

2. ____Roger Clemens   .406

3. ____Jimmie Foxx   67

4. ____Mel Parnell   .301

5. ____Pedro Martinez   34

6. ____Earl Webb   20

7. ____Ted Williams   313

8. ____Smokey Joe Wood   511

9. ____Carl Yastrzemski   175

10. ____Cy Young   240

"WHAT HAPPENS WHEN OUR THIRD BASEMAN IS REALLY TIRED?"

Answer: "Wade boggs down."

Here's a little just-for-fun quiz in which the logical answers incorporate great Red Sox names. If you hate puns and think ESPN's Chris Berman and his fanciful player nicknames are a yawn, skip this. If you have a slightly bent sense of the ridiculous, read on.

1. "How do you open a great second baseman?"
2. "What does a slugging left fielder eat for breakfast?"
3. "What should you call a brilliant center fielder in the U.S. House of Representatives?"
4. "Where did a premier reliever of the 1950s start to school?"
5. "Speaking of schools, whose parent-teacher meetings does the 1973 A.L. base-stealing champ attend?"

6. "How should you measure radioactivity on a speedy center fielder of the early 1960s?"
7. "What cowboy song does a pre-World War I infielder and manager sing?"
8. "Meanwhile, what is that blues a good-hitting second sacker and utility man of the 1950s is singing?"
9. "What does a 25-game winner from 1946 go around on?"
10. "Do you think that 1975's 19-game winner is a smart aleck?"

Answers to Pilgrims' Progress, 1901–1909

1. d. Pilgrims
2. b. Jimmy Collins
3. d. Charles Somers
4. a. Huntington Avenue Grounds
5. b. Chicago White Stockings
6. c. Buck Freeman
7. a. Deacon Phillippe
8. b. Bill Dinneen
9. d. "Tessie"
10. c. Happy Jack Chesbro
11. d. No one
12. c. Cy Young
13. a. Owner John I. Taylor
14. b. Rube Waddell
15. b. Chick Stahl

Answers to the Best of Times, 1910–1918

1. c. Stahls
2. b. Harry Hooper
3. d. Chick Stahl
4. b. 16
5. d. Fred Snodgrass
6. c. Smokey Joe Wood
7. a. Catcher
8. b. Grover Alexander

9. b. Braves Field
10. d. Cleveland Indians
11. a. Babe Ruth
12. b. Ernie Shore
13. c. It ended on September 1
14. b. Chicago Cubs
15. c. Ed Barrow

Answers to the Worst of Times, 1919–1932

1. a. *No, No, Nanette*
2. c. Howard Ehmke
3. b. Fenway Park
4. b. Ned Williamson
5. a. Everett Scott
6. c. Yankees
7. c. Joe Tinker and Johnny Evers
8. b. Howard Ehmke
9. c. St. Louis Browns
10. b. George Burns
11. d. Smead Jolley
12. a. Rough Carrigan
13. b. Red Ruffing
14. c. Earl Webb
15. b. Dale Alexander

Buy Me a Champion, 1933–1946

1. d. Detroit Tigers
2. a. Eddie Collins
3. b. Rick Ferrell
4. b. Billy Werber
5. c. Connie Mack
6. c. Lefty Grove
7. d. Clark Griffith
8. a. Jimmie Foxx
9. b. Bobby Doerr
10. c. .3996

11. c. Lefty Grove
12. b. Joe Gordon
13. a. Tex Hughson
14. d. Rudy York
15. a. Harry Walker

Answers to Frustrations and a Dream, 1947–1967

1. b. Joe Dobson
2. c. St. Louis Browns
3. b. Denny Galehouse
4. b. Broke his elbow
5. d. Billy Goodman
6. b. Jimmy Piersall
7. c. Harry Agganis
8. a. Pumpsie Green
9. d. Tony Gwynn
10. a. homered
11. d. "Dr. Strangeglove"
12. b. 20
13. d. The Monster
14. b. Bob Gibson
15. a. Jim Lonborg

Answers to the Close-Call Years, 1968–1985

1. b. Skiing
2. c. "The Pitcher"
3. a. Ken Harrelson
4. a. Carlton Fisk
5. b. Orlando Cepeda
6. d. Luis Tiant
7. b. runs
8. a. Luis Tiant
9. c. Bernie Carbo
10. d. Dwight Evans
11. a. Pat Darcy
12. a. Mike Torrez

13. d. Carney Lansford
14. a. 3
15. d. Tony Armas

Answers to Pitching and Heartache, 1986–2003

1. d. Seattle Mariners
2. c. Dave Henderson
3. b. Bruce Hurst
4. b. Mookie Wilson
5. c. 5
6. b. Joe Morgan
7. c. Five
8. a. He was ejected
9. c. Mock funeral
10. b. Rich Garces
11. c. Nomar Garciaparra
12. d. Six
13. a. John Valentin
14. b. Hideo Nomo
15. a. Jose Offerman

Answers to Reversing the Curse, 2004

1. a. Ted Williams
2. b. Losses. Wakefield has 99 while Young had 112 and Clemens 111.
3. b. Nomar Garciaparra had seven
4. d. Sandy Alomar Jr. had 19 for the Indians in 1997
5. d. Carlton Fisk (in 1975) and Trot Nixon (in 2003)
6. a. David Ortiz
7. a. Manny Ramirez, tying Yankees Derek Jeter and Hank Bauer
8. c. Pittsburgh Pirates and Steelers in 1979
9. d. Ted Williams (.634); Ramirez is second, Foxx third, and Nomar fourth
10. b. Jason Varitek with 832 games played; Nixon is second with 744
11. a. Tim Wakefield with 387

12. b. Fifteen of the 25 were acquired after Nov. 25, 2002
13. c. Trot Nixon
14. a. Sons of Sam Horn
15. b. A lunar eclipse; Hector Luna of the Cardinals pinch-hit and struck out during the eclipse

Answers to Match the Player to the Number

1. 240, Wade Boggs's hits in 1985 (club record)
2. 20, Roger Clemens's strikeouts in one game (league record)
3. 175, Jimmie Foxx's RBI in 1938 (club record)
4. 25, Mel Parnell's wins in 1949 (club record for a lefty)
5. 313, Pedro Martinez's strikeouts in 1999 (club record)
6. 67, Earl Webb's doubles in 1931 (major league record)
7. .406, Ted Williams' 1941 batting average (last .400 season)
8. 34, Smokey Joe Wood's wins in 1912 (club record)
9. .301, Carl Yastrzemski's batting average in 1968 (the lowest to ever lead a major league)
10. 511, Cy Young's career victories (192 with the Red Sox)

"What Happens When Our Third Baseman is Really Tired?" Answers

1. "With a Bobby Doerr-key."
2. "Jim Rice Krispies."
3. "Tris Speaker of the House."
4. "Ellis Kindergarten."
5. "The Tommy Harper Valley P.T.A."
6. "With a Gary Geiger counter."
7. "Jack Barry Me Not on the Lone Prairie."
8. "A Billy Goodman Is Hard to Find."
9. "A Dave Ferriss wheel."
10. "He's a real Rick Wise-acre."

4

RED SOX STATISTICAL LEADERS, RECORD HOLDERS, AWARD WINNERS, AND HALL-OF-FAMERS

RED SOX WITH 600 OR MORE AT BATS IN A SEASON

AB	PLAYER	YEAR	AB	PLAYER	YEAR
684	Nomar Garciaparra	1997	622	Dom DiMaggio	1948
677	Jim Rice	1976	621	Joe Vosmik	1938
673	Bill Buckner	1985	621	Johnny Pesky	1946
663	Rick Burleson	1977	621	Wade Boggs	1989
661	Doc Cramer	1940	621	Johnny Damon	2004
658	Doc Cramer	1938	620	Johnny Pesky	1942
658	Nomar Garciaparra	2003	619	Frank Malzone	1962
657	Jim Rice	1984	619	Jim Rice	1979
653	Wade Boggs	1985	619	Wade Boggs	1990
648	Dom DiMaggio	1948	618	Reggie Smith	1971
646	Tom Oliver	1930	618	Jim Rice	1986
646	Chuck Schilling	1961	618	Jody Reed	1991
646	Carl Yastrzemski	1962	617	Dwight Evans	1985
644	Jim Rice	1977	612	Dick Stuart	1963
644	Rick Burleson	1980	612	Marty Barrett	1988
643	Doc Cramer	1936	611	Troy O'Leary	1998
639	Dom DiMaggio	1951	610	Vern Stephens	1949
639	Tony Armas	1984	610	Mike Greenwell	1990
636	Johnny Pesky	1947	609	Jimmy Piersall	1957
636	Bill Wambsganss	1924	609	Dwight Evans	1982
636	Jerry Remy	1982	609	Mo Vaughn	1998
635	Vern Stephens	1948	608	Tony Lupien	1943
635	Mo Vaughn	1996	608	Johnny Damon	2003
635	Nomar Garciaparra	2002	607	Del Pratt	1922
634	Frank Malzone	1957	607	Mel Almada	1935
634	Shea Hillenbrand	2002	605	Dom DiMaggio	1949
633	Jimmy Collins	1904	604	Bobby Doerr	1943
630	Dwight Evans	1984	604	Johnny Pesky	1949
629	Bill Buckner	1986	604	Frank Malzone	1959
628	Vern Stephens	1950	604	Nomar Garciaparra	1998
627	Frank Malzone	1958	603	Dick Stuart	1964
627	Rick Burleson	1979	603	Carl Yastrzemski	1969
626	Rick Burleson	1978	602	Freddy Parent	1905
626	Jim Rice	1983	601	Jimmy Piersall	1956
625	Wade Boggs	1984	601	George Scott	1966
625	Marty Barrett	1986	601	Mike Easler	1984
623	Billy Werber	1934	600	Freddy Parent	1906
623	Johnny Damon	2002			

RED SOX WITH 175 OR MORE HITS IN A SEASON

H	PLAYER	YEAR	H	PLAYER	YEAR
240	Wade Boggs	1985	190	Nomar Garciaparra	1999
222	Tris Speaker	1912	189	Tom Oliver	1930
214	Wade Boggs	1988	189	Dom DiMaggio	1951
213	Jim Rice	1978	189	Carl Yastrzemski	1967
210	Wade Boggs	1983	189	Johnny Damon	2004
209	Nomar Garciaparra	1997	188	Doc Cramer	1936
208	Johnny Pesky	1946	188	Ted Williams	1948
207	Johnny Pesky	1947	188	Mike Easler	1984
207	Wade Boggs	1986	187	Wade Boggs	1990
207	Mo Vaughn	1996	186	Ted Williams	1942
206	Jim Rice	1977	186	Dom DiMaggio	1949
205	Johnny Pesky	1942	186	Carl Yastrzemski	1970
205	Wade Boggs	1989	186	Dwight Evans	1984
205	Mo Vaughn	1998	186	Shea Hillenbrand	2002
203	Wade Boggs	1984	185	Jimmy Collins	1901
201	Joe Vosmik	1938	185	Ted Williams	1939
201	Jim Rice	1979	185	Ted Williams	1941
201	Bill Buckner	1985	185	Dom DiMaggio	1948
200	Bill Werber	1934	185	Johnny Pesky	1949
200	Doc Cramer	1940	185	Vern Stephens	1950
200	Jim Rice	1986	185	Frank Malzone	1957
200	Wade Boggs	1987	185	Frank Malzone	1958
198	Jimmie Foxx	1936	185	Manny Ramirez	2003
198	Doc Cramer	1938	184	Jim Rice	1984
198	Nomar Garciaparra	2003	183	Tris Speaker	1910
197	Jimmie Foxx	1938	183	Del Pratt	1922
197	Nomar Garciaparra	2000	183	Doc Cramer	1939
197	Nomar Garciaparra	2002	183	Pete Runnels	1958
196	Earl Webb	1931	183	Pete Runnels	1962
195	Patsy Dougherty	1903	183	Carl Yastrzemski	1963
195	Nomar Garciaparra	1998	182	Jackie Jensen	1956
194	Ted Williams	1949	181	George Burns	1923
194	Rick Burleson	1977	181	Ted Williams	1947
193	Tris Speaker	1914	181	Mike Greenwell	1990
193	Ted Williams	1940	181	Wade Boggs	1991
193	Dom DiMaggio	1950	180	Walt Dropo	1950
192	Mike Greenwell	1988	179	Stuffy McInnis	1921
191	Carl Yastrzemski	1962	179	Rick Burleson	1980
191	Jim Rice	1983	179	Marty Barrett	1986
190	Tris Speaker	1913	179	Johnny Damon	2002

H	PLAYER	YEAR	H	PLAYER	YEAR
178	Dom DiMaggio	1942	176	Billy Goodman	1955
178	Dwight Evans	1982	176	Jimmy Piersall	1956
178	Jerry Remy	1982	176	Pete Runnels	1959
178	Mike Greenwell	1989	176	Reggie Smith	1970
177	Buck Freeman	1902	176	John Valentin	1997
177	Vern Stephens	1949	175	Joe Cronin	1937
177	Fred Lynn	1979	175	Reggie Smith	1971
177	Jim Rice	1982	175	Fred Lynn	1975
176	Tris Speaker	1915	175	Jody Reed	1991
176	Mel Almada	1935	175	Manny Ramirez	2004
176	Ted Williams	1946	175	David Ortiz	2004

RED SOX WITH 25 OR MORE HOME RUNS IN A SEASON

HR	PLAYER	YEAR	HR	PLAYER	YEAR
50	Jimmie Foxx	1938	33	Manny Ramirez	2002
46	Jim Rice	1978	32	Ted Williams	1947
44	Carl Yastrzemski	1967	32	Tony Conigliaro	1965
44	Mo Vaughn	1996	32	Dwight Evans	1982
43	Ted Williams	1949	32	Dwight Evans	1984
43	Tony Armas	1984	31	Ted Williams	1939
43	Manny Ramirez	2004	31	Don Baylor	1986
42	Dick Stuart	1963	31	David Ortiz	2003
41	Jimmie Foxx	1936	30	Vern Stephens	1950
41	Manny Ramirez	2001	30	Ted Williams	1951
41	David Ortiz	2004	30	Felix Mantilla	1964
40	Carl Yastrzemski	1969	30	Reggie Smith	1971
40	Rico Petrocelli	1969	30	Butch Hobson	1977
40	Carl Yastrzemski	1970	30	Nick Esasky	1989
40	Mo Vaughn	1998	30	Nomar Garciaparra	1997
39	Vern Stephens	1949	29	Babe Ruth	1919
39	Jim Rice	1977	29	Vern Stephens	1948
39	Fred Lynn	1979	29	Ted Williams	1954
39	Jim Rice	1979	29	Ted Williams	1960
39	Jim Rice	1983	29	Rico Petrocelli	1970
39	Mo Vaughn	1995	29	Dwight Evans	1985
38	Ted Williams	1946	29	Mo Vaughn	1993
38	Ted Williams	1957	28	Ted Williams	1950
37	Ted Williams	1941	28	Ted Williams	1955
37	Manny Ramirez	2003	28	Jackie Jensen	1959
36	Jimmie Foxx	1937	28	Tony Conigliaro	1966
36	Jimmie Foxx	1940	28	Rico Petrocelli	1971
36	Ted Williams	1942	28	Carl Yastrzemski	1977
36	Tony Conigliaro	1970	28	Butch Hobson	1979
36	Tony Armas	1963	28	Jim Rice	1984
35	Jimmie Foxx	1939	28	Jack Clark	1991
35	Jackie Jensen	1958	28	Jose Canseco	1996
35	Ken Harrelson	1968	28	Troy O'Leary	1999
35	Mo Vaughn	1997	28	Trot Nixon	2003
35	Nomar Garciaparra	1998	28	Nomar Garciaparra	2003
34	Walt Dropo	1950	27	Bobby Doerr	1948
34	Dwight Evans	1987	27	Bobby Doerr	1950
34	Carl Everett	2000	27	Norm Zauchin	1955
33	Dick Stuart	1964	27	George Scott	1966
33	George Scott	1977	27	Mike Easler	1984

HR	PLAYER	YEAR	HR	PLAYER	YEAR
27	Jim Rice	1985	26	Mo Vaughn	1994
27	John Valentin	1995	25	Ted Williams	1948
27	Nomar Garciaparra	1999	25	Jackie Jensen	1954
27	Trot Nixon	2001	25	Reggie Smith	1969
26	Jackie Jensen	1955	25	Jim Rice	1976
26	Ted Williams	1958	25	Tony Perez	1980
26	Carlton Fisk	1973	25	Jason Varitek	2003
26	Carlton Fisk	1977	25	Kevin Millar	2003
26	Dwight Evans	1986			

RED SOX WITH 100 OR MORE RBI IN A SEASON

RBI	PLAYER	YEAR	RBI	PLAYER	YEAR
175	Jimmie Foxx	1938	116	Tony Conigliaro	1970
159	Vern Stephens	1949	115	Mo Vaughn	1998
159	Ted Williams	1949	114	Buck Freeman	1901
145	Ted Williams	1939	114	Babe Ruth	1919
144	Walt Dropo	1950	114	Ted Williams	1947
144	Vern Stephens	1950	114	Dick Stuart	1964
143	Jimmie Foxx	1936	114	Jim Rice	1977
143	Mo Vaughn	1996	113	Ted Williams	1940
139	Jim Rice	1978	112	Jackie Jensen	1959
139	David Ortiz	2004	112	Butch Hobson	1977
137	Ted Williams	1942	111	Joe Cronin	1940
137	Vern Stephens	1948	111	Bobby Doerr	1948
130	Jim Rice	1979	111	Carl Yastrzemski	1969
130	Manny Ramirez	2004	111	Dwight Evans	1988
127	Jimmie Foxx	1937	110	Joe Cronin	1937
127	Ted Williams	1948	110	Bill Buckner	1985
126	Ted Williams	1951	110	Jim Rice	1986
126	Jim Rice	1983	109	Duffy Lewis	1912
126	Mo Vaughn	1995	109	Bobby Doerr	1949
125	Manny Ramirez	2001	109	Ken Harrelson	1968
123	Ted Williams	1946	108	Nick Esasky	1989
123	Tony Armas	1984	108	Carl Everett	2000
123	Dwight Evans	1987	107	Joe Cronin	1939
122	Jackie Jensen	1958	107	Tony Armas	1983
122	Fred Lynn	1979	107	Manny Ramirez	2002
122	Jim Rice	1984	106	Pinky Higgins	1937
122	Nomar Garciaparra	1998	106	Pinky Higgins	1938
121	Buck Freeman	1902	106	Bob Johnson	1944
121	Carl Yastrzemski	1967	105	Jimmie Foxx	1939
120	Ted Williams	1941	105	Bobby Doerr	1940
120	Bobby Doerr	1950	105	Jimmie Foxx	1941
120	Nomar Garciaparra	2002	105	Fred Lynn	1975
119	Roy Johnson	1934	105	Tony Perez	1980
119	Jimmie Foxx	1940	105	Nomar Garciaparra	2003
119	Rudy York	1946	104	Buck Freeman	1903
119	Mike Greenwell	1988	104	Dwight Evans	1984
118	Dick Stuart	1963	104	Nomar Garciaparra	1999
117	Jackie Jensen	1954	104	Manny Ramirez	2003
116	Bobby Doerr	1946	103	Earl Webb	1931
116	Jackie Jensen	1955	103	Jackie Jensen	1957

RBI	PLAYER	YEAR	RBI	PLAYER	YEAR
103	Frank Malzone	1957	102	Carlton Fisk	1977
103	Vic Wertz	1960	102	Carl Yastrzemski	1977
103	Rico Petrocelli	1970	102	Bill Buckner	1986
103	Jim Rice	1985	102	John Valentin	1995
103	Troy O'Leary	1999	101	Jim Tabor	1941
102	Bobby Doerr	1942	101	Mo Vaughn	1993
102	Carl Yastrzemski	1970	101	David Ortiz	2003
102	Jim Rice	1975	100	Del Pratt	1921
102	Carl Yastrzemski	1976	100	Dwight Evans	1989

RED SOX WITH 100 OR MORE RUNS SCORED IN A SEASON

RUNS	PLAYER	YEAR	RUNS	PLAYER	YEAR
150	Ted Williams	1949	113	John Valentin	1998
142	Ted Williams	1946	112	Johnny Pesky	1950
141	Ted Williams	1942	112	Carl Yastrzemski	1967
139	Jimmie Foxx	1938	111	Jimmie Foxx	1937
136	Tris Speaker	1912	111	Johnny Pesky	1949
135	Ted Williams	1941	111	Nomar Garciaparra	1998
134	Ted Williams	1940	110	Doc Cramer	1939
131	Ted Williams	1939	110	Dom DiMaggio	1942
131	Dom DiMaggio	1950	110	Dwight Evans	1985
130	Jimmie Foxx	1936	109	Jimmy Collins	1901
130	Jimmie Foxx	1939	109	Ted Williams	1951
129	Billy Werber	1934	109	Reggie Smith	1970
128	Wade Boggs	1988	109	Wade Boggs	1984
127	Dom DiMaggio	1948	109	Dwight Evans	1987
126	Dom DiMaggio	1949	108	Tris Speaker	1915
125	Ted Williams	1947	108	Wade Boggs	1987
125	Vern Stephens	1950	108	John Valentin	1995
125	Carl Yastrzemski	1970	108	Manny Ramirez	2004
124	Ted Williams	1948	107	Tony Armas	1984
124	Johnny Pesky	1948	107	Wade Boggs	1985
123	Johnny Damon	2004	107	Wade Boggs	1986
122	Dwight Evans	1982	107	Mo Vaughn	1998
122	Nomar Garciaparra	1997	107	Jose Offerman	1999
121	Joe Vosmik	1938	106	Chick Stahl	1901
121	Jim Rice	1978	106	Patsy Dougherty	1903
121	Dwight Evans	1984	106	Ira Flagstead	1924
120	Nomar Garciaparra	2003	106	Jimmie Foxx	1940
118	Mo Vaughn	1996	106	Bob Johnson	1944
118	Johnny Damon	2002	106	Johnny Pesky	1947
117	Dom DiMaggio	1941	106	Carlton Fisk	1977
117	Jim Rice	1979	105	Johnny Pesky	1942
117	Manny Ramirez	2003	104	Tommy Dowd	1901
116	Doc Cramer	1938	104	Joe Cronin	1940
116	Fred Lynn	1979	104	Jim Rice	1977
115	Johnny Pesky	1946	104	Nomar Garciaparra	2000
114	Vern Stephens	1948	103	Babe Ruth	1919
113	Vern Stephens	1949	103	Bobby Doerr	1950
113	Dom DiMaggio	1951	103	Jimmy Piersall	1957
113	Wade Boggs	1989	103	Pete Runnels	1958

RUNS	PLAYER	YEAR	RUNS	PLAYER	YEAR
103	Fred Lynn	1975	101	Jackie Jensen	1959
103	George Scott	1977	101	Nomar Garciaparra	2002
103	Nomar Garciaparra	1999	100	Harry Hooper	1913
103	Johnny Damon	2003	100	Billy Goodman	1955
102	Joe Cronin	1937	100	Wade Boggs	1983
101	Tris Speaker	1914	100	Trot Nixon	2001
101	Walt Dropo	1950			

RED SOX WITH 90 OR MORE BASES ON BALLS IN A SEASON

BB	PLAYER	YEAR	BB	PLAYER	YEAR
162	Ted Williams	1947	100	Johnny Pesky	1949
162	Ted Williams	1949	99	Jimmie Foxx	1937
156	Ted Williams	1946	99	Johnny Pesky	1948
145	Ted Williams	1941	99	Billy Goodman	1955
145	Ted Williams	1942	99	Jackie Jensen	1958
144	Ted Williams	1951	99	Dwight Evans	1989
136	Ted Williams	1954	98	Ted Williams	1958
128	Carl Yastrzemski	1970	98	Rico Petrocelli	1969
126	Ted Williams	1948	97	Dwight Evans	1986
125	Wade Boggs	1988	97	Manny Ramirez	2003
119	Jimmie Foxx	1938	96	Ted Williams	1940
119	Ted Williams	1957	96	Bob Johnson	1944
119	Carl Yastrzemski	1968	96	Dom DiMaggio	1949
114	Dwight Evans	1985	96	Carl Yastrzemski	1961
112	Dwight Evans	1982	96	Dwight Evans	1984
107	Ted Williams	1939	96	Wade Boggs	1985
107	Wade Boggs	1989	96	Jack Clark	1991
106	Topper Rigney	1926	96	Jose Offerman	1999
106	Eddie Lake	1945	95	Pete Runnels	1959
106	Carl Yastrzemski	1971	95	Carl Yastrzemski	1963
106	Dwight Evans	1987	95	Mo Vaughn	1996
105	Jimmie Foxx	1936	93	Jimmie Foxx	1941
105	Carl Yastrzemski	1973	92	Don Buddin	1959
105	Wade Boggs	1986	92	Wade Boggs	1983
105	Wade Boggs	1987	91	Joe Cronin	1938
104	Johnny Pesky	1950	91	Ted Williams	1955
104	Carl Yastrzemski	1974	91	Gary Geiger	1961
102	Ted Williams	1956	91	Joe Foy	1966
101	Babe Ruth	1919	91	Carl Yastrzemski	1967
101	Jimmie Foxx	1940	91	Rico Petrocelli	1971
101	Dom DiMaggio	1948	90	Dom DiMaggio	1941
101	Vern Stephens	1949	90	Billy Klaus	1956
101	Carl Yastrzemski	1969			

RED SOX BATTERS WITH 100 OR MORE STRIKEOUTS IN A SEASON

SO	PLAYER	YEAR	SO	PLAYER	YEAR
177	Mark Bellhorn	2004	118	Lu Clinton	1963
162	Butch Hobson	1977	117	Dwight Evans	1986
156	Tony Armas	1984	117	Nick Esasky	1988
154	Mo Vaughn	1996	116	Tony Conigliaro	1965
154	Mo Vaughn	1997	115	Dwight Evans	1984
152	George Scott	1966	113	Carl Everett	2000
150	Mo Vaughn	1995	113	Trot Nixon	2001
147	Manny Ramirez	2001	112	Tony Conigliaro	1966
144	Dick Stuart	1963	112	George Scott	1977
144	Mo Vaughn	1998	112	Mo Vaughn	1994
134	Mike Easler	1984	111	Tony Conigliaro	1969
133	Jack Clark	1991	111	Don Baylor	1986
133	David Ortiz	2004	109	Trot Nixon	2002
131	Tony Armas	1983	108	Rico Petrocelli	1971
130	Dick Stuart	1964	108	Troy O'Leary	1998
130	Mo Vaughn	1993	108	Brian Daubach	2001
130	Brian Daubach	2000	108	Kevin Millar	2003
129	Mike Easler	1985	106	Don Buddin	1958
126	Jim Rice	1978	106	Jason Varitek	2003
126	Brian Daubach	2002	105	Norm Zauchin	1955
126	Jason Varitek	2004	105	Dwight Evans	1985
124	Manny Ramirez	2004	105	Tom Brunansky	1990
123	Jim Rice	1976	104	Tommy Harper	1972
122	Jim Rice	1975	104	Carl Everett	2001
122	Butch Hobson	1978	103	Jimmie Foxx	1941
122	Wil Cordero	1997	102	George Scott	1971
119	Jimmie Foxx	1936	102	Jim Rice	1983
119	Dwight Evans	1978	102	Jim Rice	1984
119	George Scott	1978	102	Darren Bragg	1997
118	Ed Bressoud	1962			

RED SOX WITH 20 OR MORE STOLEN BASES IN A SEASON

SB	PLAYER	YEAR	SB	PLAYER	YEAR
54	Tommy Harper	1973	26	Joe Foy	1968
52	Tris Speaker	1912	25	Fred Parent	1905
46	Tris Speaker	1913	25	Tris Speaker	1911
42	Tris Speaker	1914	25	Larry Gardner	1912
42	Otis Nixon	1994	25	Tommy Harper	1972
40	Harry Hooper	1910	25	Ellis Burks	1988
40	Bill Werber	1934	24	Fred Parent	1903
38	Harry Hooper	1911	24	Clyde Engle	1911
36	Harry Lord	1909	24	Harry Hooper	1918
35	Patsy Dougherty	1903	23	Harry Lord	1908
35	Tris Speaker	1909	23	Harry Hooper	1919
35	Tris Speaker	1910	23	Mike Menosky	1920
33	Tommy Dowd	1901	23	Jack Rothrock	1929
31	Amby McConnell	1908	23	Bill Werber	1936
31	Johnny Damon	2002	23	Carl Yastrzemski	1970
30	Buddy Myer	1928	22	Jimmy Collins	1903
30	Jerry Remy	1978	22	Jake Stahl	1910
30	Johnny Damon	2003	22	Duffy Lewis	1914
29	Chick Stahl	1901	22	Harry Hooper	1915
29	Harry Hooper	1912	22	Pete Fox	1943
29	Hal Janvrin	1914	22	Jackie Jensen	1954
29	Tris Speaker	1915	22	Reggie Smith	1968
29	Bill Werber	1935	22	Nomar Garciaparra	1997
29	Darren Lewis	1998	21	Heinie Wagner	1912
28	Clyde Engle	1913	21	Harry Hooper	1917
28	Tommy Harper	1974	21	Ellis Burks	1989
27	Harry Niles	1909	20	Patsy Dougherty	1902
27	Larry Gardner	1911	20	Fred Parent	1904
27	Harry Hooper	1916	20	Heinie Wagner	1907
27	Ben Chapman	1937	20	Heinie Wagner	1908
27	Ellis Burks	1987	20	Amos Strunk	1918
26	Amby McConnell	1909	20	Mel Almada	1935
26	Heinie Wagner	1910	20	John Valentin	1995
26	Harry Hooper	1913			

RED SOX WITH BATTING AVERAGES OF .315 OR BETTER FOR A SEASON

BA	PLAYER	YEAR	BA	PLAYER	YEAR
.406	Ted Williams	1941	.331	Fred Lynn	1975
.388	Ted Williams	1957	.330	Ike Boone	1925
.383	Tris Speaker	1912	.330	Wade Boggs	1989
.372	Nomar Garciaparra	2000	.329	Jimmy Collins	1901
.369	Ted Williams	1948	.329	Carl Yastrzemski	1970
.368	Wade Boggs	1985	.328	George Burns	1923
.366	Wade Boggs	1988	.328	Dom DiMaggio	1950
.363	Tris Speaker	1913	.328	Ted Williams	1958
.363	Wade Boggs	1988	.328	Mike Greenwell	1987
.361	Wade Boggs	1983	.327	Ted Williams	1939
.360	Jimmie Foxx	1939	.326	Pete Runnels	1962
.357	Wade Boggs	1986	.326	Carl Yastrzemski	1967
.357	Nomar Garciaparra	1999	.326	Mo Vaughn	1996
.356	Ted Williams	1942	.326	Bill Mueller	2003
.354	Billy Goodman	1950	.325	Jimmy Collins	1902
.349	Jimmie Foxx	1938	.325	Joe Cronin	1938
.349	Manny Ramirez	2002	.325	Bobby Doerr	1944
.346	Buck Freeman	1901	.325	Al Zarilla	1950
.345	Ted Williams	1954	.325	Jim Rice	1979
.345	Ted Williams	1956	.325	Wade Boggs	1984
.344	Ted Williams	1940	.325	Mike Greenwell	1988
.343	Ted Williams	1947	.325	Manny Ramirez	2003
.343	Ted Williams	1949	.324	Del Pratt	1921
.342	Patsy Dougherty	1902	.324	Joe Vosmik	1928
.342	Ted Williams	1946	.324	Bob Johnson	1944
.340	Tris Speaker	1910	.324	Johnny Pesky	1947
.340	Ben Chapman	1938	.324	Jim Rice	1986
.338	Tris Speaker	1914	.323	Earl Webb	1930
.338	Jimmie Foxx	1936	.323	Nomar Garciaparra	1998
.337	Mo Vaughn	1998	.322	Tris Speaker	1915
.336	Carney Lansford	1981	.322	Babe Ruth	1919
.335	Joe Harris	1923	.322	Walt Dropo	1950
.334	Tris Speaker	1911	.322	Pete Runnels	1958
.333	Ike Boone	1924	.321	Bill Werber	1934
.333	Earl Webb	1931	.321	Carl Yastrzemski	1963
.333	Fred Lynn	1979	.321	Dave Stapleton	1980
.332	Wade Boggs	1991	.320	Roy Johnson	1934
.331	Patsy Dougherty	1903	.320	Lou Finney	1940
.331	Johnny Pesky	1942	.320	Pete Runnels	1960

BA	PLAYER	YEAR	BA	PLAYER	YEAR
.320	Jim Rice	1977	.315	Roy Johnson	1935
.319	Reggie Jefferson	1997	.315	Pete Fox	1944
.318	Chick Stahl	1902	.315	Jackie Jensen	1956
.318	Bobby Doerr	1939	.315	Carlton Fisk	1977
.318	Ted Williams	1951	.315	Jim Rice	1978
.316	Joe Harris	1922	.315	Mike Greenwell	1993
.316	Dom DiMaggio	1946	.315	Mo Vaughn	1997
.315	Larry Gardner	1912			

RED SOX WITH .525 OR BETTER SLUGGING AVERAGE

SLG	PLAYER	YEAR	SLG	PLAYER	YEAR
.735	Ted Williams	1941	.583	Walt Dropo	1950
.731	Ted Williams	1957	.583	Mo Vaughn	1996
.704	Jimmie Foxx	1938	.581	Jimmie Foxx	1940
.694	Jimmie Foxx	1939	.578	Trot Nixon	2003
.667	Ted Williams	1946	.576	Mo Vaughn	1994
.657	Babe Ruth	1919	.575	Mo Vaughn	1995
.648	Ted Williams	1942	.570	Mike Greenwell	1987
.647	Manny Ramirez	2002	.569	Dwight Evans	1987
.637	Fred Lynn	1979	.567	Tris Speaker	1912
.635	Ted Williams	1954	.566	Fred Lynn	1975
.634	Ted Williams	1947	.560	Mo Vaughn	1997
.631	Jimmie Foxx	1936	.556	Ted Williams	1951
.622	Carl Yastrzemski	1967	.555	Babe Ruth	1918
.615	Ted Williams	1948	.550	Jim Rice	1983
.613	Manny Ramirez	2004	.540	Bill Mueller	2003
.609	Ted Williams	1939	.539	Vern Stephens	1949
.609	Manny Ramirez	2001	.538	Jimmie Foxx	1937
.605	Ted Williams	1956	.538	Carlton Fisk	1972
.603	Nomar Garciaparra	1999	.536	Joe Cronin	1938
.603	David Ortiz	2004	.536	Carl Yastrzemski	1965
.600	Jim Rice	1978	.535	Jackie Jensen	1958
.599	Nomar Garciaparra	2000	.534	Dwight Evans	1982
.596	Jim Rice	1979	.534	Nomar Garciaparra	1997
.594	Ted Williams	1940	.533	John Valentin	1995
.593	Jim Rice	1977	.532	Dwight Evans	1984
.592	Carl Yastrzemski	1970	.531	Tony Armas	1984
.592	David Ortiz	2003	.531	Mike Greenwell	1987
.591	Mo Vaughn	1998	.530	Tony Conigliaro	1964
.589	Rico Petrocelli	1969	.528	Earl Webb	1931
.588	Wade Boggs	1987	.528	Bobby Doerr	1944
.587	Carl Everett	2000	.528	Bob Johnson	1944
.587	Manny Ramirez	2003	.528	Nomar Garciaparra	2002
.584	Ted Williams	1958	.527	Reggie Smith	1969
.584	Nomar Garciaparra	1998	.525	Mo Vaughn	1993

RED SOX WITH 50 OR MORE GAMES PITCHED IN A SEASON

GP	PITCHER	YEAR	GP	PITCHER	YEAR
80	Greg Harris	1993	62	Rich Garces	2001
79	Dick Radatz	1964	61	Ugueth Urbina	2002
76	Mike Timlin	2004	60	John Wyatt	1967
75	Heathcliff Slocumb	1996	60	Tony Fossas	1992
74	Rob Murphy	1989	60	Rheal Cormier	1999
74	Derek Lowe	1999	59	Mike Stanton	1996
74	Derek Lowe	2000	59	Jim Corsi	1998
73	Tom Gordon	1998	58	Diego Segui	1974
72	Mike Timlin	2003	57	Mike Fornieles	1961
72	Keith Foulke	2004	57	Arnie Earley	1965
71	Sparky Lyle	1969	57	Bob Stanley	1984
71	Tony Fossas	1993	57	Bob Stanley	1988
71	Alan Embree	2004	57	Jeff Reardon	1991
70	Mike Fornieles	1960	55	Bob Heffner	1964
70	Greg Harris	1992	55	Mark Clear	1982
69	Ellis Kinder	1953	54	Joe Willoughby	1976
69	Bill Campbell	1977	53	Wilcy Moore	1931
68	Rob Murphy	1990	53	Arnie Earley	1963
68	Rod Beck	2001	53	Dick Drago	1979
67	Derek Lowe	2001	53	Joe Sambito	1986
66	Dick Radatz	1963	53	Greg Harris	1991
66	Bob Stanley	1986	53	John Wasdin	1997
65	Jack Lamabe	1963	52	Murray Wall	1958
65	Alan Embree	2003	52	Vicente Romo	1969
64	Bob Stanley	1983	52	Bob Bolin	1971
64	Lee Smith	1988	52	Bob Stanley	1978
64	Lee Smith	1989	52	Bob Stanley	1980
64	Tony Fossas	1991	52	Jim Corsi	1997
64	Rich Garces	2000	51	Jack Wilson	1937
64	Rheal Cormier	2000	51	Dennis Lamp	1991
63	Ellis Kinder	1951	51	Danny Darwin	1992
63	Dick Radatz	1965	51	Jeff Russell	1993
63	Sparky Lyle	1970	51	Tim Wakefield	2000
63	Stan Belinda	1995	50	Jose Santiago	1967
63	Derek Lowe	1998	50	Lee Stange	1968
62	Dick Radatz	1962	50	Sparky Lyle	1971
62	Tom Burgmeier	1980	50	Jeff Gray	1991
62	Calvin Schiraldi	1987	50	Dennis Eckersley	1998

RED SOX PITCHERS WITH 34 OR MORE STARTS IN A SEASON

GS	PITCHER	YEAR	GS	PITCHER	YEAR
43	Cy Young	1902	35	Bill Monbouquette	1964
42	Bill Dinneen	1902	35	Bill Monbouquette	1965
41	Cy Young	1901	35	Marty Pattin	1972
41	Cy Young	1904	35	Luis Tiant	1973
40	Babe Ruth	1916	35	Rick Wise	1975
39	Howard Ehmke	1923	35	Luis Tiant	1975
39	Jim Lonborg	1967	35	Dennis Eckersley	1978
38	Smokey Joe Wood	1912	35	Oil Can Boyd	1985
38	Babe Ruth	1917	35	Roger Clemens	1988
38	Sad Sam Jones	1921	35	Roger Clemens	1989
38	Wes Ferrell	1935	35	Roger Clemens	1991
38	Wes Ferrell	1936	35	Frank Viola	1992
38	Luis Tiant	1974	34	Ted Lewis	1901
38	Luis Tiant	1976	34	Cy Young	1905
37	Bill Dinneen	1904	34	Cy Young	1906
37	Cy Young	1907	34	Buck O'Brien	1912
37	Bill Lee	1974	34	Dutch Leonard	1916
36	Dutch Leonard	1917	34	Red Ruffing	1928
36	Howard Ehmke	1924	34	Milt Gaston	1930
36	Bill Monbouquette	1963	34	Mel Parnell	1953
36	Earl Wilson	1967	34	Earl Wilson	1963
36	Mike Torrez	1978	34	Gary Peters	1970
36	Mike Torrez	1979	34	Bill Lee	1975
36	Roger Clemens	1987	34	Rick Wise	1976
35	Cy Young	1903	34	John Tudor	1983
35	Bill Dinneen	1903	34	Mike Boddicker	1989
35	Boo Ferriss	1946	34	Mike Boddicker	1990
35	Tex Hughson	1946	34	Danny Darwin	1993
35	Frank Sullivan	1955	34	Roger Clemens	1996
35	Bill Monbouquette	1962	34	Tom Gordon	1996

RED SOX PITCHERS WITH 20 OR MORE COMPLETE GAMES IN A SEASON

CG	PITCHER	YEAR	CG	PITCHER	YEAR
41	Cy Young	1902	25	Tom Hughes	1903
40	Cy Young	1904	25	Smokey Joe Wood	1911
39	Bill Dinneen	1902	25	Sad Sam Jones	1921
38	Cy Young	1901	25	Red Ruffing	1928
37	Bill Dinneen	1904	25	Luis Tiant	1974
35	Smokey Joe Wood	1912	24	George Winter	1905
35	Babe Ruth	1917	23	Bill Dinneen	1905
34	Cy Young	1903	23	Babe Ruth	1916
33	Cy Young	1907	23	Luis Tiant	1973
32	Bill Dinneen	1902	22	Bill Dinneen	1906
32	Cy Young	1905	22	Rube Foster	1915
31	Ted Lewis	1901	22	Howard Ehmke	1922
31	Wes Ferrell	1935	22	Lefty Grove	1936
30	Jesse Tannehill	1904	22	Tex Hughson	1942
30	Carl Mays	1918	22	Jim Lonborg	1968
29	Norwood Gibson	1904	21	George Winter	1907
28	Cy Young	1906	21	Sad Sam Jones	1919
28	Howard Ehmke	1923	21	Lefty Grove	1937
26	Wes Ferrell	1936	21	Tex Hughson	1946
27	Jesse Tannehill	1905	21	Mel Parnell	1950
27	Carl Mays	1917	20	Joe Harris	1906
27	Mel Parnell	1949	20	Eddie Cicotte	1910
26	George Winter	1901	20	Sad Sam Jones	1920
26	Buck O'Brien	1912	20	Bullet Joe Bush	1921
26	Dutch Leonard	1917	20	Ed Morris	1928
26	Babe Ruth	1918	20	Milt Gaston	1929
26	Howard Ehmke	1924	20	Milt Gaston	1930
26	Boo Ferriss	1945	20	Tex Hughson	1943
26	Boo Ferriss	1946			

RED SOX PITCHERS WITH 18 OR MORE WINS IN A SEASON

GW	PITCHER	YEAR	GW	PITCHER	YEAR
34	Smokey Joe Wood	1912	20	Ray Collins	1914
33	Cy Young	1901	20	Howard Ehmke	1923
32	Cy Young	1902	20	Lefty Grove	1935
28	Cy Young	1903	20	Wes Ferrell	1936
26	Cy Young	1904	20	Tex Hughson	1946
25	Wes Ferrell	1935	20	Bill Monbouquette	1963
25	Boo Ferriss	1946	20	Luis Tiant	1973
25	Mel Parnell	1949	20	Dennis Eckersley	1978
24	Babe Ruth	1917	20	Roger Clemens	1987
24	Roger Clemens	1986	20	Pedro Martinez	2002
23	Bill Dinneen	1904	19	Ray Collins	1913
23	Smokey Joe Wood	1911	19	Dutch Leonard	1914
23	Babe Ruth	1916	19	Ernie Shore	1915
23	Sam Jones	1921	19	Howard Ehmke	1924
23	Ellis Kinder	1949	19	Ed Morris	1928
23	Pedro Martinez	1999	19	Dick Newsome	1941
22	Jesse Tannehill	1905	19	Tom Brewer	1956
22	Cy Young	1907	19	Rick Wise	1975
22	Carl Mays	1917	19	Pedro Martinez	1998
22	Tex Hughson	1942	18	Cy Young	1905
22	Jim Lonborg	1967	18	Babe Ruth	1915
22	Luis Tiant	1974	18	Dutch Leonard	1916
21	Bill Dinneen	1902	18	Carl Mays	1916
21	Bill Dinneen	1903	18	Tex Hughson	1944
21	Jesse Tannehill	1904	18	Joe Dobson	1947
21	Cy Young	1908	18	Jack Kramer	1948
21	Carl Mays	1918	18	Mel Parnell	1950
21	Boo Ferriss	1945	18	Mel Parnell	1951
21	Mel Parnell	1953	18	Mickey McDermott	1953
21	Luis Tiant	1976	18	Frank Sullivan	1955
21	Roger Clemens	1990	18	Luis Tiant	1975
21	Derek Lowe	2002	18	Roger Clemens	1988
21	Curt Schilling	2004	18	Bruce Hurst	1988
20	Tom Hughes	1903	18	Roger Clemens	1991
20	Hugh Bedient	1912	18	Roger Clemens	1992
20	Buck O'Brien	1912	18	Pedro Martinez	2000

RED SOX PITCHERS WITH 15 OR MORE LOSSES IN A SEASON

GL	PITCHER	YEAR	GL	PITCHER	YEAR
25	Red Ruffing	1928	16	George Winter	1905
22	Red Ruffing	1929	16	George Winter	1907
21	Bill Dinneen	1902	16	Dutch Leonard	1913
21	Joe Harris	1906	16	Sad Sam Jones	1920
21	Cy Young	1906	16	Sad Sam Jones	1921
21	Slim Harriss	1927	16	Alex Ferguson	1922
20	Sad Sam Jones	1919	16	Jack Quinn	1922
20	Howard Ehmke	1925	16	Ted Wingfield	1926
20	Milt Gaston	1930	16	Bob Weiland	1932
20	Jack Russell	1930	16	Fritz Ostermueller	1936
19	Cy Young	1905	16	Jim Bagby	1940
19	Bill Dinneen	1906	16	Frank Sullivan	1960
19	Ted Wingfield	1925	16	Earl Wilson	1963
19	Milt Gaston	1929	16	Ray Culp	1971
18	George Winter	1906	16	Mike Torrez	1980
18	Red Ruffing	1925	15	Cy Young	1907
18	Paul Zahniser	1926	15	Eddie Cicotte	1911
18	Hal Wiltse	1927	15	Bullet Joe Bush	1918
18	Danny MacFayden	1929	15	Bullet Joe Bush	1920
18	Jack Russell	1929	15	Curt Fullerton	1923
18	Jack Russell	1931	15	Hal Wiltse	1926
18	Bill Monbouquette	1965	15	Red Ruffing	1926
18	Dave Morehead	1965	15	Ed Morris	1928
17	Smokey Joe Wood	1911	15	Danny MacFayden	1928
17	Dutch Leonard	1917	15	Ed Durham	1930
17	Herb Pennock	1922	15	Gordon Rhodes	1933
17	Howard Ehmke	1923	15	Johnny Welch	1934
17	Jack Quinn	1923	15	Wes Ferrell	1936
17	Bill Piercy	1923	15	Jack Wilson	1938
17	Alex Ferguson	1924	15	Tex Hughson	1943
17	Howard Ehmke	1924	15	Tom Brewer	1960
17	Hod Lisenbee	1930	15	Don Schwall	1962
17	Jim Lonborg	1965	15	Dave Morehead	1964
17	Marty Pattin	1973	15	Bob Stanley	1987
17	Bill Lee	1974	15	Tim Wakefield	1997
16	Ted Lewis	1901	15	Frank Castillo	2002
16	Cy Young	1904			

RED SOX PITCHERS WITH A WINNING PERCENTAGE OF .667 OR BETTER IN A SEASON (MINIMUM OF 15 DECISIONS)

PCT.	PITCHER	W–L	YEAR
.882	Bob Stanley	15–2	1978
.872	Smokey Joe Wood	34–5	1912
.867	Roger Moret	13–2	1973
.857	Roger Clemens	24–4	1986
.852	Pedro Martinez	23–4	1999
.833	Pedro Martinez	20–4	2002
.824	Roger Moret	14–3	1975
.806	Boo Ferriss	25–6	1946
.793	Ellis Kinder	23–6	1949
.792	Dutch Leonard	19–5	1914
.789	Lefty Grove	15–4	1939
.786	Tex Hughson	22–6	1942
.783	Tex Hughson	18–5	1944
.783	Jack Kramer	18–5	1948
.781	Mel Parnell	25–7	1949
.778	Roger Clemens	21–6	1990
.778	Curt Schilling	21–6	2004
.778	Lefty Grove	14–4	1938
.778	Pedro Martinez	14–4	2003
.767	Cy Young	33–10	1901
.762	Sad Sam Jones	16–5	1918
.757	Cy Young	29–9	1903
.750	Babe Ruth	18–6	1915
.750	Bruce Hurst	18–6	1988
.750	Pedro Martinez	18–6	2000
.750	Erik Hanson	15–5	1995
.750	Jose Santiago	12–4	1967
.750	Joe Hesketh	12–4	1991
.744	Cy Young	32–11	1902
.741	Tom Hughes	20–7	1903
.737	Smokey Joe Wood	14–5	1915
.737	Wes Ferrell	14–5	1934
.731	Pedro Martinez	19–7	1998
.727	Ray Culp	16–6	1968
.724	Mel Parnell	21–8	1953
.724	Derek Lowe	21–8	2002
.722	Eddie Cicotte	13–5	1909
.722	Fritz Ostermueller	13–5	1938

PCT.	PITCHER	W–L	YEAR
.714	Rube Foster	20–8	1915
.714	Dennis Eckersley	20–8	1978
.714	Dick Radatz	15–6	1963
.714	Luis Tiant	15–6	1972
.710	Carl Mays	22–9	1917
.710	Jim Lonborg	22–9	1967
.708	Derek Lowe	17–7	2003
.706	Joe Dobson	12–5	1941
.704	Ray Collins	19–8	1913
.704	Ernie Shore	19–8	1915
.696	Dick Ellsworth	16–7	1968
.692	Joe Dobson	18–8	1947
.690	Hugh Bedient	20–9	1912
.690	Roger Clemens	20–9	1987
.688	Jesse Tannehill	22–10	1905
.688	Smokey Joe Wood	11–5	1913
.688	Rick Wise	11–5	1977
.688	Tim Wakefield	11–5	2002
.662	Don Schwall	15–7	1961
.680	Ray Culp	17–8	1969
.680	Mike Boddicker	17–8	1990
.680	Tim Wakefield	17–8	1998
.679	Tom Brewer	19–9	1956
.677	Boo Ferriss	21–10	1945
.667	Bill Monbouquette	20–10	1963
.667	Herb Pennock	16–8	1919
.667	Tim Wakefield	16–8	1995
.667	Dutch Leonard	14–7	1915
.667	Frank Sullivan	14–7	1956
.667	Charlie Smith	12–6	1910
.667	Jack Wilson	12–6	1940
.667	Mike Fornieles	10–5	1960
.667	Mike Paxton	10–5	1977
.667	Tom Bolton	10–5	1990
.667	Roger Clemens	10–5	1995

RED SOX WITH 250 OR MORE INNINGS PITCHED IN A SEASON

IP	PLAYER	YEAR	IP	PLAYER	YEAR
385	Cy Young	1902	273	Bullet Joe Bush	1918
380	Cy Young	1904	273	Milt Gaston	1930
371	Cy Young	1901	273	Lefty Grove	1935
371	Bill Dinneen	1902	273	Jim Lonborg	1967
344	Smokey Joe Wood	1912	272	Jesse Tannehill	1905
343	Cy Young	1907	272	Ray Collins	1914
342	Cy Young	1903	272	Luis Tiant	1973
336	Bill Dinneen	1904	271	Roger Clemens	1991
326	Babe Ruth	1917	269	Denny MacFayden	1930
324	Babe Ruth	1916	266	Dennis Eckersley	1978
322	Wes Ferrell	1935	267	Bill Monbouquette	1963
321	Cy Young	1905	266	Tex Hughson	1943
317	Howard Ehmke	1923	265	Boo Ferriss	1945
316	Ted Lewis	1901	264	George Winter	1905
315	Howard Ehmke	1924	264	Roger Clemens	1988
311	Luis Tiant	1974	262	Lefty Grove	1937
301	Wes Ferrell	1936	261	Howard Ehmke	1925
299	Bill Dinneen	1903	260	Frank Sullivan	1955
299	Cy Young	1908	260	Luis Tiant	1975
299	Sad Sam Jones	1921	260	Bill Lee	1975
295	Mel Parnell	1949	259	Hugh Bedient	1913
294	Dutch Leonard	1917	259	Dutch Leonard	1913
293	Carl Mays	1918	258	Ed Morris	1928
289	Carl Mays	1917	257	George Winter	1907
289	Red Ruffing	1928	256	Jack Quinn	1922
288	Cy Young	1906	255	Rube Foster	1915
285	Bill Lee	1973	255	Rick Wise	1975
282	Jesse Tannehill	1904	254	Bullet Joe Bush	1921
282	Bill Lee	1974	254	Ted Wingfield	1925
282	Roger Clemens	1987	254	Roger Clemens	1986
281	Tex Hughson	1942	253	Lefty Grove	1936
279	Luis Tiant	1976	253	Marty Pattin	1972
278	Tex Hughson	1946	253	Roger Clemens	1989
277	Smokey Joe Wood	1911	252	Ellis Kinder	1949
276	Buck O'Brien	1912	252	Mike Torrez	1979
274	Dutch Leonard	1916	251	Ray Culp	1970
274	Sad Sam Jones	1920	250	Eddie Cicotte	1910
274	Boo Ferriss	1946	250	Mike Torrez	1978
273	Norwood Gibson	1904			

RED SOX PITCHERS WITH 140 OR MORE STRIKEOUTS IN A SEASON

SO	PITCHER	YEAR	SO	PITCHER	YEAR
313	Pedro Martinez	1999	166	Bruce Hurst	1988
291	Roger Clemens	1988	164	Earl Wilson	1965
284	Pedro Martinez	2000	163	Dave Morehead	1965
258	Smokey Joe Wood	1912	163	Pedro Martinez	2001
257	Roger Clemens	1996	162	Dick Radatz	1963
256	Roger Clemens	1987	162	Dennis Eckersley	1978
251	Pedro Martinez	1998	161	Bill Monbouquette	1961
246	Jim Lonborg	1967	160	Cy Young	1902
241	Roger Clemens	1991	160	Roger Clemens	1993
239	Pedro Martinez	2002	159	Tom Gordon	1997
238	Roger Clemens	1986	158	Cy Young	1901
231	Smokey Joe Wood	1911	155	Ken Brett	1970
230	Roger Clemens	1989	155	Gary Peters	1970
227	Pedro Martinez	2004	154	Oil Can Boyd	1985
220	Hideo Nomo	2001	153	Bill Dinneen	1904
210	Cy Young	1905	153	Lefty Grove	1937
209	Roger Clemens	1990	153	Bill Monbouquette	1962
206	Roger Clemens	1992	151	Ray Culp	1971
206	Luis Tiant	1973	151	Tim Wakefield	1997
206	Pedro Martinez	2003	150	Cy Young	1908
203	Curt Schilling	2004	150	Dennis Eckersley	1979
200	Cy Young	1904	148	Bill Dinneen	1903
197	Ray Culp	1970	148	Tim Wakefield	2001
190	Ray Culp	1968	147	Cy Young	1907
190	Bruce Hurst	1987	146	John Tudor	1982
189	Bruce Hurst	1985	146	Tim Wakefield	1998
181	Dick Radatz	1964	145	Mike Boddicker	1988
176	Cy Young	1903	144	Dutch Leonard	1913
176	Luis Tiant	1974	144	Dutch Leonard	1916
175	Dutch Leonard	1914	144	Dutch Leonard	1917
174	Bill Monbouquette	1963	144	Dick Radatz	1962
172	Tex Hughson	1946	143	Mike Boddicker	1990
172	Ray Culp	1969	142	Sonny Siebert	1970
171	Tom Gordon	1996	142	Luis Tiant	1975
170	Babe Ruth	1916	142	Ferguson Jenkins	1976
169	Tim Wakefield	2003	142	Bronson Arroyo	2004
168	Marty Pattin	1972	141	Rick Wise	1975
168	Roger Clemens	1994	140	Cy Young	1906
167	Bruce Hurst	1986	140	Tim Wakefield	1996
166	Earl Wilson	1964			

RED SOX PITCHERS WITH 90 OR MORE BASES ON BALLS IN A SEASON

BB	PITCHER	YEAR	BB	PITCHER	YEAR
134	Mel Parnell	1949	98	Mill Gaston	1930
121	Don Schwall	1962	98	Gordon Rhodes	1934
121	Mike Torrez	1979	97	Bob Weiland	1932
119	Howard Ehmke	1923	97	Joe Dobson	1949
119	Wes Ferrell	1936	96	Red Ruffing	1928
119	Bobo Newsom	1937	96	Tracy Stallard	1961
119	Jack Wilson	1937	96	Bob Ojeda	1984
118	Babe Ruth	1916	96	Hideo Nomo	2001
118	Red Ruffing	1929	95	Sad Sam Jones	1919
117	Emmett O'Neill	1945	95	Ed Morris	1929
116	Mel Parnell	1953	95	Charlie Wagner	1942
113	Dave Morehead	1965	95	Tom Brewer	1954
112	Tom Brewer	1956	94	Dutch Leonard	1913
112	Dave Morehead	1964	94	Bullet Joe Bush	1920
111	Earl Wilson	1962	93	Bullet Joe Bush	1921
110	Don Schwall	1961	93	Danny MacFayden	1930
109	Mickey McDermott	1953	93	Gordon Rhodes	1933
108	Babe Ruth	1917	93	Tom Brewer	1957
108	Alex Ferguson	1924	93	Tom Brewer	1958
108	Wes Ferrell	1935	93	Roger Clemens	1989
106	Mel Parnell	1950	92	Ted Wingfield	1925
106	Mike Nagy	1969	92	Boo Ferriss	1947
106	Roger Clemens	1996	92	Joe Dobson	1948
105	Earl Wilson	1963	92	Mickey McDermott	1951
105	Tom Gordon	1996	92	Mickey McDermott	1952
103	Rip Collins	1922	91	Ted Lewis	1901
100	Bob Weiland	1933	91	Bullet Joe Bush	1918
100	Frank Sullivan	1955	91	Jack Wilson	1938
100	Bill Monbouquette	1961	91	Ray Culp	1970
99	Bill Dinneen	1902	90	Cy Morgan	1908
99	Hal Wiltse	1926	90	Jim Bagby	1938
99	Fritz Ostermueller	1934	90	Oscar Judd	1942
99	Ellis Kinder	1944	90	Mel Parnell	1948
99	Dave Morehead	1963	90	Tim Wakefield	1996
99	Mike Torrez	1978			

RED SOX PITCHERS WITH 4 OR MORE SHUTOUTS IN A SEASON

SH	PITCHER	YEAR	SH	PITCHER	YEAR
10	Cy Young	1904	5	Joe Dobson	1948
10	Smokey Joe Wood	1912	5	Mel Parnell	1953
9	Babe Ruth	1916	5	Bill Monbouquette	1964
8	Carl Mays	1918	5	Luis Tiant	1978
8	Roger Clemens	1988	5	Bob Ojeda	1984
7	Cy Young	1903	5	Roger Clemens	1992
7	Ray Collins	1914	4	Jesse Tannehill	1904
7	Dutch Leonard	1914	4	George Winter	1907
7	Bullet Joe Bush	1918	4	Smokey Joe Wood	1909
7	Luis Tiant	1974	4	Ray Collins	1910
7	Roger Clemens	1987	4	Ray Collins	1912
6	Bill Dinneen	1903	4	Ernie Shore	1915
6	Jesse Tannehill	1905	4	Dutch Leonard	1917
6	Cy Young	1907	4	Herb Pennock	1920
6	Rube Foster	1914	4	Jack Quinn	1922
6	Dutch Leonard	1914	4	Howard Ehmke	1924
6	Babe Ruth	1917	4	Danny MacFayden	1929
6	Lefty Grove	1936	4	Tex Hughson	1942
6	Boo Ferriss	1946	4	Tex Hughson	1943
6	Tex Hughson	1946	4	Mel Parnell	1949
6	Ellis Kinder	1949	4	Mickey McDermott	1953
6	Ray Culp	1968	4	Tom Brewer	1956
6	Luis Tiant	1972	4	Bill Monbouquette	1962
5	Cy Young	1901	4	Gary Peters	1970
5	Tom Hughes	1903	4	Sonny Siebert	1971
5	Bill Dinneen	1904	4	Marty Pattin	1972
5	Cy Young	1905	4	John Curtis	1973
5	Smokey Joe Wood	1911	4	Bill Lee	1975
5	Rube Foster	1915	4	Rick Wise	1976
5	Sad Sam Jones	1918	4	Bob Stanley	1979
5	Herb Pennock	1919	4	Bruce Hurst	1986
5	Sad Sam Jones	1919	4	Roger Clemens	1990
5	Sad Sam Jones	1921	4	Roger Clemens	1991
5	Boo Ferriss	1945	4	Pedro Martinez	2000

RED SOX PITCHERS WITH ERAS OF 2.70 OR LESS IN A SEASON

ERA	PITCHER	YEAR	ERA	PITCHER	YEAR
1.00	Dutch Leonard	1914	2.22	Ernie Shore	1917
1.26	Cy Young	1908	2.22	Babe Ruth	1918
1.49	Smokey Joe Wood	1915	2.22	Pedro Martinez	2003
1.62	Ray Collins	1910	2.23	Bill Dinneen	1903
1.63	Cy Young	1901	2.25	Sad Sam Jones	1918
1.64	Ernie Shore	1915	2.26	Tex Hughson	1944
1.65	Rube Foster	1914	2.26	Pedro Martinez	2002
1.68	Smokey Joe Wood	1910	2.30	Charlie Smith	1910
1.74	Carl Mays	1917	2.32	Ralph Glaze	1907
1.74	Pedro Martinez	2000	2.36	Dutch Leonard	1915
1.75	Babe Ruth	1916	2.36	Dutch Leonard	1916
1.82	Cy Young	1905	2.39	Ray Collins	1911
1.91	Charley Hall	1910	2.39	Dutch Leonard	1913
1.91	Smokey Joe Wood	1912	2.39	Carl Mays	1916
1.91	Luis Tiant	1972	2.41	Roger Clemens	1992
1.93	Roger Clemens	1990	2.43	Eddie Cicotte	1908
1.97	Cy Young	1904	2.44	Babe Ruth	1915
1.97	Eddie Cicotte	1909	2.46	Cy Morgan	1908
1.99	Cy Young	1907	2.46	Larry Pape	1911
2.02	Smokey Joe Wood	1911	2.48	Ray Collins	1914
2.02	Babe Ruth	1917	2.48	Jesse Tannehill	1905
2.04	Jesse Tannehill	1904	2.48	Carl Mays	1919
2.07	George Winter	1907	2.48	Roger Clemens	1986
2.07	Pedro Martinez	1999	2.54	Ray Collins	1912
2.08	Cy Young	1903	2.54	Lefty Grove	1939
2.11	Bullet Joe Bush	1918	2.57	Tom Hughes	1903
2.12	Rube Foster	1915	2.57	Buck O'Brien	1912
2.15	Cy Young	1902	2.58	Derek Lowe	2002
2.17	Dutch Leonard	1917	2.59	Tex Hughson	1942
2.18	Frank Arellanes	1909	2.63	Ray Collins	1913
2.20	Bill Dinneen	1904	2.63	Ernie Shore	1916
2.21	Norwood Gibson	1904	2.64	Tex Hughson	1943
2.21	Smokey Joe Wood	1909	2.70	Lefty Grove	1935
2.21	Carl Mays	1918			

RED SOX PITCHERS WITH 10 OR MORE SAVES IN A SEASON

SV	PITCHER	YEAR	SV	PITCHER	YEAR
46	Tom Gordon	1998	15	Bobby Bolin	1973
42	Derek Lowe	2000	15	Dick Drago	1975
40	Jeff Reardon	1991	15	Derek Lowe	1999
40	Ugueth Urbina	2002	15	Tim Wakefield	1999
33	Bob Stanley	1983	14	Ellis Kinder	1951
33	Jeff Russell	1993	14	Mike Fornieles	1960
32	Keith Foulke	2004	14	Bob Stanley	1980
31	Bill Campbell	1977	14	Mark Clear	1982
31	Heathcliff Slocumb	1996	14	Bob Stanley	1982
29	Dick Radatz	1964	13	Dick Drago	1979
29	Lee Smith	1988	13	Ken Ryan	1994
27	Ellis Kinder	1953	12	Leo Kiely	1958
27	Jeff Reardon	1992	12	Lee Stange	1968
25	Dick Radatz	1963	12	Steve Crawford	1985
25	Lee Smith	1989	12	Joe Sambito	1986
24	Dick Radatz	1962	12	Jeff Russell	1994
24	Tom Burgmeier	1980	11	Ike Delock	1957
24	Derek Lowe	2001	11	Mike Fornieles	1959
22	Dick Radatz	1965	11	Sparky Lyle	1968
22	Bob Stanley	1984	11	Vicente Romo	1969
21	Jeff Reardon	1990	11	Bob Veale	1973
20	John Wyatt	1967	11	Tom Gordon	1997
20	Sparky Lyle	1970	11	Tom Gordon	1999
20	Rick Aguilera	1995	10	Wilcy Moore	1931
18	Ellis Kinder	1955	10	Murray Wall	1958
17	Sparky Lyle	1969	10	Diego Segui	1974
17	Heathcliff Slocumb	1997	10	Jim Willoughby	1976
16	Sparky Lyle	1971	10	Bob Stanley	1978
16	Bob Stanley	1986	10	Bob Stanley	1985
16	Byung-Hyun Kim	2003	10	Wes Gardner	1987
15	Ellis Kinder	1954	10	Stan Belinda	1995
15	Mike Fornieles	1961			

RED SOX ALL-STAR SELECTIONS

1933	Rick Ferrell, C*			Tex Hughson, P
1934	Rick Ferrell, C			Bob Johnson, OF*
1935	Joe Cronin, SS*		1945	No game
	Rick Ferrell, C		1946	Dom DiMaggio, OF*
	Lefty Grove, P			Bobby Doerr, 2B*
1936	Joe Cronin, SS			Boo Ferriss, P
	Rick Ferrell, C*			Mickey Harris, P
	Jimmie Foxx, 1B			Johnny Pesky, SS*
	Lefty Grove, P*			Hal Wagner, C
1937	Doc Cramer, OF			Ted Williams, OF* (MVP)
	Joe Cronin, SS*			Rudy York, 1B
	Jimmie Foxx, 1B		1947	Bobby Doerr, 2B
	Lefty Grove, P			Ted Williams, OF*
1938	Doc Cramer, OF		1948	Joe Dobson, P
	Joe Cronin, SS*			Bobby Doerr, 2B
	Jimmie Foxx, 1B*			Vern Stephens, SS
	Lefty Grove, P			Birdie Tebbetts, C
1939	Doc Cramer, OF*			Ted Williams, OF
	Joe Cronin, SS*		1949	Dom DiMaggio, OF*
	Jimmie Foxx, 1B			Billy Goodman, 1B
	Lefty Grove, P			Mel Parnell, P*
1940	Doc Cramer, OF			Vern Stephens, SS
	Lou Finney, OF			Birdie Tebbetts, C*
	Jimmie Foxx, 1B*			Ted Williams, OF*
	Ted Williams, OF*		1950	Dom DiMaggio, OF
1941	Joe Cronin, SS*			Bobby Doerr, 2B*
	Dom DiMaggio, OF			Walt Drogo, 1B*
	Bobby Doerr, 2B*			Vern Stephens, SS
	Jimmie Foxx, 1B			Ted Williams, OF*
	Ted Williams, OF* (MVP)		1951	Dom DiMaggio, OF*
1942	Dom DiMaggio, OF			Bobby Doerr, 2B
	Bobby Doerr, 2B			Mel Parnell, P
	Tex Hughson P			Vern Stephens, SS
	Ted Williams, OF*			Ted Williams, OF*
1943	Bobby Doerr, 2B* (MVP)		1952	Dom DiMaggio, OF
	Tex Hughson, P			George Kell, 3B
	Oscar Judd, P		1953	Billy Goodman, 2B*
1944	Bobby Doerr, 2B*			George Kell, 3B
	Pete Fox, OF			Sammy White, C

*Starter

1954	Jimmy Piersall, OF		Carl Yastrzemski, OF
	Ted Williams, OF	1964	Eddie Bressoud, SS
1955	Jackie Jensen, OF		Frank Malzone, 3B
	Frank Sullivan, P		Dick Radatz, P
	Ted Williams, OF*	1965	Felix Mantilla, 2B*
1956	Tom Brewer, P		Carl Yastrzemski, OF
	Jimmy Piersall, OF	1966	George Scott, 1B*
	Frank Sullivan, P		Carl Yastrzemski, OF
	Mickey Vernon, 1B*	1967	Tony Conigilaro, OF*
	Ted Williams, OF*		Jim Lonborg, P
1957	Frank Malzone, 3B		Rico Petrocelli, SS*
	Ted Williams, OF*		Carl Yastrzemski, OF*
1958	Jackie Jensen, OF*	1968	Ken Harrelson, OF
	Frank Malzone, 3B*		Jose Santiago, P
	Ted Williams, OF		Gary Bell, P
1958	Jackie Jensen, OF*		Carl Yastrzemski, OF*
	Frank Malzone, 3B*	1969	Mike Andrews, 2B
	Ted Williams, OF		Ray Culp, P
1959	Frank Malzone, 3B		Rico Petrocelli, SS*
(July 7)	Pete Runnels, 1B		Reggie Smith, OF
	Ted Williams, OF		Carl Yastrzemski OF*
1959	Frank Malzone, 3B*	1970	Jerry Moses, C
(August 3)	Pete Runnels, 1B*		Carl Yastrzemski OF*
	Ted Williams, OF*		(MVP)
1960	Frank Malzone, 3B*	1971	Luis Aparicio, SS*
(July 11)	Bill Monbouquette, P*		Bill Siebert, P
	Pete Runnels, 2B*		Carl Yastrzemski, OF*
	Ted Williams, OF	1972	Luis Aparicio, SS
1960	Frank Malzone, 3B*		Carlton Fisk, C
(July 13)	Bill Monbouquette, P		Reggie Smith, OF
	Pete Runnels, 2B*		Carl Yastrzemski, OF*
	Ted Williams, OF	1973	Carlton Fisk, C*
1961	Mike Fornieles, P		Bill Lee, P
(July 11)			Carl Yastrzemski, OF
1961	Don Schwall, P	1974	Carlton Fisk, C
(July 31)			Luis Tiant, P
1962	Bill Monbouquette, P		Carl Yastrzemski, OF
(July 10)		1975	Fred Lynn, OF
1962	Pete Runnels, 2B		Carl Yastrzemski, OF
(July 30)		1976	Carlton Fisk, C
1963	Frank Malzone, 3B*		Fred Lynn, OF*
	Bill Monbouquette, P		Luis Tiant, P
	Dick Radatz, P		Carl Yastrzemski, OF

1977	Rick Burleson, SS*		Bruce Hurst, P
	Bill Campbell, P	1988	Wade Boggs, 3B*
	Carlton Fisk, C*		Roger Clemens, P
	Fred Lynn, OF		Mike Greenwell, OF
	Jim Rice, OF	1989	Wade Boggs, 3B*
	George Scott, 1B	1990	Wade Boggs, 3B*
	Carl Yastrzemski, OF*		Ellis Burks, OF
1978	Rick Burleson, SS		Roger Clemens, P
	Dwight Evans, OF	1991	Wade Boggs, 3B*
	Carlton Fisk, C*		Roger Clemens P
	Fred Lynn, OF*		Jeff Reardon, P
	Jerry Remy, 2B	1992	Wade Boggs, 3B*
	Jim Rice, OF*		Roger Clemens, P
	Carl Yastrzemski, OF	1993	Scott Cooper, 3B
1979	Rick Burleson, SS	1994	Scott Cooper, 3B
	Fred Lynn, OF*	1995	Erik Hanson, P
	Jim Rice, OF*		Mo Vaughn, 1B
	Bob Stanley, P	1996	Mo Vaughn, 1B*
	Carl Yastrzemski, 1B*	1997	Nomar Garciaparra, SS
1980	Tom Burgmeier, P	1998	Tom Gordon, P
	Carlton Fisk, C*		Pedro Martinez, P
	Fred Lynn, OF*		Mo Vaughn, P
	Jim Rice, OF	1999	Nomar Garciaparra, SS*
1981	Dwight Evans, OF		Pedro Martinez, P*
1982	Mark Clear, P		(MVP)
	Dennis Eckersley, P*		Jose Offerman, 2B
	Carl Yastrzemski, 1B	2000	Carl Everett, OF
1983	Jim Rice, OF*		Nomar Garciaparra, SS
	Bob Stanley, P		Derek Lowe, P
	Carl Yastrzemski, 1B	2001	Manny Ramirez, OF*
1984	Tony Amas, OF	2002	Johnny Damon, OF
	Jim Rice, OF		Nomar Garciaparra, SS
1985	Wade Boggs, 3B		Shea Hillenbrand, 3B*
	Rich Gedman, C		Derek Lowe, P*
	Jim Rice, OF*		Pedro Martinez, P
1986	Wade Boggs, 3B*		Manny Ramirez, OF*
	Roger Clemens, P*		Ugueth Urbina, P
	(MVP)	2003	Nomar Garciapprra, SS
	Rich Gedman, C		Manny Ramirez, OF*
	Jim Rice, OF		Jason Varitek, C
1987	Wade Boggs, 3B*	2004	David Ortiz, IB
	Dwight Evans, OF		Manny Ramirez, OF*
			Curt Schilling, P

*Starter

RED SOX HALL-OF-FAMERS

PLAYER	ACTIVE YEARS	ENSHRINEMENT YEAR
Luis Aparicio	1971–1973	1984
Ed Barrow	1918–1920(m)	1953
Wade Boggs	1982–1992	2005
Lou Boudreau	1951–1952	1970
	1952–1954(m)	
Jesse Burkett	1905	1946
Orlando Cepeda	1973	1999
Frank Chance	1923(m)	1946
Jack Chesbro	1909	1946
Eddie Collins	1933–1951(e)	1939
Jimmy Collins	1901–1907	1945
	1901–1906(m)	
Joe Cronin	1935–1945	1956
	1935–1947(m)	
Bobby Doerr	1937–1951	1986
Hugh Duffy	1921–1922(m)	1945
Dennis Eckersley	1978–1984, 1998	2004
Rick Ferrell	1933–1937	1984
Carlton Fisk	1969–1980	2000
Jimmie Foxx	1936–1942	1951
Lefty Grove	1934–1941	1947
Bucky Harris	1934(m)	1975
Billy Herman	1964–1966(m)	1975
Harry Hooper	1909–1920	1971
Waite Hoyt	1919–1920	1969
Ferguson Jenkins	1976–1977	1991
George Kell	1952–1954	1983
Heinie Manush	1936	1964
Juan Marichal	1974	1983
Joe McCarthy	1948–1950(m)	1957
Herb Pennock	1915–1922	1948
Tony Perez	1980–1982	2000
Red Ruffling	1924–1930	1967
Babe Ruth	1914–1919	1936
Tom Seaver	1986	1992
Al Simmons	1943	1953
Tris Speaker	1907–1915	1937
Ted Williams	1939–1960	1966
Carl Yastrzemski	1961–1983	1989
Tom Yawkey	1933–1976(e)	1980
Cy Young	1901–1908	1937
	1907(m)	

m = Red Sox manager
e = Red Sox executive

THE RED SOX HALL OF FAME

The Red Sox Hall of Fame was instituted in 1995 to recognize the outstanding careers of former Red Sox players. Players must have played a minimum of three seasons with the Boston Red Sox and must also have been out of uniform as an active player a minimum of three years. Non-uniformed persons are chosen only by a unanimous vote of the 15-member selection committee. Former Red Sox personnel in the National Baseball Hall of Fame are automatically enshrined into the Boston Red Sox Hall of Fame.

Wade Boggs	1982–92	2004
Rick Burleson	1974–80	2002
Bill Carrigan	1906, 08–16, 27–29(m)	2004
Ken Coleman	1966–74, 79–89(b)	2000
Jimmy Collins	1901–07	2004
Tony Conigliaro	1964–67, 69–70, 75	1995
Dom DiMaggio	1940–42, 46–53	1995
Dennis Eckersley	1978–84, 98	2004
Dwight Evans	1972–90	2000
Boo Ferriss	1945–50	2002
Carlton Fisk	1969, 71–80	1997
Larry Gardner	1908–17	2000
Billy Goodman	1947–57	2004
Lou Gorman	1984–present(e)	2002
John Harrington	1973–2002(e)	2002
Tex Hughson	1941–44, 46–49	2002
Bruce Hurst	1980–88	2004
Jackie Jensen	1954–59, 61	2000
Duffy Lewis	1910–17	2002
Jim Lonborg	1965–71	2002
Fred Lynn	1974–80	2002
Frank Malzone	1955–65	1995
Ned Martin	1961–92(b)	2000
Bill Monbouquette	1958–65	2000
Dick O'Connell	1949–77(e)	1997
Mel Parnell	1947–56	1997
Johnny Pesky	1942, 46–52	1995
Rico Petrocelli	1963, 65–76	1997
Dick Radatz	1963–66	1997
Jim Rice	1974–89	1995
Pete Runnels	1958–62	2004
Reggie Smith	1966–73	2000
Bob Stanley	1977–89	2000

RED SOX STATISTICS

Haywood Sullivan	1955, 57, 59–60, 66–83(e)	2004
Luis Tiant	1971–78	1997
Smokey Joe Wood	1908–15	1995
Jean R. Yawkey		1995

b=Red Sox broadcaster
e=Red Sox executive
m=Rex Sox manager

RED SOX PLAYERS ON THE ALL-CENTURY TEAM

(25-man All-Century team selected by fans; 5 additional names chosen by a special panel

Roger Clemens, P
Babe Ruth, OF
Ted Williams, OF
Cy Young, P

RED SOX ALL-TIME TEAMS VOTED BY THE FANS

1969

C	Birdie Tebbetts
1B	Jimmie Foxx
2B	Bobby Doerr
3B	Frank Malzone
SS	Joe Cronin
OF	Ted Williams
OF	Carl Yastrzemski
OF	Tris Speaker
RHP	Cy Young
LHP	Lefty Grove
	Ted Williams—Greatest player

1982

	FIRST TEAM		SECOND TEAM
C	Carlton Fisk	C	Birdie Tebbetts
1B	Jimmie Foxx	1B	George Scott
2B	Bobby Doerr	2B	Jerry Remy
3B	Rico Petrocelli	3B	Frank Malzone
SS	Rick Burleson	SS	Johnny Pesky
OF	Ted Williams	OF	Jim Rice
OF	Carl Yastrzemski	OF	Dom DiMaggio
OF	Dwight Evans	OF	Fred Lynn
RHP	Cy Young	RHP	Luis Tiant
LHP	Babe Ruth	LHP	Lefty Grove
REL P	Dick Radatz	REL P	Sparky Lyle
MGR	Dick Williams	MGR	Joe Cronin
	Ted Williams—Greatest player		

2001 (FAN BALLOTS IN BOSTON GLOBE VOTE)

FIRST TEAM

C	Carlton Fisk	OF	Jim Rice
1B	Jimmie Foxx	SP	Cy Young
2B	Bobby Doerr	SP	Pedro Martinez
3B	Wade Boggs	SP	Roger Clemens
SS	Nomar Garciaparra	SP	Smokey Joe Wood
OF	Ted Williams	REL P	Dick Radatz
OF	Carl Yastrzemski	MGR	Joe Cronin

RED SOX SILVER SLUGGER AWARD WINNERS (CHOSEN BY THE SPORTING NEWS; 1980–2000)

1981	Carney Lansford, 3B	1989	Wade Boggs, 3B
1981	Dwight Evans, RF	1990	Ellis Burks, CF
1983	Wade Boggs, 3B	1991	Wade Boggs, 3B
1983	Jim Rice, LF	1995	John Valentin, 3B
1984	Tony Armas, CF	1995	Mo Vaughn, 1B
1984	Jim Rice, LF	1997	Nomar Garciaparra, SS
1986	Wade Boggs, 3B	2001	Manny Ramirez, OF
1986	Don Baylor, DH	2002	Manny Ramirez, OF
1987	Wade Boggs, 3B	2003	Bill Mueller, 3B
1987	Dwight Evans, RF–1B	2003	Manny Ramirez, OF
1988	Wade Boggs, 3B	2004	Manny Ramirez, OF
1988	Mike Greenwell, LF	2004	David Ortiz, 1B

RED SOX RAWLINGS GOLD GLOVE AWARD WINNERS

1957	Frank Malzone, 3B	1976	Dwight Evans, OF
1958	Frank Malzone, 3B (2)	1977	Carl Yastrzemski, OF (7)
	Jim Piersall, CF	1978	Dwight Evans, OF (2)
1959	Frank Malzone, 3B (3)		Fred Lynn, OF (2)
	Jackie Jensen, RF	1979	Rick Burleson, SS
1963	Carl Yastrzemski, OF		Dwight Evans, OF (3)
1965	Carl Yastrzemski OF (2)		Fred Lynn, OF (3)
1967	George Scott, 1B	1980	Fred Lynn, OF (4)
	Carl Yastrzemski, OF (3)	1981	Dwight Evans, OF (4)
1968	George Scott, 1B (2)	1982	Dwight Evans, OF (5)
	Reggie Smith, OF	1983	Dwight Evans, OF (6)
	Carl Yastrzemski, OF (4)	1984	Dwight Evans, OF (7)
1969	Carl Yastrzemski, OF (5)	1985	Dwight Evans, OF (8)
1971	Carl Yastrzemski, OF (6)	1990	Mike Boddicker, P
1972	Carlton Fisk, C		Ellis Burks, OF
	Doug Griffin, 2B	1991	Tony Pena, C
1975	Fred Lynn, OF		

RED SOX RETIRED NUMBERS

#9—Ted Williams—Number formally retired May 29, 1984
#4—Joe Cronin—Number formally retired May 29, 1984
#1—Bobby Doerr—Number formally retired May 21, 1988
#8—Carl Yastrzemski—Number formally retired August 6, 1989
#27—Carlton Fisk—Number formally retired September 4, 2000

BOSTON WRITERS MVP AWARD (THOMAS A. YAWKEY AWARD)

From 1937 through 1952, the Boston chapter of the Baseball Writers Association of America (the BBWAA) voted the award to either a Red Sox player or a Boston Braves player. The Braves moved to Milwaukee after the 1952 season. After club owner Tom Yawkey's death in 1976, the writers renamed the award in his honor.

1937	Jim Turner*	1973	Tommy Harper
1938	Jimmie Foxx	1974	Carl Yastrzemski
1939	Joe Cronin	1975	Fred Lynn
1940	Johnny Cooney*	1976	Carl Yastrzemski
1941	Ted Williams	1977	Carlton Fisk
1942–1944	No award	1978	Jim Rice
1945	Tommy Holmes*	1979	Rick Burleson
1946	Ted Williams	1980	Rick Burleson
1947	Bob Elliott*	1981	Dwight Evans
1948	Johnny Sain*	1982	Dwight Evans
1949	Ted Williams	1983	Jim Rice
1950	Billy Goodman	1984	Dwight Evans and
1951	Ellis Kinder		Tony Armas
1952	Walker Cooper*	1985	Wade Boggs
1953	Ellis Kinder	1986	Roger Clemens
1954	Jackie Jensen	1987	Dwight Evans
1955	Ted Williams	1988	Mike Greenwell
1956	Jim Piersall	1989	Nick Esasky
1957	Frank Malzone	1990	Roger Clemens
1958	Jackie Jensen	1991	Roger Clemens
1959	Frank Malzone	1992	Roger Clemens
1960	Vic Wertz	1993	Mo Vaughn
1961	Chuck Schilling	1994	Mo Vaughn
1962	Eddie Bressoud	1995	Mo Vaughn
1963	Carl Yastrzemski	1996	Mo Vaughn
1964	Dick Radatz	1997	Nomar Garciaparra
1965	Carl Yastrzemski	1998	Nomar Garciaparra
1966	Tony Conigliaro	1999	Pedro Martinez
1967	Carl Yastrzemski	2000	Pedro Martinez
1968	Ken Harrelson	2001	Trot Nixon
1969	Rico Petrocelli	2002	Derek Lowe and
1970	Carl Yastrzemski		Pedro Martinez
1971	Reggie Smith	2003	Jason Varitek
1972	Carlton Fisk	2004	David Ortiz

*Boston Brave

RED SOX AMERICAN LEAGUE MVP AWARDS
(VOTED BY BBWAA)

YEAR	PLAYER	BA	HR	RBI
1912	**Tris Speaker, OF	.383	*10	98
1938	Jimmie Foxx, 1B	*.349	50	*175
1946	Ted Williams, LF	.342	38	123
1949	Ted Williams, LF	.343	*43	*159
1958	Jackie Jensen, RF	.286	35	*122
1967	Carl Yastrzemski, LF	*.326	*44	*121
1975	Fred Lynn, CF	.331	21	105
1978	Jim Rice, LF	.315	*46	*139
1995	Mo Vaughn, 1B	.300	39	*126

		W–L	ERA	SO
1986	Roger Clemens, P	*24–4	*2.48	238

*Led league
**From 1910–14, this award was officially called the Chalmers Award.

RED SOX CY YOUNG AWARD WINNERS
(VOTED BY BBWAA)

YEAR	PLAYER	W–L	ERA	SO
1967	Jim Lonborg	*22–9	3.16	*246
1986	Roger Clemens	*24–4	*2.48	238
1987	Roger Clemens	*20–9	2.56	256
1991	Roger Clemens	18–10	*2.62	*241
1999	Pedro Martinez	*23–4	*2.07	*313
2000	Pedro Martinez	18–6	*1.74	*284

*Led league

RED SOX ROOKIE OF THE YEAR AWARD WINNERS (VOTED BY BBWAA)

YEAR	PLAYER	BA	HR	RBI
1950	Walt Dropo, 1B	.322	34	**144
1972	Carlton Fisk, C	.293	22	61
1975	Fred Lynn, CF	.331	21	105
1997	Nomar Garciaparra, SS	.306	30	98

YEAR	PLAYER	W–L	ERA	SO
1961	Don Schwall, P	15–7	3.22	91

*Led league
**Tied for league lead

RED SOX MANAGER OF THE YEAR AWARD WINNERS

YEAR	MANAGER	W–L	%
1986	John McNamara	95–66	.590
1999	Jimy Williams	94–68	.580

ANNUAL MAN OF THE YEAR AWARD
(CHOSEN BY THE BOSOX CLUB OF BOSTON)

The annual Man of the Year is selected for his contributions to the success of the Red Sox and for his cooperation in community endeavors.

1967	Rico Petrocelli, SS	1987	Bruce Hurst, P
1968	Mike Andrews, 2B	1988	Bill Fischer, Coach
1969	Lee Stange, P	1989	Dennis Lamp, P
1970	Jerry Moses, C	1990	Tony Pena, C
1971	John Kennedy, INF	1991	Tony Fossas, P
1972	Bob Montgomery, C	1992	Roger Clemens, P
1973	Tommy Harper, LF	1993	Mo Vaughn, 1B
1974	Rick Miller, CF	1994	Ken Ryan, P
1975	Denny Doyle, 2B	1995	Tim Naehring, 3B
1976	Reggie Cleveland, P	1996	Heathcliff Slocumb, P
1977	Butch Hobson, 3B	1997	Wendell Kim, Coach
1978	Bill Campbell, P	1998	Tim Wakefield, P
1979	Tom Burgmeier, P	1999	Trot Nixon, OF
1980	Steve Renko, P	2000	John Harrington, CEO
1981	Jerry Remy, 2B	2001	Ben Mondor, PawSox CEO
1982	Bob Stanley, P		
1983	Carl Yastrzemski, DH	2002	Carlos Baerga, INF
1984	Mike Easler, DH	2003	Ron Jackson, Coach
1985	Wade Boggs, 3B	2004	Jason Varitek, C
1986	Marty Barrett, 2B		

RED SOX NO-HITTERS

May 5, 1904	Cy Young (H)	vs. Philadelphia 3–0*
Aug 17, 1904	Jesse Tannehill (A)	vs. Chicago 6–0
Sep 27, 1905 (G1)	Bill Dinneen (H)	vs. Chicago 2–0
Jun 30, 1908	Cy Young (A)	vs. New York 8–0
Jul 29, 1911 (G1)	Smokey Joe Wood (H)	vs. St. Louis 5–0
Jun 21, 1916	Rube Foster (H)	vs. New York 2–0
Aug 30, 1916	Dutch Leonard (H)	vs. St. Louis 4–0
Jun 23, 1917 (G1)	Ernie Shore (H)	vs. Washington 4–0*

(Shore didn't start the game. Babe Ruth walked the first batter and was ejected for arguing with the umpire. Shore relieved. The base runner was out attempting to steal. Shore was given credit for a perfect game in facing only 26 batters.)

Jun 3, 1918	Dutch Leonard (A)	vs. Detroit 5–0
Sep 7, 1923	Howard Ehmke (A)	vs. Philadelphia 4–0
Jul 14, 1956	Mel Parnell (H)	vs. Chicago 4–0
Jun 26, 1962	Earl Wilson (H)	vs. Los Angeles 2–0
Aug 1, 1962	Bill Monbouquette (A)	vs. Chicago 1–0
Sep 16, 1965	Dave Morehead (H)	vs. Cleveland 2–0
Apr 4, 2001	Hideo Nomo (A)	vs. Baltimore 3–0
Apr 27, 2002	Derek Lowe (H)	vs. Tampa Bay 10–0

H = Home
A = Away
* = Perfect game

NO-HITTERS PITCHED AGAINST THE SOX

Sep 18, 1908	Dusty Rhoads, Cleveland (A) 2–1
Aug 17, 1911	Ed Walsh, Chicago (A) 5–0
Apr 24, 1917	George Mogridge, New York (H) 2–1
Jul 1, 1920	Walter Johnson, Washington (H) 1–0
Aug 21, 1926	Ted Lyons, Chicago (H) 6–0
Aug 8, 1931	Bob Burke, Washington (A) 5–0
Sep 18, 1934	Bobo Newson, St. Louis (A) 1–2
	(Lost in 10th but pitched 9 hitless innings)
Sep 28, 1951 (G1)	Allie Reynolds, New York (A) 8–0
Jul 20, 1958 (G1)	Jim Bunning, Detroit (H) 3–0
Aug 6, 1967	Dean Chance, Minnesota (5 innings) (A) 2–0
Apr 27, 1968	Tom Phoebou, Baltimore (A) 6–0
Jul 4, 1983	Dave Righetti, New York (A) 4–0
Apr 22, 1993	Chris Bosio, Seattle (A) 7–0

H = Home
A = Away

RED SOX CYCLES

Buck Freeman	June 21, 1903 at Clev.
Patsy Dougherty	July 29, 1903 vs. N.Y.
Tris Speaker	June 9, 1912 at St. L.
Roy Carlyle	July 21, 1925 at Chi. (1st G.)
Julius Solters	Aug. 19, 1934 at Det. (1st G.)
Joe Cronin	Aug. 2, 1940 at Det.
Leon Culberson	July 3, 1943 at Clev.
Bobby Doerr	May 17, 1944 vs. St. L. (2nd G.)
Bob Johnson	July 6, 1944 vs. Det.
Ted Williams	July 21, 1946 vs. St. L. (2nd G.)
Bobby Doerr (2)	May 13, 1947 vs. Chi.
Lu Clinton	July 13, 1962 at K.C.
Carl Yastrzemski	May 14, 1965 vs. Det.
Bob Watson	Sept. 15, 1979 at Balt.
Fred Lynn	May 13, 1980 vs. Minn.
Dwight Evans	June 28, 1984 vs. Sea.
Rich Gedman	Sept. 18, 1985 vs. Tor.
Mike Greenwell	Sept. 14, 1988 vs. Balt.
Scott Cooper	Apr. 12, 1994 at K.C.
John Valentin	June 6, 1996 vs. Chi.

RED SOX TRIPLE CROWN WINNERS

1942	Ted Williams	36 home runs 137 runs batted in .356 batting average
1947	Ted Williams	32 home runs 114 runs batted in .343 batting average
1967	Carl Yastrzemski	44 home runs 121 runs batted in .326 batting average

Almost—2 of 3

1903	Buck Freeman	13 home runs 104 runs batted in (.287 batting average)
1919	Babe Ruth	19 home runs 114 runs batted in (.322 batting average)
1938	Jimmie Foxx	(50 home runs) 175 runs batted in .349 batting average
1941	Ted Williams	37 home runs (120 runs batted in) .406 batting average
1949	Ted Williams	43 home runs 159 runs batted in (.343 batting average)
1978	Jim Rice	46 home runs 139 runs batted in (.315 batting average)
1984	Tony Armas	43 home runs 123 runs batted in (.268 batting average)

10 OR MORE YEARS WITH THE RED SOX

Only 11 Red Sox have played 10 or more seasons in the major leagues, exclusively with Boston.

	YEARS	GAMES
Bill Carrigan, C	1906–16	706
Dom DiMaggio, CF–RF	1940–53	1,399
Bobby Doerr, 2B	1937–51	1,865
Mike Greenwell, LF	1985–96	1,269
Bob Montgomery, C	1970–79	387
Mel Parnell, P	1947–56	289
Rico Petrocelli, SS–3B	1963–76	1,553
Jim Rice, LF–DH	1974–89	2,089
Bob Stanley, P	1977–89	637
John Valentin, SS–3B	1992–01	991
Tim Wakefield, P	1995–04	387
Ted Williams, LF–RF	1939–60	2,292
Carl Yastrzemski, LF–1B–DH	1961–83	3,308

RED SOX GRAND SLAMS

In 104 seasons the Red Sox have hit 321 grand slams; 183 have come at Fenway Park and 3 at the old Huntington Avenue Grounds. Not surprisingly, Ted Williams holds the BoSox career grand-slam record with 17. The season mark was set by Babe Ruth in 1919 when he blasted 4 slams, all on the road. Those were the only grand slams the Bambino hit in a Red Sox uniform. Jim Tabor (July 4, 1939), Rudy York (July 22, 1946), Nomar Garciaparra (May 10, 1999), and Bill Mueller (July 29, 2003) all hit two in a single game, and Jimmie Foxx (May 20–21, 1940) hit slams in consecutive games.

CAREER	NO.
Ted Williams	17
Rico Petrocelli	9
Bobby Doerr	8
Jim Rice	8
Jimmie Foxx	7
Jackie Jensen	7
Mo Vaughn	7
Carl Yastrzemski	7
Trot Nixon	7
Ellis Burks	6
Jim Tabor	6
Tony Conigliaro	5
Dom DiMaggio	5
Dwight Evans	5
Joe Foy	5
Vern Stephens	5
Vic Wertz	5
Nomar Garciaparra	5

SEASON	NO.	YEAR
Babe Ruth	4	1919
Jimmie Foxx	3	1938
Jimmie Foxx	3	1940
Ted Williams	3	1955
Vic Wertz	3	1960
Dick Stuart	3	1964
Carl Yastrzemski	3	1969
Rico Petrocelli	3	1972
Mo Vaughn	3	1995

CLUB, SEASON

9	1941, 1950, 1987, 2001
8	1952, 1964
7	1938, 1940, 1955, 1986, 1992, 1995, 1999

RED SOX INDIVIDUAL SEASON RECORDS

BATTING

GAMES, most ....163, Jim Rice, 1978
AT-BATS: Left-handed, most ....673, Bill Buckner, 1985
  Right-handed, most..............................684, Nomar Garciaparra, 1997
PLATE APPEARANCES, most ....758*, Wade Boggs, 1985
HITS, most...240, Wade Boggs, 1985
GAMES HIT SAFELY IN, most......................135****, Wade Boggs, 1985
MULTIPLE-HIT GAMES, most.............................72, Wade Boggs, 1985
HITTING STREAKS, longest ....34, Dom DiMaggio, 1949
  Longest start of season ....20, Eddie Bressoud, 1964
BATTING AVERAGE
  Left-handed, highest .... .406, Ted Williams, 1941
  Right-handed, highest .... .372, Nomar Garciaparra, 2000

SINGLES, most ....187, Wade Boggs, 1985
DOUBLES, most...67***, Earl Webb, 1931
TRIPLES, most..22, Tris Speaker, 1913
HOME RUNS, most...50, Jimmie Foxx, 1938
  At home ....35, Jimmie Foxx, 1938
  At home by left-handed hitter ....28, Fred Lynn, 1979
  On road ....26, Ted Williams, 1957
  One month ....14, Jackie Jensen, June, 1958
  By position, 1B ....50, Jimmie Foxx, 1938
    2B...27, Bobby Doerr, 1948 and 1950
    SS ....40, Rico Petrocelli, 1969
    3B ....30, Butch Hobson, 1977
    LF...44, Carl Yastrzemski, 1967
    CF ....38#, Fred Lynn, 1979 ##, Tony Armas, 1984
    RF ....36, Tony Conigliaro, 1970
    C....................................26, Carlton Fisk, 1973 and 1977
    DH ....33###, David Ortiz, 2004
    P...7, Wes Ferrell, 1935

Multi-homer games ....10, Jimmie Foxx, 1938
Two consecutive games ....5****, Carl Yastrzemski, May 19–20, 1976
                    Nomar Garciaparra, July 21, 23 (1st G.), 2002
First 2 major-league games ....2**, Sam Horn, 1987
                    Dave Stapleton, 1980
Grand slams ....4, Babe Ruth, 1919
LONG HITS, most ....92, Jimmie Foxx, 1938
EXTRA BASES ON LONG HITS ....201, Jimmie Foxx, 1938
TOTAL BASES, most...406, Jim Rice, 1978
SLUGGING PERCENTAGE
  Left-handed, highest ....735, Ted Williams, 1941
  Right-handed, highest ....704, Jimmie Foxx, 1938
ON-BASE PERCENTAGE, highest....................552*, Ted Williams, 1941

RUNS, most...150, Ted Williams, 1949
RUNS BATTED IN, most ....175, Jimmie Foxx, 1938
STOLEN BASES, most...54, Tommy Harper, 1973
  Most caught stealing ....19, Mike Menosky, 1920
BASES ON BALLS, most ....162, Ted Williams, 1947 and 1949
  Intentional..33*, Ted Williams, 1957
STRIKEOUTS, Left-handed, most..........154, Mo Vaughn, 1996 and 1997
  Right-handed, most ....162, Butch Hobson, 1977
  Switch-hitter, most..177, Mark Bellhorn, 2004
  Fewest..9, Stuffy McInnis (584 AB), 1921
GROUNDED INTO DOUBLE PLAYS,
Left-handed, most ....30***, Carl Yastrzemski, 1964
  Right-handed, most..36***, Jim Rice, 1984
  Fewest...1, Ellis Burks (558 AB), 1987
HIT BY PITCHER, most..35*, Don Baylor, 1986
SACRIFICES, most, including flies ....54, Jack Barry, 1917
  Most, no flies ....35, Fred Parent, 1905
  Most, flies..........12, Jackie Jensen, 1955 and 1959, Jim Piersall, 1956

MANAGING, most games won at the start ....12, Joe Morgan, 1988

#Plus 1 HR as DH
##Plus 5 HR as DH
###Plus 8 HR as 1B

PITCHING

GAMES, most ....80, Greg Harris, 1993
   Most by left-hander.............................74, Rob Murphy, 1989
   Started, most.......................................43, Cy Young, 1902
   Complete, most ....41, Cy Young, 1902
   Finished, most ....69, Tom Gordon, 1998

WINS, most..34, Smokey Joe Wood, 1912
   Wins, left-hander ....25, Mel Parnell, 1949
   Won consecutively ....16**, Smokey Joe Wood, 1912
   Won consecutively, at home ..13, Tex Hughson, 1944, Boo Ferriss, 1946
   Won consecutively, start of season ....14, Roger Clemens, 1986
   Won, most at home ....19, Cy Young, 1901
   Won, most at Fenway Park.....................18, Smokey Joe Wood, 1912
   Won, most on road................................16, Smokey Joe Wood, 1912
   Won, most in relief...............................16, Dick Radatz, 1964
LOSSES, most.......................................25, Red Ruffing, 1928
   Lost, consecutively ....14, Joe Harris, 1906
WINNING PERCENTAGE, highest .... .882, Bob Stanley (15–2), 1978

INNINGS, most ....384.2, Cy Young, 1902
   Relief, most ....168.1*, Bob Stanley, 1982
   Consecutive hitless, most...................25.1***, Cy Young, 1904
   Batters, most retired without a hit ....76***, Cy Young, 1904
   Consecutive scoreless, most.............................45.2, Cy Young, 1904

HITS, most ....350, Cy Young, 1902
BATTING AVERAGE AGAINST, lowest..... .167***, Pedro Martinez, 2000
RUNS, most ....172, Ted Lewis, 1901
EARNED RUNS, most..140, Wes Ferrell, 1936
EARNED RUN AVERAGE, lowest ....0.96***, Dutch Leonard (224.2
   innings), 1914
STRIKEOUTS, most.......................................313, Pedro Martinez, 1999
   Left-hander, most ....190, Bruce Hurst, 1987
   Most per 9 IP.....................................13.2***, Pedro Martinez, 1999
   Most games, 10 or more ....19, Pedro Martinez, 1999
   Consecutive games, most, 10 or more ....8, Pedro Martinez, 1999
   Three consecutive games of 9 IP, most...................46, Pedro Martinez
   (24 IP), 1999

BASES ON BALLS, most ....134, Mel Parnell, 1949
   Right-hander, most............121, Don Schwall, 1962, Mike Torrez, 1979

SHUTOUTS, most won...10, Cy Young, 1904, Smokey Joe Wood, 1912
   Left-hander, most won ....9**, Babe Ruth, 1916
   Most lost ....8, Joe Harris, 1906
   Most lost by 1–0 ....5**, Bullet Joe Bush, 1918

HIT BATSMEN, most ....20, Howard Ehmke, 1923
WILD PITCHES, most ....21, Earl Wilson, 1963
HOME RUNS, most...38, Tim Wakefield, 1996

SAVES, most ....46, Tom Gordon, 1998
   Most, left-handed ....24, Tom Burgmeier, 1980

*A.L. record
**Tied A.L. record
***Major-league record
****Tied major-league record

ROOKIE RECORDS

GAMES . . . . 162****, George Scott, 1966
AT-BATS . . . . 684, Nomar Garciaparra, 1997
HITS . . . . 209, Nomar Garciaparra, 1997
SINGLES. . . . . 165, Johnny Pesky, 1942
DOUBLES . . . . 47*, Fred Lynn, 1975
TRIPLES. . . . . 17, Russ Scarritt, 1929
HOME RUNS . . . . 34, Walt Dropo, 1950
TOTAL BASES. . . . . 364, Nomar Garciaparra, 1997
RUNS . . . . 131, Ted Williams, 1939
RUNS BATTED IN . . . . 145***, Ted Williams, 1939
BATTING AVERAGE . . . . .342 Pat Dougherty, 1902, .349,
                                        Wade Boggs, 1982, 104G[2]
SLUGGING AVERAGE . . . . .609*, Ted Williams, 1939
BASES ON BALLS . . . . 107***, Ted Williams, 1939
MOST INTENTIONAL WALKS . . . . 13, George Scott, 1966
STRIKEOUTS . . . . 152, George Scott, 1966
STOLEN BASES . . . . 35, Tris Speaker, 1909
WINS . . . . 21, Dave Ferriss, 1945
LOSSES, most. . . . . 19, Ted Wingfield, 1925
INNINGS PITCHED . . . . 275.2, Buck O'Brien, 1912
STRIKEOUTS. . . . . 155, Ken Brett, 1970
  Right-handed, most . . . 144, Dutch Leonard, 1913, Dick Radatz, 1962
EARNED RUN AVERAGE . . . . 1.89 Ernie Shore, 1914
GAMES. . . . . 47, Ed Morris, 1928
GAMES STARTED . . . . 34, Buck O'Brien, 1912
COMPLETE GAMES . . . 26, George Winter, 1901, Buck O'Brien, 1912,
                                         Dave Ferriss, 1945
HITS ALLOWED, most . . . . 263, Dave Ferriss, 1945
BASES ON BALLS, most . . . . 110, Don Schwall, 1961
RUNS ALLOWED, most. . . . . 149, Ted Wingfield, 1925
EARNED RUNS ALLOWED, most . . . . 101, Ed Morris, 1928
SHUTOUTS . . . . 5, Dave Ferriss, 1945

*A.L. record
***Major-league record
****Tied major-league record
[2]Did not qualify for batting title but A.L. record, 100 games

INDIVIDUAL GAME AND INNING RECORDS

BATTING, GAME

Most Times Faced Pitcher ..8****, Clyde Vollmer, June 8, 1950, vs. St. L.

Most Times Faced Pitcher, No At-Bats ....6**** (6 BB), Jimmie Foxx, June 16, 1936, at St. L.

Most Runs ....6****, Johnny Pesky, May 8, 1946, vs. Chi.
Spike Owen, Aug. 21, 1986, at Clev.

Most Hits ..6** (1 double, 5 singles) Jim Piersall, June 10, 1953, at St. L.
(1 double, 5 singles) Pete Runnels, Aug. 30, 1960, 15 innings vs. Det.
(6 singles) Jerry Remy, Sept. 3–4, 1981, 20 innings vs. Sea.
(6 singles) Nomar Garciaparra, June 21, 2003, 13 innings, at Phi. NL

Most Singles ....6 Jerry Remy, Sept. 3–4, 1981, 20 innings vs. Sea.
Nomar Garciaparra, June 21, 2003, 13 innings, at Phi. NL

Most Doubles.............4****, Billy Werber, July 17, 1935, 1st G. vs. Clev.
Al Zarilla, June 8, 1950, vs. St. L.
Orlando Cepeda, Aug. 8, 1973, at K. C.
Rick Miller, May 11, 1981, at Tor.

Most Consecutive Doubles.................4****, Billy Werber, July 17, 1935,
1st G. vs. Clev.

Most Triples.....................3****, Patsy Dougherty, Sept. 5, 1903, vs. Phil.

Most Home Runs ....3, Jim Tabor, July 4, 1939 at Phil.
Ted Williams, July 14, 1946, 1st G. vs. Clev.
Bobby Doerr, June 8, 1950, vs. St. L.
Clyde Vollmer, July 26, 1951, vs. Chi.
Norm Zauchin, May 27, 1955, vs. Wash
Ted Williams, May 8, 1957, at Chi.
Ted Williams, June 13, 1957, at Clev.
Ken Harrelson, June 14, 1966, at Clev.
Joe Lahoud, June 11, 1969, at Minn.
Fred Lynn, June 18, 1975, at Det.
Carl Yastrzemski, May 19, 1976, at Det.
Jim Rice, Aug. 29, 1977, vs. Oak.
Jim Rice, Aug. 29, 1983, 2nd G. at Tor
Tom Brunansky, Sept. 29, 1990, vs. Tor.
Jack Clark, July 31, 1991, 14 innings vs. Oak.
John Valentin, June 2, 1995, vs. Sea.
Mo Vaughn, Sept. 24, 1996, vs. Bal.
Mo Vaughn, May 30, 1997, vs. NYY.
Nomar Garciaparra, May 10, 1999, vs. Sea.

Trot Nixon, July 24, 1999, at Det.

Jason Varitek, May 20, 2001, at K.C.

Nomar Garciaparra, July 23, 2002, 1st G., vs. T.B.

Bill Mueller, July 29, 2003, at Tex.

Kevin Millar, July 23, 2004, vs. NYY

Most Consecutive Home Runs.........3, Ken Harrelson, June 14, 1968, at Clev., Mo Vaughn, Sept. 24, 1996, vs. Bal.

Nomar Garciaparra, July 23, 2002, 1st G., vs. T.B.

Most Grand Slam Home Runs........2****, Jim Tabor, July 4, 1939, at Phil.

Rudy York, July 27, 1946, at St. L.

Nomar Garciaparra, May 10, 1999, vs. Sea.

Bill Mueller, July 29, 2003, at Tex.

Most Total Bases.........................16**, Fred Lynn, June 18, 1975, at Det.

Most RBI.......................................10, Rudy York, July 27, 1946, at St. L.

Norm Zauchin, May 27, 1946, vs. Wash.

Fred Lynn, June 18, 1975, at Det.

Nomar Garciaparra, May 10, 1999, vs. Sea.

Batting in All Club's Runs (Most)...........................9***, Mike Greenwell, Sept. 2, 1996, 10 innings at Sea.

Most Walks..........................6****, Jimmie Foxx, June 16, 1938, at St. L.

Most International Walks ......**4, Manny Ramirez, June 5, 2001, vs. Det.

Most Strikeouts (9 innings) .....5****, Ray Jarvis, April 20, 1969, vs. Clev.

Phil Plantier, Oct. 1, 1991, vs. Det.

Most Strikeouts (Extra innings)................................6****, Cecil Cooper, June 14, 1974, at Calif.

Most Stolen Bases ....4, Jerry Remy, June 14, 1980, at Cal.

Most Sacrifices......................4****, Jack Barry, Aug. 21, 1916, vs. Clev.

Most Sacrifice Flies for RBI ..3****, Russ Nixon, Aug. 31, 1965, at Wash.

PITCHING, GAME

Shutout in First Major-League Game........................Done 9 times, last 3:
Boo Ferriss, April 29, 1945, at Phil.
Dave Morehead, April 13, 1963, at Wash.
Billy Rohr, April 14, 1967, at N.Y.
Least Hits Allowed First Game.....1****, Billy Rohr, April 14, 1967, at N.Y.
Most Balks ....4**, John Dopson, June 13, 1989, vs. Det.
Most Strikeouts.......20****, Roger Clemens, April 29, 1986 (N), vs. Sea.
and Sept. 18, 1996 (N) at Det.
Most Consecutive Strikeouts.....8**, Roger Clemens, April 29, 1986 (N),
vs. Sea. (3 in 4th and 5th innings, 2 in 6th).
Most Innings..................24**, Joe Harris, Sept. 1, 1906 (L 4–1), vs. Phil.
Most Innings in Relief..................11, Ted Lewis, July 27, 1901 (L), at Chi
Babe Ruth, May 15, 1919 (W), at Chi.
Most Consecutive Scoreless....................20*, Joe Harris, Sept. 1, 1906,
(4th thru 23rd), vs. Phil.

BATTING, INNING

Most Times Faced Pitcher.......3****, Ted Williams, July 4, 1948 (7th), vs.
Phil., Sammy White, Gene Stephens, Tom Umphlett, Johnny Lipon,
George Kell, all on June 18, 1953 (7th), vs. Det.
Most Runs..................3****, Sammy White, June 18, 1953 (7th), vs. Det.
Most Hits..................3****, Gene Stephens, June 18, 1953 (7th), vs. Det.
Most Pinch Hits................2****, Russ Nixon, May 4, 1962 (4th), vs. Chi.
Most Doubles......2****, Smokey Joe Wood, July 4, 1913 (4th inning, 1st
G.), vs. Phil.
Hal Janvrin, June 9, 1914 (6th), at Clev.
Grover Hartley, May 28, 1957 (5th inning, 1st G.), vs. Phil.
Joe Cronin, Aug. 3, 1939 (8th), vs. Clev.
Jody Reed, Sept. 8, 1991 (3rd), vs. Sea.
Mo Vaughn, June 21, 1994 (1st), at Tor.
Most Home Runs...............2****, Bill Regan, June 16, 1928 (4th), at Chi.
Ellis Burks, Aug. 27, 1990 (4th), at Clev.
Nomar Garciaparra, July 23, 2002, (3rd inning, 1st G.) vs. T.B.
Most RBI.........6****, Tom McBride, Aug. 4, 1945 (4th inning, 2nd G.), at
Wash., Carlos Quintana, July 30, 1991 (3rd), vs. Tex.
Home Run, First Major-League Plate Appearance................Bill LeFebvre,
June 10, 1938, vs. Chi.
Eddie Pellagrini, April 22, 1946, vs. Wash.

PITCHING, INNING

Most Batters Faced ....16****, Merle Adkins, July 8, 1902 (6th), vs. Phil.

Lefty O'Doul, July 7, 1923 (6th), vs. Clev.

Howard Ehmke, Sept. 28, 1923 (6th), vs. N.Y.

Most Hits Allowed................12***, Merle Adkins, July 8, 1902 (6th), vs. Phil.

Most Runs Allowed ....13***, Lefty O'Doul, July 7, 1923 (6th), vs. Clev.

Most Walks Allowed..................6, Lefty O'Doul, July 7, 1923 (6th), vs. Clev.

Most Strikeouts ....4****, Tim Wakefield, Aug. 10, 1999 (9th), at K.C.

*A.L. record

**Tied A.L. record

***Major-league record

****Tied major-league record

CLUB SEASON RECORDS

GENERAL

Most Players ....55 in 1996
Fewest Players ....18*** in 1904
Most Games ....163 in 1961, 1978, and 1985
Most Consecutive Games Without a Tie ....3,868***(6/6/61 thru 7/30/85)
Most Extra-Inning Games Played in a Season ....31*** in 1943
Fewest Games Lost by 1 Run, Season ....10*** in 1986 (won 24)
Most Games Won ....105 in 1912
Most Consecutive Games Won, Start of Season ....6 in 1916
Most Consecutive Games Won, Following All-Star Break ....12 in 1988
Most Games Won, End of Season ....8 in 1905
Most Games Lost ....111 in 1932
Highest Percentage Games Won .... .691 in 1912 (won 105, lost 47)
Lowest Percentage Games Won ....279 in 1932 (won 43, lost 111)
Games Won, league ....8,263 in 104 years
Games Lost, league..7,817 in 104 years
Most Shutouts Won, Season ....26 in 1918
Most Shutouts Lost, Season ....26 in 1906
Most 1–0 Games Won ....8 in 1918
Most 1–0 Games Lost ....7 in 1909
Most 1-run games...59 in 1961 (32–27)
Most 1-run games won ....35 in 1953 (lost 16)
Most Consecutive Games Won, Season ....15 in 1946
Most Consecutive Games Lost, Season..20 in 1906
Most Consecutive Games Won, Home..*24 in 1988
Most Times Finished First 13
Most Times Finished Second 21
Most Times Finished Last..11

BATTING

Most At-Bats	5,781*** in 1997 (162 games)
Most Runs	1,027 in 1950 (154 games)
Fewest Runs	463 in 1906 (154 games)
Most Hits	1,684 in 1997 (162 games)
Fewest Hits	990 in 1918 (126 games)
	1,177 in 1905 (153 games)
Most Doubles	373**** in 1997 (162 games)
	373**** in 2004 (162 games)
Most Triples	112** in 1903 (141 games)
Most Home Runs	283 in 2003 (162 games)
Most Consecutive Games 1 or More Home Runs	19 (30 home runs) in 1996
Most Grand-Slam Home Runs	9 in 1941, 1950, 1987, 2001
Most Home Runs by Pinch Hitters	6 in 1953
Most Times 5 or More Home Runs in 1 Game	8***, in 1977 (161 games)
Most Times 2 or More Consecutive Home Runs	16****, in 1977 (161 games)
Most Long Hits	649 in 2003 (162 games)
Most Extra Bases on Long Hits	1,165 in 2003 (162 games)
Most Total Bases	2,832*** in 2003 (162 games)
Most Sacrifice Flies	64 in 2003 (162 games)
Most Stolen Bases	215 in 1909 (151 games)
Most Bases on Balls	835 in 1949 (155 games)
Most Strikeouts	1,189 in 2004 (162 games)
Fewest Strikeouts	324 in 1918 (126 games)
	329 in 1921 (154 games)
Most Hit by Pitcher	72 in 2002 (162 games)
Fewest Hit by Pitcher	11 in 1934 (153 games)
Most Runs Batted in	974 in 1950 (154 games)
Highest Batting Average	.302 in 1950 (154 games)
Lowest Batting Average	.234 in 1905 (153 games)
	1907 (155 games)
Highest Slugging Average	.491* in 2003 (162 games)
Lowest Slugging Average	.292 in 1907 (149 games)
Most Grounded into Double Plays	174***, in 1990 (162 games)
Fewest Grounded into Double plays	94 in 1942 (152 games)
Most Left on Base	1,308 in 1989 (162 games)
	1,304 in 1948 (155 games)

Fewest Left on Base ....1,015 in 1929 (155 games)
Most .300 Hitters ....9 in 1950
Most Players 100 Hits ....9**** in 1984, 1991, 1999, 2003

PITCHING

Bases on Balls, most..748 in 1950
ERA, lowest..2.12 in 1904
ERA, highest...5.02 in 1932
Home Runs Allowed, Most..190 in 1987
Home Runs Allowed, Least...6* in 1913
Home Runs Allowed, Least Since 1946 ....82 in 1949
Saves, Most...53 in 1998
Strikeouts, Most..1,259 in 2001 (161 games)

FIELDING

Most Putouts...4,418 in 1978 (163 games)
Fewest Putouts ....3,949 in 1938 (150 games)
Most Assists ....2,195 in 1907 (155 games)
Fewest Assists ....1,555 in 1964 (162 games)
Most Chances Accepted........................6,425 in 1907 (155 games)
Fewest Chances Accepted....................5,667 in 1938 (150 games)
Most Errors ....373 in 1901 (137 games)
Fewest Errors ....93 in 1988 (162 games)
Most Errorless Games ....92 in 1998 (162 games)
Most Consecutive Errorless Games...............................10 in 1986
Most Double plays ....207 in 1949 (155 games)
Fewest Double plays ....74 in 1913 (151 games)
Most Consecutive Games, 1 or More
    Double Plays ....25**** (38 double plays), 1951
Most DPs in Consecutive Games in Which DPs Were Made................38****
                                              (25 games), 1951
Most Triple Plays ....3**** in 1924 (156 games) and 1979 (160 games)
Most Passed Balls...................................35 in 1998 (162 games)
Fewest Passed Balls ....3 in 1975 (160 games)
                                              1933 (149 games)
Highest Fielding Average .... .984 in 1988 (162 games)
Lowest Fielding Average........................ .942 in 1901 (137 games)

Note: Several records were set for some "fewest" categories in 1981.
*A.L. record
**Tied A.L. record
***Major-league record
****Tied major-league record

CLUB GAME, INNING RECORDS

BATTING, GAME

Most Times Faced Pitcher.......................64, vs. St. L., June 8, 1950

Most Runs, One Club ....Boston 29**, St. Louis 4, June 8, 1950

Most Runs, Both Clubs........................36*, Boston 22, Philadelphia
14, June 29, 1950

Most Runs, Shutout........................Boston 19, Philadelphia 0, April 30, 1950

Most Runs by Opponent.......................Cleveland 27, Boston 3, July 7, 1929

Most Runs, Shutout by Opponent............................Cleveland 19, Boston 0,
May 18, 1955

Most Innings Scored, 9-Inning Game
(Scoring in every inning) ....8**, vs. Cleveland,
Sept. 16, 1903 (did not bat in 9th)

Most Innings Scored, 9-Inning Game
(Scoring in every Inning) by Opponent.......................8**, by Chicago at Chi.,
May 11, 1949 (did not bat in 9th)

Most Runs to Overcome and Win ...11 down, 1–12 vs. Clev., Aug. 28, 1950,
won 15–14

Most Spectacular Rally to Win ..down 5–12 vs. Wash., 1 on and 1 out in 9th,
June 18, 1961 (1st G.), won 13–12

Largest Lead Lost ....10 runs up, vs. Tor., June 4, 1989, 10–0 after 6 innings,
lost 13–11 in 12 innings

Most Hits, 1 Club...............................28, vs. St. L., June 8, 1950

Most Hits, Both Clubs ....45**, Phil. 27, Boston 18, July 8, 1902

Most Consecutive Hits, 1 Club.........................10**, vs. Milw., June 2, 1901,
9th inning

Most Players 4 or More Hits ....4**, vs. St. L., June 8, 1950

Most Singles, 1 Club ....24, vs. Det., June 18, 1953

Most Singles, Both Clubs...............................36****, Chicago 21, Boston 15,
Aug. 15, 1922

Most Doubles, 1 Club...........................12**, at Det., July 29, 1990

Most Home Runs, 1 Club.............................8, vs. Tor., July 4, 1977

Most HR, Season Opener, 1 Club ....5**, vs. Wash. April 12, 1965

Most HR, Season Opener, Both Clubs ....7****, vs. Wash.
April 12, 1965

Most Players 2 or More HR, 1 Club ....3****, vs. St. L., June 8, 1950

Most Players 1 or More HR, Both Clubs...................9****, Min. 5, Boston 4,
May 25, 1965, Balt. 7, Boston 2, May 17, 1967,
Boston 5, Milw. 4, May 22, 1977

Most HR Start of Game...2**, vs. Minn.,
May 1, 1971 (Aparicio, Smith)
at Milw., June 20, 1973 (Miller, Smith)
vs. N.Y., June 17, 1977 (Burleson, Lynn)
vs. Clev., Sept. 5, 1985, 1st G. (Evans, Boggs)
vs. Minn., July 21, 1995 (O'Leary, Valentin)

Most HR, 9 Innings, None On ....7***, vs. Tor., July 4, 1977

Most Grand Slams, 1 Club ....2****, vs. Chi., May 13, 1934
(Walters, Morgan)
vs. Phil., June 4, 1939 (Tabor 2)
vs. St. L., July 27, 1946 (York 2)
vs. Chi., May 10, 1960 (Wertz, Repulski)
vs. Det., Aug. 7, 1984, 1st G. (Armas, Buckner)
at Balt., June 10, 1967 (Burks, Barrett)
at N.Y., May 2, 1995 (Valentin, Vaughn)
at Tex., July 29, 2003 (Mueller 2)

Most Runners Left on Base (9 Innings, ShO)..............................14, vs. Oak.,
May 16, 1988 (L 3–0)

Most Total Bases..60***, vs. St. L., June 8, 1950

Most Extra Base Hits ....17***, vs. St. L., June 8, 1950

Most RBI...29***, vs. St. L., June 8, 1950

Most Strikeouts, 9 Innings ....19 vs. Calif., Aug. 12, 1974

Most Batters Walked, None Scored ....13 vs. Tex., May 18, 1986

Most Double plays Hit Into ....6**, vs. Minn., July 18, 1990

Most Triple Plays Hit Into ....2***, vs. Minn., July 17, 1990

BATTING, INNING

Most Batters Facing Pitcher ....23***, vs. Det., June 18, 1953 (7th)

Most Runs ....17*, vs. Det., June 18, 1953 (7th)

Most Runs With 2 Out ....11, at Clev., Aug. 21, 1986 (6th)

Most Runs With 2 Out, None On...................9, vs. Milw., June 2, 1901 (9th)

Most Hits ....14*, vs. Det., June 18, 1953 (7th)

Most Consecutive Hits ....10****, vs. Milw., June 2, 1901 (9th)

Most Batters Reaching First Base, Consecutive ....12, vs. Det.,
June 18, 1953 (7th)

Most Batters Reaching First Base..........20***, vs. Det., June 18, 1953 (7th)

Most Doubles ....5, at Tor., June 21, 1994 (1st)
at Tor., June 1, 2003 (3rd)

Most Triples ....4, vs. Det., May 6, 1934 (4th)

Most Triples, Consecutive...........................4***, vs. Det., May 6, 1934 (4th)

Most Home Runs...4, vs. Phil., Sept. 24, 1940, 1st G. (6th)
vs. Cleve., May 27, 1957 (6th), at K.C., Aug. 26,1957 (7th)
vs. N.Y., June 17, 1977 (1st), vs. Tor., July 4, 1977 (8th)
vs. Milw., May 31, 1980 (4th), at Det., July 8, 1998 (4th)
at Minn., July 3, 2000 (4th)
vs. T.B., July 23, 2002, 1st G. (3rd)

Most Consecutive Home Runs ....3, vs. Phil. Sept. 24, 1940, 1st G. (6th)
vs. Phil., April 19, 1948 (1st), vs. Det., June 6, 1948 (6th)
vs. N.Y., Sept. 7, 1959 (7th), vs. Tor., July 4, 1977 (8th)
vs. Sea., Aug. 13, 1977 (6th), vs. Milw., May 31, 1980 (4th)

Most Total Bases...25*, vs. Phil., Sept. 24, 1940, G–1 (6th)

Most Extra Base Hits......................................7****, vs. Phil., Sept. 24, 1940, G–1 (6th)

*A.L. record
**Tied A.L. record
***Major-league record
****Tied major-league record

YEARLY RESULTS

YEAR	PLACE	W–L	%	GAMES BEHIND OR AHEAD	ATTEN- DANCE	MANAGER	MULTI- MANAGER YEAR W–L
1901	2	79–59	.581	4	289,448	Jimmy Collins	
1902	3	77–60	.562	6.5	348,567	Jimmy Collins	
1903	1	91–47	.659	14.5	379,338	Jimmy Collins	
1904	1	95–59	.617	1.5	*623,295	Jimmy Collins	
1905	4	78–74	.513	16	466,828	Jimmy Collins	
1906	8	49–105	.318	45.5	410,209	Jimmy Collins,	35–79
						Chick Stahl	14–26
1907	7	59–90	.396	32.5	436,777	Cy Young,	3–3
						George Huff,	2–6
						Bob Unglaub,	9–20
						Deacon McGuire	45–61
1908	5	75–79	.487	15.5	473,048	Deacon McGuire	53–62
						Fred Lake	22–17
1909	4	88–83	.583	9.5	668,965	Fred Lake	
1910	4	81–72	.529	22.5	584,619	Patsy Donovan	
1911	5	78–75	.510	24	503,961	Patsy Donovan	
1912	1	105–47	.691	14	597,096	Jake Stahl	
1913	4	79–71	.527	15.5	437,194	Jake Stahl,	39–41
						Bill Carrigan	40–30
1914	2	91–62	.595	8.5	*481,359	Bill Carrigan	
1915	1	101–50	.669	2.5	*539,885	Bill Carrigan	
1916	1	91–63	.591	2	496,397	Bill Carrigan	
1917	2	90–62	.592	9	387,856	Jack Barry	
1918	1	75–51	.595	2.5	249,513	Ed Barrow	
1919	6	66–71	.482	20.5	417,291	Ed Barrow	
1920	5	72–81	.471	25.5	402,445	Ed Barrow	
1921	5	75–79	.487	23.5	279,273	Hugh Duffy	
1922	8	61–93	.396	33	259,184	Hugh Duffy	
1923	8	61–91	.401	37	229,666	Frank Chance	
1924	7	67–87	.436	25	448,556	Lee Fohl	
1925	8	47–105	.309	49.5	267,782	Lee Fohl	
1926	8	46–107	.301	44.5	285,155	Lee Fohl	
1927	8	51–103	.331	59	305,275	Bill Carrigan	
1928	8	57–96	.373	43.5	396,920	Bill Carrigan	
1929	8	58–96	.377	48	394,820	Bill Carrigan	
1930	8	52–102	.338	50	444,045	Heinie Wagner	
1931	6	62–90	.408	45	350,975	Shano Collins	

YEAR	PLACE	W–L	%	GAMES BEHIND OR AHEAD	ATTEN- DANCE	MANAGER	MULTI- MANAGER YEAR W–L
1932	8	43–111	.279	64	182,150	Shano Collins	11–44
						Marty McManus	32–67
1933	7	63–86	.423	34.5	268,715	Marty McManus	
1934	4	76–76	.500	24	610,640	Bucky Harris	
1935	4	78–75	.516	16	558,568	Joe Cronin	
1936	6	74–80	.481	28.5	626,895	Joe Cronin	
1937	5	80–72	.526	21	559,659	Joe Cronin	
1938	2	88–61	.591	9.5	646,459	Joe Cronin	
1939	2	89–62	.589	17	573,070	Joe Cronin	
1940	4t	82–72	.532	8	716,234	Joe Cronin	
1941	2	84–70	.545	17	718,497	Joe Cronin	
1942	2	93–59	.612	9	730,340	Joe Cronin	
1943	7	68–84	.447	29	358,275	Joe Cronin	
1944	4	77–77	.500	12	506,975	Joe Cronin	
1945	7	71–83	.461	17.5	603,794	Joe Cronin	
1946	1	104–50	.675	12	1,416,944	Joe Cronin	
1947	3	83–71	.539	14	1,427,315	Joe Cronin	
1948	2***	96–59	.619	1	1,558,798	Joe McCarthy	
1949	2	96–58	.623	1	1,596,650	Joe McCarthy	
1950	3	94–60	.610	4	1,344,060	Joe McCarthy	32–30
						Steve O'Neill	62–30
1951	3	87–67	.565	11	1,312,282	Steve O'Neill	
1952	6	76–78	.494	19	1,115,750	Lou Boudreau	
1953	4	84–69	.549	16	1,026,133	Lou Boudreau	
1954	4	69–85	.448	42	931,127	Lou Boudreau	
1955	4	84–70	.545	12	1,203,200	Pinky Higgins	
1956	4	84–70	.545	13	1,137,156	Pinky Higgins	
1957	3	82–72	.532	16	1,181,067	Pinky Higgins	
1958	3	79–75	.513	13	1,077,047	Pinky Higgins	
1959	5	75–79	.487	19	984,102	Pinky Higgins	31–41
						Rudy York	0–1
						Billy Jurges	44–38
1960	7	65–89	.422	32	1,129,866	Billy Jurges	34–47
						Pinky Higgins	31–42
1961	6	76–86	.469	33	850,589	Pinky Higgins	
1962	8	76–84	.475	19	733,080	Pinky Higgins	
1963	7	76–85	.472	28	942,642	Johnny Pesky	
1964	8	72–90	.444	27	883,276	Johnny Pesky	70–90
						Billy Herman	2–0

YEAR	PLACE	W–L	%	GAMES BEHIND OR AHEAD	ATTEN-DANCE	MANAGER	MULTI-MANAGER YEAR W–L
1965	9	62–100	.383	40	652,201	Billy Herman	
1966	9	72–90	.444	26	811,172	Billy Herman	64–82
						Pete Runnels	8–8
1967	1	92–70	.568	1	1,727,632*	Dick Williams	
1968	4	86–76	.531	17	1,940,788	Dick Williams	
1969	3**	87–75	.537	22	1,833,246*	Dick Williams	82–71
						Eddie Popowski	5–4
1970	3	87–75	.537	21	1,595,278*	Eddie Kasko	
1971	3	85–77	.525	18	1,678,732*	Eddie Kasko	
1972	2	85–70	.548	0.5	1,441,716	Eddie Kasko	
1973	2	89–73	.549	8	1,481,002	Eddie Kasko	88–73
						Eddie Popowski	1–0
1974	3	84–78	.519	7	1,566,411*	Darrell Johnson	
1975	1	95–65	.594	4.5	1,748,567*	Darrell Johnson	
1976	3	83–79	.512	15.5	1,895,846	Darrell Johnson	41–45
						Don Zimmer	42–34
1977	2t	97–64	.602	2.5	2,074,549	Don Zimmer	
1978	2	99–64	.607	1	2,320,643	Don Zimmer	
1979	3	91–69	.589	11.5	2,353,114	Don Zimmer	
1980	4	83–77	.519	19	1,956,092	Don Zimmer	82–73
						Johnny Pesky	1–4
1981[2]	5	30–26	.536	4			
	2	29–23	.558	1.5	1,060,379	Ralph Houk	....
1982	3	89–73	.549	6	1,950,124	Ralph Houk	
1983	6	78–84	.481	20	1,782,285	Ralph Houk	
1984	4	86–76	.531	18	1,661,818	Ralph Houk	
1985	5	81–81	.500	18.5	1,786,833	John McNamara	
1986	1	95–66	.590	5.5	2,147,641	John McNamara	
1987	5	78–84	.481	20	2,231,551	John McNamara	
1988	1	89–73	.549	1	2,464,851	John McNamara	43–42
						Joe Morgan	46–31
1989	3	83–79	.512	6	2,510,012	Joe Morgan	
1990	1	88–74	.543	2	2,528,985	Joe Morgan	
1991	2t	84–78	.519	7	2,562,435	Joe Morgan	
1992	7	73–89	.451	23	2,468,574	Butch Hobson	
1993	5	80–82	.494	15	2,422,021	Butch Hobson	
1994	4****	54–61	.470	17	1,775,818	Butch Hobson	
1995	1	86–58	.597	7	2,164,410	Kevin Kennedy	
1996	3	85–77	.525	7	2,315,231	Kevin Kennedy	

1997	4	78–84	.481	20	2,226,136	Jimy Williams	
1998	2[22]	92–70	.568	22	2,343,947	Jimy Williams	
1999	2[22]	94–68	.580	4	2,446,162	Jimy Williams	
2000	2	85–77	.525	2.5	2,586,024	Jimy Williams	
2001	2	82–79	.509	13.5	2,625,333	Jimy Williams	65–53
						Joe Kerrigan	17–26
2002	2	93–69	.574	10.5	2,650,063	Grady Little	
2003	2[22]	95–67	.586	6	2,724,162	Grady Little	
2004	2[22]	98–64	.605	3	2,837,294	Terry Francona	

*Led league in attendance
**Beginning in 1969 the A.L. was split into two divisions with Boston in the Eastern Division
***Boston tied Cleveland for first but lost 1-game playoff
****Beginning in 1994 the A.L. was split into three divisions with Boston in the Eastern Division
[2]1981 season split into first and second halves
[22]Boston won the Wild Card

YEARLY RESULTS

Manager Records (by wins)

		SEASONS	W–L–T	%
1	Joe Cronin	13	1,071–916–20	.539
2	Pinky Higgins	8	560–556–3	.502
3	Bill Carrigan	6	489–500–14	.494
4	Jimmy Collins	6	455–376–11	.548
5	Jimy Williams	4	414–352	.540
6	Don Zimmer	5	411–304	.575
7	Eddie Kasko	4	346–295	.540
8	Ralph Houk	4	312–282	.525
9	Joe Morgan	3	301–262	.535
10	John McNamara	4	297–273–1	.521
11	Dick Williams	3	260–217	.545
12	Lou Boudreau	3	229–232–2	.497
13	Joe McCarthy	3	223–145–1	.606
14	Darrell Johnson	3	220–188	.539
15	Ed Barrow	3	213–203–2	.512
16	Butch Hobson	3	207–232	.472
17	Grady Little	2	188–136	.580
18	Kevin Kennedy	2	171–135	.559
19	Lee Fohl	3	160–299–3	.346
20	Patsy Donovan	2	159–147–5	.520
21	Steve O'Neill	2	150–99	.602
22	Johnny Pesky	3	147–179	.451
23	Jake Stahl	2	144–88–3	.621
24	Hugh Duffy	2	136–172	.442
25	Billy Herman	3	128–182	.413
26	Fred Lake	2	110–80–2	.579
27	Terry Francona	1	98–64	.605
28	Deacon McGuire	2	98–123–6	.443
29	Marty McManus	2	95–153	.383
30	Jack Barry	1	90–62–5	.592
31	Bucky Harris	1	76–76–1	.500
32	Shano Collins	2	73–134–1	.353
33	Frank Chance	1	61–91–2	.401
34	Billy Jurges	2	59–63	.484
35	Heinie Wagner	1	52–102	.338
36	Joe Kerrigan	1	17–26	.395
37	Chick Stahl	1	14–26	.350
38	Bob Unglaub	1	9–20	.310

39	Pete Runnels	1	8–8	.500
40	Eddie Popowski	2	6–4	.600
41	Cy Young	1	3–3	.500
42	George Huff	1	2–6	.250
43	Rudy York	1	0–1	.000

BOSTON RED SOX TOP 10 IN BATTING

GAMES		AT BATS	
Carl Yastrzemski	3,308	Carl Yastrzemski	11,988
Dwight Evans	2,505	Dwight Evans	8,726
Ted Williams	2,292	Jim Rice	8,225
Jim Rice	2,089	Ted Williams	7,706
Bobby Doerr	1,865	Bobby Doerr	7,093
Harry Hooper	1,647	Harry Hooper	6,270
Wade Boggs	1,625	Wade Boggs	6,213
Rico Petrocelli	1,553	Dom DiMaggio	5,640
Dom DiMaggio	1,399	Rico Petrocelli	5,390
Frank Malzone	1,359	Frank Malzone	5,273

HITS		RUNS	
Carl Yastrzemski	3,419	Carl Yastrzemski	1,816
Ted Williams	2,654	Ted Williams	1,798
Jim Rice	2,452	Dwight Evans	1,435
Dwight Evans	2,373	Jim Rice	1,249
Wade Boggs	2,098	Bobby Doerr	1,094
Bobby Doerr	2,042	Wade Boggs	1,067
Harry Hooper	1,707	Dom DiMaggio	1,046
Dom DiMaggio	1,680	Harry Hooper	988
Frank Malzone	1,454	Johnny Pesky	776
Mike Greenwell	1,400	Jimmie Foxx	721

DOUBLES		TRIPLES	
Carl Yastrzemski	646	Harry Hooper	130
Ted Williams	525	Tris Speaker	106
Dwight Evans	474	Buck Freeman	90
Wade Boggs	422	Bobby Doerr	89
Bobby Doerr	381	Larry Gardner	87
Jim Rice	373	Jim Rice	79
Dom DiMaggio	308	Hobe Ferris	77
Nomar Garciaparra	279	Dwight Evans	72
Mike Greenwell	275	Ted Williams	71
Joe Cronin	270	Jimmy Collins	65

HOME RUNS		RBI	
Ted Williams	521	Carl Yastrzemski	1,844
Carl Yastrzemski	452	Ted Williams	1,839
Jim Rice	382	Jim Rice	1,451
Dwight Evans	379	Dwight Evans	1,346
Mo Vaughn	230	Bobby Doerr	1,247
Bobby Doerr	223	Jimmie Foxx	788
Jimmie Foxx	222	Rico Petrocelli	773
Rico Petrocelli	210	Joe Cronin	737
Nomar Garciaparra	178	Jackie Jensen	733
Jackie Jensen	170	Mike Greenwell	726

BATTING AVERAGE (1,500 AT BATS)		STOLEN BASES	
Ted Williams	.344	Harry Hooper	300
Wade Boggs	.338	Tris Speaker	267
Tris Speaker	.337	Carl Yastrzemski	168
Nomar Garciaparra	.323	Heinie Wagner	141
Manny Ramirez	.321	Larry Gardner	134
Jimmie Foxx	.320	Fred Parent	129
Pete Runnels	.320	Tommy Harper	107
Roy Johnson	.313	Billy Werber	107
Johnny Pesky	.313	Chick Stahl	105
Fred Lynn	.308	Jimmy Collins	102
		Duffy Lewis	102

BOSTON RED SOX TOP 10 PITCHING

GAMES		GAMES STARTED	
Bob Stanley	637	Roger Clemens	382
Tim Wakefield	387	Cy Young	297
Derek Lowe	384	Tim Wakefield	250
Roger Clemens	383	Luis Tiant	238
Ellis Kinder	365	Mel Parnell	232
Cy Young	327	Bill Monbouquette	228
Ike Delock	322	Tom Brewer	217
Bill Lee	321	Bruce Hurst	217
Mel Parnell	289	Joe Dobson	202
Greg Harris	287	Frank Sullivan	201
		Pedro Martinez	201

COMPLETE GAMES		WINS	
Cy Young	276	Roger Clemens	192
Bill Dinneen	156	Cy Young	192
George Winter	141	Mel Parnell	123
Smokey Joe Wood	121	Luis Tiant	122
Lefty Grove	119	Pedro Martinez	117
Mel Parnell	113	Smokey Joe Wood	117
Luis Tiant	113	Bob Stanley	115
Babe Ruth	105	Tim Wakefield	114
Roger Clemens	100	Joe Dobson	106
Tex Hughson	99	Lefty Grove	105

LOSSES		WINNING PERCENTAGE (100 DECISIONS)	
Cy Young	112	Pedro Martinez	.760
Roger Clemens	111	Smokey Joe Wood	.676
Tim Wakefield	99	Babe Ruth	.659
Bob Stanley	97	Tex Hughson	.640
George Winter	97	Roger Clemens	.634
Red Ruffing	96	Cy Young	.632
Jack Russell	94	Lefty Grove	.629
Bill Monbouquette	91	Ellis Kinder	.623
Bill Dinneen	85	Mel Parnell	.621
Tom Brewer	82	Jesse Tannehill	.620

INNINGS PITCHED		SHUTOUTS	
Roger Clemens	2,776.0	Roger Clemens	38
Cy Young	2,728.1	Cy Young	38
Tim Wakefield	1,846.1	Smokey Joe Wood	28
Luis Tiant	1,774.0	Luis Tiant	26
Mel Parnell	1,752.2	Dutch Leonard	25
Bob Stanley	1,707.0	Mel Parnell	20
Bill Monbouquette	1,622.0	Ray Collins	19
George Winter	1,599.2	Tex Hughson	19
Joe Dobson	1,544.0	Sad Sam Jones	18
Lefty Grove	1,539.2	Joe Dobson	17
		Babe Ruth	17

STRIKEOUTS		WALKS	
Roger Clemens	2,590	Roger Clemens	856
Pedro Martinez	1,683	Mel Parnell	758
Cy Young	1,341	Tim Wakefield	719
Tim Wakefield	1,329	Tom Brewer	669
Luis Tiant	1,075	Joe Dobson	604
Bruce Hurst	1,043	Jack Wilson	564
Smokey Joe Wood	986	Willard Nixon	530
Bill Monbouquette	969	Ike Delock	514
Frank Sulivan	821	Mickey McDermott	504
Ray Culp	794	Luis Tiant	501

ERA (1,000 IP)		SAVES	
Smokey Joe Wood	1.99	Bob Stanley	132
Cy Young	2.00	Dick Radatz	104
Dutch Leonard	2.13	Ellis Kinder	91
Babe Ruth	2.19	Jeff Reardon	88
Carl Mays	2.21	Derek Lowe	85
Ray Collins	2.51	Sparky Lyle	69
Pedro Martinez	2.52	Tom Gordon	68
Bill Dinneen	2.81	Lee Smith	58
George Winter	2.91	Bill Campbell	51
Tex Hughson	2.94	Ugueth Urbina	49

RED SOX YEARLY BASE-HIT LEADERS

YEAR	PLAYER	HITS	YEAR	PLAYER	HITS
1901	Jimmy Collins	185	1939	Ted Williams	185
1902	Buck Freeman	177	1940	Doc Cramer	*200
1903	Patsy Dougherty	*195	1941	Ted Williams	185
1904	Chick Stahl	173	1942	Johnny Pesky	*205
1905	Jesse Burkett	147	1943	Bobby Doerr	163
1906	Chick Stahl	170	1944	Bob Johnson	170
1907	Bunk Congalton	142	1945	Bob Johnson	148
1908	Harry Lord	145	1946	Johnny Pesky	*208
1909	Tris Speaker	168	1947	Johnny Pesky	*207
1910	Tris Speaker	183	1948	Ted Williams	188
1911	Tris Speaker	167	1949	Ted Williams	194
1912	Tris Speaker	222	1950	Dom DiMaggio	193
1913	Tris Speaker	190	1951	Dom DiMaggio	189
1914	Tris Speaker	*193	1952	Billy Goodman	157
1915	Tris Speaker	176	1953	Billy Goodman	161
1916	Harry Hooper	156	1954	Jackie Jensen	160
1917	Duffy Lewis	167	1955	Billy Goodman	176
1918	Harry Hooper	137	1956	Jackie Jensen	182
1919	Everett Scott	141	1957	Frank Malzone	185
1920	Harry Hooper	167	1958	Frank Malzone	185
1921	Stuffy McInnis	179	1959	Pete Runnels	176
1922	Del Pratt	183	1960	Pete Runnels	169
1923	George Burns	181	1961	Chuck Schilling	167
1924	Bill Wambsganss	174	1962	Carl Yastrzemski	191
1925	Ira Flagstead	160	1963	Carl Yastrzemski	*183
1926	Phil Todt	153	1964	Dick Stuart	168
1927	Buddy Myer	135	1965	Carl Yastrzemski	154
1928	Buddy Myer	168	1966	Carl Yastrzemski	165
1929	Russ Scarritt	159	1967	Carl Yastrzemski	*189
1930	Tom Oliver	189	1968	Carl Yastrzemski	162
1931	Earl Webb	196	1969	Reggie Smith	168
1932	Smead Jolley	164	1970	Carl Yastrzemski	186
1933	Roy Johnson	151	1971	Reggie Smith	175
1934	Billy Werber	200	1972	Tommy Harper	141
1935	Mel Almada	176	1973	Carl Yastrzemski	160
1936	Jimmie Foxx	198	1974	Carl Yastrzemski	155
1937	Joe Cronin	176	1975	Fred Lynn	175
1938	Joe Vosmik	*201	1976	Jim Rice	164

*Led league

YEAR	PLAYER	HITS	YEAR	PLAYER	HITS
1977	Jim Rice	206	1990	Wade Boggs	187
1978	Jim Rice	*213	1991	Wade Boggs	181
1979	Jim Rice	201	1992	Jody Reed	136
1980	Rick Burleson	179	1993	Mike Greenwell	170
1981	Carney Lansford	134	1994	Mo Vaughn	122
1982	Dwight Evans		1995	Mo Vaughn	165
	Jerry Remy	178	1996	Mo Vaughn	207
1983	Wade Boggs	210	1997	Nomar Garciaparra	*209
1984	Wade Boggs	203	1998	Mo Vaughn	205
1985	Wade Boggs	*240	1999	Nomar Garciaparra	190
1986	Wade Boggs	207	2000	Nomar Garciaparra	197
1987	Wade Boggs	200	2001	Manny Ramirez	162
1988	Wade Boggs	214	2002	Nomar Garciaparra	197
1989	Wade Boggs	205	2003	Nomar Garciaparra	198
			2004	Johnny Damon	189

*Led league

RED SOX YEARLY LEADERS IN RUNS SCORED

YEAR	PLAYER	RUNS	YEAR	PLAYER	RUNS
1901	Jimmy Collins	109	1938	Jimmie Foxx	139
1902	Chick Stahl	92	1939	Ted Williams	131
1903	Patsy Dougherty	*106	1940	Ted Williams	*134
1904	Jimmy Collins		1941	Ted Williams	*135
	Fred Parent	85	1942	Ted Williams	*141
1905	Jesse Burkett	78	1943	Bobby Doerr	78
1906	Fred Parent	67	1944	Bob Johnson	106
1907	Denny Sullivan	73	1945	Eddie Lake	81
1908	Amby McConnell	77	1946	Ted Williams	*142
1909	Harry Lord	86	1947	Ted Williams	*125
1910	Tris Speaker	92	1948	Dom DiMaggio	127
1911	Harry Hooper	93	1949	Ted Williams	*150
1912	Tris Speaker	136	1950	Dom DiMaggio	*131
1913	Harry Hooper	100	1951	Dom DiMaggio	*113
1914	Tris Speaker	101	1952	Dom DiMaggio	81
1915	Tris Speaker	108	1953	Jimmy Piersall	76
1916	Harry Hooper	75	1954	Ted Williams	93
1917	Harry Hooper	89	1955	Billy Goodman	100
1918	Harry Hooper	81	1956	Billy Klaus	
1919	Babe Ruth	*103		Jimmy Piersall	91
1920	Harry Hooper	91	1957	Jimmy Piersall	103
1921	Nemo Leibold	88	1958	Pete Runnels	103
1922	Del Pratt	73	1959	Jackie Jensen	101
1923	George Burns	91	1960	Pete Runnels	80
1924	Ira Flagstead	106	1961	Chuck Schilling	87
1925	Ira Flagstead	84	1962	Carl Yastrzemski	99
1926	Topper Rigney	71	1963	Carl Yastrzemski	91
1927	Ira Flagstead	63	1964	Eddie Bressoud	86
1928	Ira Flagstead	84	1965	Tony Conigliaro	82
1929	Jack Rothrock	70	1966	Joe Foy	97
1930	Tom Oliver	86	1967	Carl Yastrzemski	*112
1931	Earl Webb	96	1968	Carl Yastrzemski	90
1932	Roy Johnson	70	1969	Carl Yastrzemski	96
1933	Roy Johnson	88	1970	Carl Yastrzemski	*125
1934	Billy Werber	129	1971	Reggie Smith	85
1935	Mel Almada	85	1972	Tommy Harper	92
1936	Jimmie Foxx	130	1973	Tommy Harper	92
1937	Jimmie Foxx	111	1974	Carl Yastrzemski	*93

*Led league

YEAR	PLAYER	RUNS	YEAR	PLAYER	RUNS
1975	Fred Lynn	103	1990	Wade Boggs	
1976	Carlton Fisk,			Ellis Burks	89
	Fred Lynn	76	1991	Wade Boggs	93
1977	Carlton Fisk	106	1992	Jody Reed	64
1978	Jim Rice	121	1993	Mo Vaughn	86
1979	Jim Rice	117	1994	Mo Vaughn	65
1980	Rick Burleson	89	1995	John Valentin	108
1981	Dwight Evans	84	1996	Mo Vaughn	118
1982	Dwight Evans	122	1997	Nomar Garciaparra	122
1983	Wade Boggs	100	1998	John Valentin	113
1984	Dwight Evans	*121	1999	Jose Offerman	107
1985	Dwight Evans	110	2000	Nomar Garciaparra	104
1986	Wade Boggs	107	2001	Trot Nixon	100
1987	Dwight Evans	109	2002	Johnny Damon	118
1988	Wade Boggs	*128	2003	Nomar Garciaparra	120
1989	Wade Boggs	*113	2004	Johnny Damon	123

*Led league

RED SOX YEARLY LEADERS IN DOUBLES

YEAR	PLAYER	2B	YEAR	PLAYER	2B
1901	Jimmy Collins	42	1937	Joe Cronin	40
1902	Buck Freeman	37	1938	Joe Cronin	*51
1903	Buck Freeman	39	1939	Ted Williams	44
1904	Jimmy Collins	32	1940	Ted Williams	43
1905	Jimmy Collins	25	1941	Joe Cronin	38
1906	Hobe Ferris	25	1942	Dom DiMaggio	37
1907	Hobe Ferris	25	1943	Bobby Doerr	32
1908	Harry Lord	15	1944	Bob Johnson	40
1909	Tris Speaker	26	1945	Skeeter Newsome	30
1910	Duffy Lewis	29	1946	Johnny Pesky	43
1911	Tris Speaker	34	1947	Ted Williams	40
1912	Tris Speaker	*53	1948	Ted Williams	*44
1913	Tris Speaker	35	1949	Ted Williams	*39
1914	Tris Speaker	*46	1950	Vern Stephens	34
1915	Duffy Lewis	31	1951	Dom DiMaggio	34
1916	Duffy Lewis		1952	Billy Goodman	27
	Tilly Walker	29	1953	George Kell	41
1917	Duffy Lewis	29	1954	Billy Goodman	
1918	Harry Hooper			Jackie Jensen	25
	Babe Ruth	26	1955	Billy Goodman	31
1919	Babe Ruth	34	1956	Jimmy Piersall	*40
1920	Harry Hooper	30	1957	Frank Malzone	31
1921	Del Pratt	36	1958	Pete Runnels	32
1922	Del Pratt	44	1959	Frank Malzone	34
1923	George Bums	47	1960	Frank Malzone	30
1924	Bill Wambsganss	41	1961	Carl Yastrzemski	31
1925	Ira Flagstead	38	1962	Carl Yastrzemski	43
1926	Baby Doll Jacobson	36	1963	Carl Yastrzemski	*40
1927	Bill Regan	37	1964	Eddie Bressoud	41
1928	Ira Flagstead	41	1965	Carl Yastrzemski	*45
1929	Phil Todt	38	1966	Carl Yastrzemski	*39
1930	Bill Regan	35	1967	Carl Yastrzemski	31
1931	Earl Webb	*67	1968	Reggie Smith	*37
1932	Urban Pickering	28	1969	Rico Petrocelli	32
1933	Dusty Cooke	35	1970	Reggie Smith	32
1934	Roy Johnson	43	1971	Reggie Smith	*33
1935	Joe Cronin	37	1972	Tommy Harper	29
1936	Eric McNair	36	1973	Orlando Cepeda,	25

*Led league

YEAR	PLAYER	2B	YEAR	PLAYER	2B
	Carl Yastrzemski	25	1989	Wade Boggs	*51
1974	Carl Yastrzemski	25	1990	Jody Reed	*45
1975	Fred Lynn	*47	1991	Jody Reed,	
1976	Dwight Evans	34		Wade Boggs	42
1977	Rick Burleson	36	1992	Tom Brunansky	31
1978	Carlton Fisk	39	1993	John Valentin	40
1979	Fred Lynn	42	1994	John Valentin	26
1980	Dwight Evans	37	1995	John Valentin	37
1981	Carney Lansford	23	1996	Reggie Jefferson	30
1982	Dwight Evans	37	1997	John Valentin	*47
1983	Wade Boggs	44	1998	John Valentin	40
1984	Dwight Evans	37	1999	Nomar Garciaparra	42
1985	Bill Buckner	46	2000	Nomar Garciaparra	51
1986	Wade Boggs	47	2001	Manny Ramirez	33
1987	Wade Boggs	40	2002	Nomar Garciaparra	*56
1988	Wade Boggs	*45	2003	Bill Mueller	45
			2004	David Ortiz	47

*Led league

RED SOX YEARLY LEADERS IN TRIPLES

YEAR	PLAYER	3B
1901	Jimmy Collins,	
	Chick Stahl	16
1902	Buck Freeman	20
1903	Buck Freeman	21
1904	Chick Stahl	*22
1905	Hobe Ferris	16
1906	Hobe Ferris	13
1907	Bob Unglaub	13
1908	Doc Gessler	14
1909	Tris Speaker	13
1910	Jake Stahl	16
1911	Tris Speaker	13
1912	Larry Gardner	18
1913	Tris Speaker	22
1914	Larry Gardner	19
1915	Harry Hooper	13
1916	Harry Hooper,	
	Tilly Walker	11
1917	Harry Hooper	11
1918	Harry Hooper	13
1919	Babe Ruth	12
1920	Harry Hooper	17
1921	Shano Collins	12
1922	Joe Harris	9
1923	Joe Harris	11
1924	Joe Harris,	
	Bobby Veach	9
1925	Phil Todt	13
1926	Phil Todt	12
1927	Buddy Myer	11
1928	Doug Taitt	14
1929	Russ Scarritt	17
1930	Bill Regan	10
1931	Tom Oliver	5
1932	Marv Olson	6
1933	Dusty Cooke	10
1934	Roy Johnson,	
	Billy Werber	10

YEAR	PLAYER	3B
1935	Joe Cronin	14
1936	Jimmie Foxx,	
	Doc Cramer	8
1937	Ben Chapman,	
	Doc Cramer	11
1938	Jimmie Foxx	9
1939	Ted Williams	11
1940	Ted Williams	14
1941	Lou Finney	10
1942	Johnny Pesky	9
1943	Tony Lupien	9
1944	Bobby Doerr	10
1945	Bob Johnson	
	Tom McBride	7
1946	Bobby Doerr	9
1947	Bobby Doerr	10
1948	Vern Stephens	8
1949	Bobby Doerr	9
1950	Dom DiMaggio	
	Bobby Doerr	*11
1951	Johnny Pesky	6
1952	Hoot Evers,	
	Clyde Vollmer	4
1953	Jimmy Piersall	9
1954	Harry Agganis	8
1955	Jackie Jensen	6
1956	Jackie Jensen	*11
1957	Frank Malzone,	
	Jimmy Piersall	5
1958	Pete Runnels	
	Jimmy Piersall	5
1959	Pete Runnels	6
1960	Don Buddin,	
	Lu Clinton	5
1961	Gary Geiger,	
	Carl Yastrzemski	6
1962	Lu Clinton	10
1963	Lu Clinton	7

*Led league

YEAR	PLAYER	3B	YEAR	PLAYER	3B
1964	Carl Yastrzemski	9	1985	Tony Armas,	
1965	Lenny Green	6		Rich Gedman	5
1966	Joe Foy	8	1986	Tony Armas,	
1967	George Scott	7		Marty Barrett	4
1968	Reggie Smith	5	1987	Spike Owen	7
1969	Reggie Smith	7	1988	Mike Greenwell	8
1970	Reggie Smith	7	1989	Wade Boggs	7
1971	John Kennedy	5	1990	Ellis Burks	8
1972	Carlton Fisk	*9	1991	Mike Greenwell	6
1973	Rick Miller	7	1992	Wade Boggs	4
1974	Dwight Evans	8	1993	Mike Greenwell	6
1975	Fred Lynn	7	1994	Scott Cooper	4
1976	Fred Lynn,		1995	Troy O'Leary	6
	Jim Rice	8	1996	Troy O'Leary	5
1977	Jim Rice	15	1997	Nomar Garciaparra	*11
1978	Jim Rice	*15	1998	Nomar Garciaparra,	
1979	Butch Hobson	7		Troy O'Leary	8
1980	Jim Rice	6	1999	Jose Offerman	*11
1981	Dwight Evans	4	2000	Trot Nixon	8
1982	Dwight Evans	7	2001	Troy O'Leary	6
1983	Wade Boggs	7	2002	Johnny Damon	*11
1984	Dwight Evans	8	2003	Nomar Garciaparra	13
			2004	Johnny Damon	6

*Led league

RED SOX YEARLY LEADERS IN HOME RUNS

YEAR	PLAYER	HR	YEAR	PLAYER	HR
1901	Buck Freeman	12	1937	Jimmie Foxx	36
1902	Buck Freeman	11	1938	Jimmie Foxx	50
1903	Buck Freeman	*13	1939	Jimmie Foxx	*35
1904	Buck Freeman	7	1940	Jimmie Foxx	36
1905	Hobe Ferris	6	1941	Ted Williams	*37
1906	Chick Stahl	4	1942	Ted Williams	*36
1907	Hobe Ferris	4	1943	Bobby Doerr	16
1908	Doc Gessler	3	1944	Bob Johnson	17
1909	Tris Speaker	7	1945	Bob Johnson	12
1910	Jake Stahl	*10	1946	Ted Williams	38
1911	Tris Speaker	8	1947	Ted Williams	*32
1912	Tris Speaker	10	1948	Vern Stephens	29
1913	Harry Hooper	4	1949	Ted Williams	*43
1914	Tris Speaker	4	1950	Walt Dropo	34
1915	Babe Ruth	4	1951	Ted Williams	30
1916	Del Gainer,		1952	Dick Gernert	19
	Babe Ruth,		1953	Dick Gernert	21
	Tilly Walker	3	1954	Ted Williams	29
1917	Harry Hooper	3	1955	Ted Williams	28
1918	Babe Ruth	*11	1956	Ted Williams	24
1919	Babe Ruth	*29	1957	Ted Williams	38
1920	Harry Hooper	7	1958	Jackie Jensen	35
1921	Del Pratt	5	1959	Jackie Jensen	28
1922	George Burns	12	1960	Ted Williams	29
1923	Joe Harris	13	1961	Gary Geiger	18
1924	Ike Boone	13	1962	Frank Malzone	21
1925	Phil Todt	11	1963	Dick Stuart	42
1926	Phil Todt	7	1964	Dick Stuart	33
1927	Phil Todt	6	1965	Tony Conigliaro	*32
1928	Phil Todt	12	1966	Tony Conigliaro	28
1929	Jack Rothrock	6	1967	Carl Yastrzemski	*44
1930	Earl Webb	16	1968	Ken Harrelson	35
1931	Earl Webb	14	1969	Rico Petrocelli,	
1932	Smead Jolley	18		Carl Yastrzemski	40
1933	Roy Johnson	10	1970	Carl Yastrzemski	40
1934	Billy Werber	11	1971	Reggie Smith	30
1935	Billy Werber	14	1972	Carlton Fisk	22
1936	Jimmie Foxx	41	1973	Carlton Fisk	26

*Led league

YEAR	PLAYER	HR	YEAR	PLAYER	HR
1974	Rico Petrocelli,		1989	Nick Esasky	30
	Carl Yastrzemski	15	1990	Ellis Burks	21
1975	Jim Rice	22	1991	Jack Clark	28
1976	Jim Rice	25	1992	Tom Brunansky	15
1977	Jim Rice	*39	1993	Mo Vaughn	29
1978	Jim Rice	*46	1994	Mo Vaughn	26
1979	Fred Lynn,		1995	Mo Vaughn	39
	Jim Rice	39	1996	Mo Vaughn	44
1980	Tony Perez	25	1997	Mo Vaughn	35
1981	Dwight Evans	*22	1998	Mo Vaughn	40
1982	Dwight Evans	32	1999	Troy O'Leary	28
1983	Jim Rice	*39	2000	Carl Everett	34
1984	Tony Armas	*43	2001	Manny Ramirez	41
1985	Dwight Evans	29	2002	Manny Ramirez	33
1986	Don Baylor	31	2003	Manny Ramirez	37
1987	Dwight Evans	34	2004	Manny Ramirez	*43
1988	Rich Gedman,				
	Mike Greenwell	22			

*Led league

RED SOX YEARLY LEADERS IN RBI

YEAR	PLAYER	RBI	YEAR	PLAYER	RBI
1901	Buck Freeman	114	1937	Jimmie Foxx	127
1902	Buck Freeman	*121	1938	Jimmie Foxx	*175
1903	Buck Freeman	*104	1939	Ted Williams	*145
1904	Buck Freeman	84	1940	Jimmie Foxx	119
1905	Jimmy Collins	65	1941	Ted Williams	120
1906	Chick Stahl	51	1942	Ted Williams	*137
1907	Bob Unglaub	62	1943	Jim Tabor	85
1908	Doc Gessler	63	1944	Bob Johnson	106
1909	Tris Speaker	77	1945	Bob Johnson	74
1910	Jake Stahl	77	1946	Ted Williams	123
1911	Duffy Lewis	86	1947	Ted Williams	*114
1912	Duffy Lewis	109	1948	Vern Stephens	137
1913	Duffy Lewis	90	1949	Vern Stephens,	
1914	Tris Speaker	90		Ted Williams	*159
1915	Duffy Lewis	76	1950	Walt Dropo,	
1916	Larry Gardner	62		Vern Stephens	*144
1917	Duffy Lewis	65	1951	Ted Williams	126
1918	Babe Ruth	66	1952	Dick Gernert	67
1919	Babe Ruth	*114	1953	George Kell	73
1920	Jim Hendryx	73	1954	Jackie Jensen	117
1921	Del Pratt	100	1955	Jackie Jensen	*116
1922	Del Pratt	86	1956	Jackie Jensen	97
1923	George Burns	82	1957	Jackie Jensen,	
1924	Bobby Veach	99		Frank Malzone	103
1925	Phil Todt	75	1958	Jackie Jensen	*122
1926	Baby Doll Jacobson,		1959	Jackie Jensen	*112
	Phil Todt	69	1960	Vic Wertz	103
1927	Ira Flagstead	69	1961	Frank Malzone	87
1928	Phil Todt	73	1962	Frank Malzone	95
1929	Russ Scarritt	72	1963	Dick Stuart	*118
1930	Earl Webb	66	1964	Dick Stuart	114
1931	Earl Webb	103	1965	Felix Mantilla	92
1932	Smead Jolley	99	1966	Tony Conigliaro	93
1933	Roy Johnson	95	1967	Carl Yastrzemski	*121
1934	Roy Johnson	119	1968	Ken Herrelson	109
1935	Joe Cronin	95	1969	Carl Yastrzemski	111
1936	Jimmie Foxx	143	1970	Tony Conigliaro	116

*Led League
**Tied for league lead

YEAR	PLAYER	RBI	YEAR	PLAYER	RBI
1971	Reggie Smith	96	1988	Mike Greenwell	119
1972	Rico Petrocelli	75	1989	Nick Esasky	108
1973	Carl Yastrzemski	95	1990	Ellis Burks	89
1974	Carl Yastrzemski	79	1991	Mike Greenwell	83
1975	Fred Lynn	105	1992	Tom Brunansky	74
1976	Carl Yastrzemski	102	1993	Mo Vaughn	101
1977	Jim Rice	114	1994	Mo Vaughn	82
1978	Jim Rice	*139	1995	Mo Vaughn	**126
1979	Jim Rice	130	1996	Mo Vaughn	143
1980	Tony Perez	105	1997	Nomar Garciaparra	98
1981	Dwight Evans	71	1998	Nomar Garciaparra	122
1982	Dwight Evans	98	1999	Nomar Garciaparra	104
1983	Jim Rice	126	2000	Carl Everett	108
1984	Tony Armas	*123	2001	Manny Ramirez	125
1985	Bill Buckner	110	2002	Nomar Garciaparra	120
1986	Jim Rice	110	2003	Nomar Garciaparra	105
1987	Dwight Evans	123	2004	David Ortiz	139

*Led League
**Tied for league lead

RED SOX YEARLY LEADERS IN BATTING

YEAR	PLAYER	BA	YEAR	PLAYER	BA
1901	Buck Freeman	.346	1937	Ben Chapman	.307
1902	Patsy Dougherty	.342	1938	Jimmie Foxx	*349
1903	Patsy Dougherty	.331	1939	Jimmie Foxx	.360
1904	Chick Stahl	.294	1940	Ted Williams	.344
1905	Jimmy Collins	.276	1941	Ted Williams	*.406
1906	Moose Grimshaw	.290	1942	Ted Williams	*.356
1907	Bunk Congalton	.286	1943	Pete Fox	.288
1908	Doc Gessler	.308	1944	Bobby Doerr	.325
1909	Harry Lord	.311	1945	Johnny Lazor	.310
1910	Tris Speaker	.340	1946	Ted Williams	.342
1911	Tris Speaker	.327	1947	Ted Williams	*.343
1912	Tris Speaker	.383	1948	Ted Williams	*.369
1913	Tris Speaker	.365	1949	Ted Williams	.343
1914	Tris Speaker	.338	1950	Billy Goodman	*.354
1915	Tris Speaker	.322	1951	Ted Williams	.318
1916	Larry Gardner	.308	1952	Billy Goodman	.306
1917	Duffy Lewis	.302	1953	Billy Goodman	.313
1918	Harry Hooper	.289	1954	Ted Williams	.345
1919	Babe Ruth	.322	1955	Billy Goodman	.294
1920	Harry Hooper	.312	1956	Ted Williams	.345
1921	Del Pratt	.324	1957	Ted Williams	*.388
1922	Joe Harris	.316	1958	Ted Williams	*.328
1923	Joe Harris	.339	1959	Pete Runnels	.314
1924	Ike Boone	.333	1960	Pete Runnels	*.320
1925	Ike Boone	.330	1961	Frank Malzone,	
1926	Ira Flagstead	.299		Carl Yastrzemski	.266
1927	Buddy Myer	.288	1962	Pete Runnels	*.326
1928	Buddy Myer	.313	1963	Carl Yastrzemski	*.321
1929	Jack Rothrock	.300	1964	Eddie Bressoud	.293
1930	Earl Webb	.323	1965	Carl Yastrzemski	.312
1931	Earl Webb	.333	1966	Carl Yastrzemski	.278
1932	Dale Alexander	*2.372	1967	Carl Yastrzemski	*.326
1933	Roy Johnson	.313	1968	Carl Yastrzemski	*.301
1934	Billy Werber	.321	1969	Reggie Smith	.309
1935	Roy Johnson	.315	1970	Carl Yastrzemski	.329
1936	Jimmie Foxx	.338	1971	Reggie Smith	.283

*Led league
*2Alexander began season with Detroit; combined BA .367

1972	Carlton Fisk	.293
1973	Carl Yastrzemski	.296
1974	Carl Yastrzemski	.301
1975	Fred Lynn	.331
1976	Fred Lynn	.314
1977	Jim Rice	.320
1978	Jim Rice	.315
1979	Fred Lynn	*.333
1980	Jim Rice	.294
1981	Carney Lansford	*.336
1982	Jim Rice	.309
1983	Wade Boggs	*.361
1984	Wade Boggs	.325
1985	Wade Boggs	*.368
1986	Wade Boggs	*.357
1987	Wade Boggs	*.363

1988	Wade Boggs	*.366
1989	Wade Boggs	.330
1990	Wade Boggs	.302
1991	Wade Boggs	.332
1992	Tom Brunansky	.266
1993	Mike Greenwell	.315
1994	Mo Vaughn	.310
1995	Tim Naehring	.307
1996	Mo Vaughn	.326
1997	Reggie Jefferson	.319
1998	Mo Vaughn	.337
1999	Nomar Garciaparra	*.357
2000	Nomar Garciaparra	*.372
2001	Manny Ramirez	.306
2002	Manny Ramirez	*.349
2003	Bill Mueller	*.326
2004	Manny Ramirez	.308

*Led league

RED SOX YEARLY LEADERS IN STOLEN BASES

YEAR	PLAYER	SB	YEAR	PLAYER	SB
1901	Tommy Dowd	33	1935	Billy Werber	*29
1902	Patsy Dougherty	20	1936	Billy Werber	23
1903	Patsy Dougherty	35	1937	Ben Chapman	*2 27
1904	Fred Parent	20	1938	Ben Chapman	13
1905	Fred Parent	25	1939	Jim Tabor	16
1906	Fred Parent	16	1940	Jim Tabor	14
1907	Heinie Wagner	20	1941	Jim Tabor	17
1908	Amby McConnell	31	1942	Dom DiMaggio	16
1909	Harry Lord	36	1943	Pete Fox	22
1910	Harry Hooper	40	1944	George Metkovich	13
1911	Harry Hooper	38	1945	George Metkovich	19
1912	Tris Speaker	52	1946	Dom DiMaggio	10
1913	Tris Speaker	46	1947	Johnny Pesky	12
1914	Tris Speaker	42	1948	Dom DiMaggio	10
1915	Tris Speaker	29	1949	Dom DiMaggio	9
1916	Harry Hooper	27	1950	Dom DiMaggio	*15
1917	Harry Hooper	21	1951	Billy Goodman	7
1918	Harry Hooper	24	1952	Faye Throneberry	16
1919	Harry Hooper	23	1953	Jimmy Piersall	11
1920	Mike Menosky	23	1954	Jackie Jensen	*22
1921	Shano Collins	15	1955	Jackie Jensen	16
1922	Mike Menosky	9	1956	Jackie Jensen	11
1923	Norm McMillan	13	1957	Jimmy Piersall	14
1924	Bill Wambsganss	14	1958	Jimmy Piersall	12
1925	Homer Ezzell,		1959	Jackie Jensen	20
	Doc Prothro	9	1960	Pete Runnels,	
1926	Fred Haney	13		Gene Stephens	5
1927	Ira Flagstead	12	1961	Gary Geiger	16
1928	Buddy Myer	*30	1962	Gary Geiger	18
1929	Jack Rothrock	23	1963	Gary Geiger	9
1930	Tom Oliver,		1964	Dalton Jones,	
	Bobby Reeves	6		Carl Yastrzemski	6
1931	Jack Rothrock	31	1965	Lenny Green,	
1932	Roy Johnson	13		Dalton Jones	8
1933	Roy Johnson	13	1966	Jose Tartabull	11
1934	Billy Werber	*40	1967	Reggie Smith	16

*Led league
*2Chapman stole 8 bases with Washington

YEAR	PLAYER	SB	YEAR	PLAYER	SB
1968	Joe Foy	26	1985	Bill Buckner	18
1969	Carl Yastrzemski	15	1986	Marty Barrett	15
1970	Carl Yastrzemski	23	1987	Ellis Burks	27
1971	Doug Griffin,		1988	Ellis Burks	25
	Reggie Smith	11	1989	Ellis Burks	21
1972	Tommy Harper	25	1990	Ellis Burks	9
1973	Tommy Harper	*54	1991	Mike Greenwell	15
1974	Tommy Harper	28	1992	Jody Reed	7
1975	Fred Lynn, Jim Rice	10	1993	Scott Fletcher	16
1976	Rick Burleson,		1994	Otis Nixon	42
	Fred Lynn	14	1995	John Valentin	20
1977	Rick Burleson	13	1996	Jeff Frye	18
1978	Jerry Remy	30	1997	Nomar Garciaparra	22
1979	Jerry Remy	14	1998	Darren Lewis	29
1980	Jerry Remy	14	1999	Jose Offerman	18
1981	Carney Lansford	15	2000	Carl Everett	11
1982	Jerry Remy	16	2001	Carl Everett	9
1983	Jerry Remy	11	2002	Johnny Damon	31
1984	Jackie Gutierrez	12	2003	Johnny Damon	30
			2004	Johnny Damon	19

*Led league

RED SOX WIN LEADERS, YEAR BY YEAR

YEAR	PITCHER	W	YEAR	PITCHER	W
1901	Cy Young	*33	1937	Lefty Grove	17
1902	Cy Young	*32	1938	Jim Bagby,	
1903	Cy Young	*28		Jack Wilson	15
1904	Cy Young	26	1939	Lefty Grove	15
1905	Jesse Tannehill	22	1940	Joe Heving,	
1906	Jesse Tannehill,			Jack Wilson	12
	Cy Young	13	1941	Dick Newsome	19
1907	Cy Young	22	1942	Tex Hughson	*22
1908	Cy Young	21	1943	Tex Hughson	12
1909	Frank Arellanes	16	1944	Tex Hughson	18
1910	Eddie Cicotte	15	1945	Boo Ferriss	21
1911	Smokey Joe Wood	23	1946	Boo Ferriss	25
1912	Smokey Joe Wood	*34	1947	Joe Dobson	18
1913	Ray Collins	19	1948	Jack Kramer	18
1914	Ray Collins	20	1949	Mel Parnell	*25
1915	Rube Foster	20	1950	Mel Parnell	18
1916	Babe Ruth	23	1951	Mel Parnell	18
1917	Babe Ruth	24	1952	Mel Parnell	12
1918	Carl Mays	21	1953	Mel Parnell	21
1919	Herb Pennock	16	1954	Frank Sullivan	15
1920	Herb Pennock	16	1955	Frank Sullivan	*18
1921	Sad Sam Jones	23	1956	Tom Brewer	19
1922	Ray Collins	14	1957	Tom Brewer	16
1923	Howard Ehmke	20	1958	Ike Delock	14
1924	Howard Ehmke	19	1959	Jerry Casale	13
1925	Ted Wingfield	12	1960	Bill Monbouquette	14
1926	Ted Wingfield	11	1961	Don Schwall	15
1927	Slim Harriss	14	1962	Gene Conley,	
1928	Ed Morris	19		Bill Monbouquette	15
1929	Ed Morris	17	1963	Bill Monbouquette	20
1930	Milt Gaston	13	1964	Dick Radatz	16
1931	Danny MacFayden	16	1965	Earl Wilson	13
1932	Bob Kline	11	1966	Jose Santiago	12
1933	Gordon Rhodes	12	1967	Jim Lonbong	*22
1934	Wes Ferrell	14	1968	Ray Culp,	
1935	Wes Ferrell	*25		Dick Ellsworth	16
1936	Wes Ferrell	20	1969	Ray Culp	17

*Led league

YEAR	PITCHER	W	YEAR	PITCHER	W
1970	Ray Culp	17	1986	Roger Clemens	*24
1971	Sonny Siebert	16	1987	Roger Clemens	*20
1972	Marty Pattin	17	1988	Roger Clemens,	
1973	Luis Tiant	20		Bruce Hurst	18
1974	Luis Tiant	22	1989	Roger Clemens	17
1975	Rick Wise	19	1990	Roger Clemens	21
1976	Luis Tiant	21	1991	Roger Clemens	18
1977	Bill Campbell	13	1992	Roger Clemens	18
1978	Dennis Eckersley	20	1993	Danny Darwin	15
1979	Dennis Eckersley	17	1994	Roger Clemens	9
1980	Dennis Eckersley	12	1995	Tim Wakefield	16
1981	Bill Stanley,		1996	Tim Wakefield	14
	Mike Torrez	10	1997	Aaron Sele	13
1982	Mark Clear	14	1998	Pedro Martinez	19
1983	John Tudor	13	1999	Pedro Martinez	*23
1984	Oil Can Boyd,		2000	Pedro Martinez	18
	Bruce Hurst,		2001	Hideo Nomo	13
	Bob Ojeda	12	2002	Derek Lowe	21
1985	Oil Can Boyd	15	2003	Derek Lowe	17
			2004	Curt Schilling	21

*Led league

RED SOX LOSS LEADERS, YEAR BY YEAR

YEAR	PITCHER	L	YEAR	PITCHER	L
1901	Ted Lewis	16	1931	Jack Russell	18
1902	Bill Dinneen	*21	1932	Bob Weiland	16
1903	Bill Dinneen,		1933	Gordon Rhodes	15
	Norwood Gibson	11	1934	Johnny Welch	15
1904	Cy Young	16	1935	Wes Ferrell	14
1905	Cy Young	19	1936	Fritz Ostermueller	16
1906	Joe Harris,		1937	Johnny Marcum	11
	Cy Young	*21	1938	Jack Wilson	15
1907	George Winter	16	1939	Jack Wilson	11
1908	George Winter	14	1940	Jim Bagby	16
1909	Frank Arellanes	12	1941	Mickey Harris	14
1910	Smokey Joe Wood	13	1942	Charlie Wagner	11
1911	Smokey Joe Wood	17	1943	Tex Hughson	15
1912	Buck O'Brien	13	1944	Emmett O'Neill	11
1913	Dutch Leonard	16	1945	Emmett O'Neill	11
1914	Ray Collins	13	1946	Tex Hughson	11
1915	Rube Foster,		1947	Boo Ferriss,	
	Ernie Shore	8		Tex Hughson,	
1916	Carl Mays	13		Earl Johnson	11
1917	Dutch Leonard	17	1948	Joe Dobson,	
1918	Bullet Joe Bush	15		Mickey Harris	10
1919	Sad Sam Jones	20	1949	Joe Dobson	12
1920	Sad Sam Jones	16	1950	Ellis Kinder	12
1921	Sad Sam Jones	16	1951	Mel Parnell	11
1922	Herb Pennock	17	1952	Mel Parnell	12
1923	Howard Ehmke,		1953	Mickey McDermott	10
	Bill Piercy,		1954	Willard Nixon,	
	Jack Quinn	17		Frank Sullivan	12
1924	Howard Ehmke,		1955	Frank Sullivan	13
	Alex Ferguson	*17	1956	Bob Porterfield	12
1925	Howard Ehmke	20	1957	Tom Brewer,	
1926	Paul Zahniser	*18		Willard Nixon	13
1927	Slim Harriss	*21	1958	Tom Brewer	12
1928	Red Ruffing	*25	1959	Tom Brewer	12
1929	Red Ruffing	*22	1960	Frank Sullivan	16
1930	Milt Gaston,		1961	Gene Conley,	
	Jack Russell	*20		Bill Monbouquette	14

*Led league
**Tied for league lead

YEAR	PITCHER	L	YEAR	PITCHER	L
1962	Don Schwall	15	1985	Oil Can Boyd,	
1963	Earl Wilson	16		Bruce Hurst	13
1964	Dave Morehead	15	1986	Al Nipper	12
1965	Bill Monbouquette,		1987	Bob Stanley	15
	Dave Morehead	*18	1988	Roger Clemens	12
1966	Jose Santiago	13	1989	Mike Smithson	14
1967	Darrell Brandon	11	1990	Greg Harris,	
1968	Gary Bell	11		Dana Kiecker	9
1969	Jim Lonborg	11	1991	Greg Harris	12
1970	Ray Culp	14	1992	Frank Viola	12
1971	Ray Culp	16	1993	Roger Clemens	14
1972	Marty Pattin	13	1994	Roger Clemens,	
1973	Marty Pattin	15		Aaron Sele	7
1974	Bill Lee	15	1995	Zane Smith,	
1975	Luis Tiant	14		Tim Wakefield	8
1976	Luis Tiant,		1996	Roger Clemens,	
	Jim Willoughby	12		Tim Wakefield	13
1977	Ferguson Jenkins	10	1997	Tim Wakefield	**15
1978	Mike Torrez	13	1998	Derek Lowe	9
1979	Mike Torrez	13	1999	Mark Portugal	12
1980	Mike Torrez	16	2000	Pete Schourek,	
1981	Frank Tanana	10		Tim Wakefield	10
1982	Dennis Eckersley	13	2001	Tim Wakefield	12
1983	Dennis Eckersley	13	2002	Frank Castillo	15
1984	Oil Can Boyd,		2003	John Burkett	9
	Bruce Hurst,		2004	Derek Lowe	12
	Bob Ojeda	12			

*Led league
**Tied for league lead

RED SOX COMPLETE GAMES LEADERS, YEAR BY YEAR

YEAR	PITCHER	CG	YEAR	PITCHER	CG
1901	Cy Young	38	1934	Wes Ferrell	17
1902	Cy Young	*41	1935	Wes Ferrell	*31
1903	Cy Young	*34	1936	Wes Ferrell	*28
1904	Cy Young	40	1937	Lefty Grove	21
1905	Cy Young	32	1938	Lefty Grove	12
1906	Cy Young	28	1939	Lefty Grove	17
1907	Cy Young	33	1940	Lefty Grove,	
1908	Cy Young	30		Jack Wilson	9
1909	Frank Arellanes	17	1941	Dick Newsome	17
1910	Eddie Cicotte	20	1942	Tex Hughson	*22
1911	Smokey Joe Wood	25	1943	Tex Hughson	*20
1912	Smokey Joe Wood	*35	1944	Tex Hughson	19
1913	Hugh Bedient,		1945	Boo Ferriss	26
	Ray Collins	19	1946	Boo Ferriss	26
1914	Rube Foster,		1947	Joe Dobson	15
	Dutch Leonard	17	1948	Joe Dobson,	
1915	Rube Foster	22		Mel Parnell	16
1916	Babe Ruth	23	1949	Mel Parnell	*27
1917	Babe Ruth	*35	1950	Mel Parnell	21
1918	Carl Mays	*30	1951	Mel Parnell	11
1919	Sad Sam Jones	21	1952	Mel Parnell	15
1920	Sad Sam Jones	20	1953	Mel Parnell	12
1921	Sad Sam Jones	25	1954	Frank Sullivan	11
1922	Jack Quinn	16	1955	Frank Sullivan	16
1923	Howard Ehmke	28	1956	Tom Brewer	15
1924	Howard Ehmke	26	1957	Tom Brewer	15
1925	Howard Ehmke	22	1958	Tom Brewer,	
1926	Hal Wiltse,			Frank Sullivan	10
	Ted Wingfield	9	1959	Tom Brewer	11
1927	Hal Wiltse	13	1960	Bill Monbouquette	12
1928	Red Ruffing	*25	1961	Bill Monbouquette	12
1929	Milt Gaston	20	1962	Bill Monbouquette	11
1930	Milt Gaston	20	1963	Bill Monbouquette	13
1931	Danny MacFayden	17	1964	Bill Monbouquette	7
1932	Ivy Andrews	8	1965	Bill Monbouquette	10
1933	Gordon Rhodes	14	1966	Lee Stange	8

*Led league

YEAR	PITCHER	CG	YEAR	PITCHER	CG
1967	Jim Lonborg	15	1987	Roger Clemens	*18
1968	Jim Lonborg	22	1988	Roger Clemens	*14
1969	Ray Culp	17	1989	Roger Clemens	8
1970	Ray Culp	15	1990	Roger Clemens	7
1971	Ray Culp,		1991	Roger Clemens	13
	Sonny Siebert	12	1992	Roger Clemens	11
1972	Marty Pattin	13	1993	Roger Clemens,	
1973	Luis Tiant	23		Danny Darwin,	
1974	Luis Tiant	25		Frank Viola	2
1975	Luis Tiant	18	1994	Roger Clemens	3
1976	Luis Tiant	19	1995	Tim Wakefield	6
1977	Ferguson Jenkins	11	1996	Roger Clemens,	
1978	Dennis Eckersley	16		Tim Wakefield	6
1979	Dennis Eckersley	17	1997	Tim Wakefield	4
1980	Dennis Eckersley	8	1998	Pedro Martinez	3
1981	Dennis Eckersley	8	1999	Pedro Martinez	5
1982	Dennis Eckersley	11	2000	Pedro Martinez	7
1983	John Tudor	7	2001	Hideo Nomo	2
1984	Oil Can Boyd	10	2002	Pedro Martinez	2
1985	Oil Can Boyd	13	2003	Pedro Martinez	3
1986	Bruce Hurst	11	2004	Curt Schilling	3

*Led league

RED SOX SHUTOUT LEADERS, YEAR BY YEAR

YEAR	PITCHER	SH	YEAR	PITCHER	SH
1901	Cy Young	*5	1930	Milt Gaston	2
1902	Cy Young	3	1931	Ed Durham	2
1903	Cy Young	*7	1932	Bob Kline,	
1904	Cy Young	*10		Johnny Welch	1
1905	Jesse Tannehill	6	1933	Lloyd Brown	
1906	Jesse Tannehill	2		George Pipgras	2
1907	Cy Young	6	1934	Wes Ferrell	3
1908	Cy Young	3	1935	Wes Ferrell	3
1909	Smokey Joe Wood	4	1936	Lefty Grove	*6
1910	Ray Collins	4	1937	Lefty Grove	2
1911	Smokey Joe Wood	5	1938	Jack Wilson	3
1912	Smokey Joe Wood	*10	1939	Lefty Grove	2
1913	Ray Collins,		1940	Jim Bagby,	
	Earl Moseley	3		Lefty Grove,	
1914	Ray Collins,			Herb Hash	1
	Dutch Leonard	7	1941	Charlie Wagner	3
1915	Rube Foster	5	1942	Tex Hughson	4
1916	Babe Ruth	*9	1943	Tex Hughson	4
1917	Babe Ruth	6	1944	Tex Hughson	2
1918	Carl Mays	*8	1945	Boo Ferriss	5
1919	Sad Sam Jones,		1946	Boo Ferriss,	
	Herb Pennock	5		Tex Hughson	6
1920	Herb Pennock	4	1947	Denny Galehouse,	
1921	Sad Sam Jones	*5		Tex Hughson,	
1922	Jack Quinn	4		Earl Johnson	3
1923	Howard Ehmke	2	1948	Joe Dobson	5
1924	Howard Ehmke	4	1949	Ellis Kinder	*6
1925	Red Ruffing	3	1950	Mel Parnell	2
1926	Howard Ehmke,		1951	Mel Parnell	3
	Slim Harriss,		1952	Mel Parnell	3
	Tony Welzer,		1953	Mel Parnell	5
	Hal Wiltse		1954	Frank Sullivan	3
	Ted Wingfield,		1955	Willard Nixon,	
	Paul Zahniser	1		Frank Sullivan	3
1927	Del Lundgren	2	1956	Tom Brewer	4
1928	Jack Russell	2	1957	Frank Sullivan	3
1929	Danny MacFayden	4	1958	Frank Sullivan	2

*Led league

YEAR	PITCHER	SH	YEAR	PITCHER	SH
1959	Tom Brewer,		1983	Bruce Hurst	2
	Jerry Casale	3		John Tudor	2
1960	Bill Monbouquette	3	1984	Bob Ojeda	5
1961	Gene Conley		1985	Oil Can Boyd	3
	Don Schwall	2	1986	Bruce Hurst	4
1962	Bill Monbouquette	4	1987	Roger Clemens	*7
1963	Earl Wilson	3	1988	Roger Clemens	*8
1964	Bill Monbouquette	5	1989	Roger Clemens	3
1965	Bill Monbouquette		1990	Roger Clemens	*4
	Dave Morehead	2	1991	Roger Clemens	*4
1966	Darrell Brandon,		1992	Roger Clemens	*5
	Lee Stange	2	1993	Roger Clemens,	
1967	Jim Lonborg	2		Danny Darwin,	
	Lee Stange	2		John Dopson,	
1968	Ray Culp	6		Paul Quantrill,	
1969	Ray Culp	2		Frank Viola	1
1970	Gary Peters	4	1994	Roger Clemens	1
1971	Sonny Siebert	4	1995	Erik Hanson,	
1972	Luis Tiant	6		Tim Wakefield	1
1973	John Curtis	4	1996	Roger Clemens	2
1974	Luis Tiant	*7	1997	Tim Wakefield	2
1975	Bill Lee	4	1998	Pedro Martinez	2
1976	Rick Wise	4	1999	Pedro Martinez	1
1977	Luis Tiant	3	2000	Pedro Martinez	*4
1978	Luis Tiant	5	2001	Hideo Nomo	2
1979	Bob Stanley	4	2002	John Burkett,	
1980	Chuck Rainey,			Derek Lowe,	
	Bob Stanley,			Darren Oliver	1
	Mike Torrez	1	2003	none	
1981	Dennis Eckersley	2	2004	Pedro Martinez	1
1982	Dennis Eckersley	3			
	Chuck Rainey	3			

*Led league

RED SOX ERA LEADERS, YEAR BY YEAR

YEAR	PITCHER	ERA	YEAR	PITCHER	ERA
1901	Cy Young	*1.63	1938	Lefty Grove	*3.07
1902	Cy Young	2.15	1939	Lefty Grove	*2.54
1903	Cy Young	2.08	1940	Lefty Grove	4.00
1904	Cy Young	1.97	1941	Charlie Wagner	3.08
1905	Cy Young	1.82	1942	Tex Hughson	2.59
1906	Bill Dinneen	2.92	1943	Tex Hughson	2.64
1907	Cy Morgan	1.97	1944	Tex Hughson	2.26
1908	Cy Young	1.26	1945	Boo Ferriss	2.95
1909	Eddie Cicotte	1.97	1946	Tex Hughson	2.75
1910	Ray Collins	1.62	1947	Joe Dobson	2.95
1911	Smokey Joe Wood	2.02	1948	Mel Parnell	3.14
1912	Smokey Joe Wood	1.91	1949	Mel Parnell	*2.78
1913	Smokey Joe Wood	2.29	1950	Mel Parnell	3.61
1914	Dutch Leonard	*1.00	1951	Mel Parnell	3.26
1915	Smokey Joe Wood	*1.49	1952	Mel Parnell	3.62
1916	Babe Ruth	*1.75	1953	Mickey McDermott	3.01
1917	Carl Mays	1.74	1954	Frank Sullivan	3.15
1918	Bullet Joe Bush	2.11	1955	Frank Sullivan	2.91
1919	Carl Mays	2.48	1956	Frank Sullivan	3.42
1920	Harry Harper	2.13	1957	Frank Sullivan	2.73
1921	Sad Sam Jones	3.22	1958	Ike Delock	3.38
1922	Jack Quinn	3.48	1959	Tom Brewer	3.77
1923	Bill Piercy	3.42	1960	Bill Monbouquette	3.64
1924	Jack Quinn	3.26	1961	Don Schwall	3.32
1925	Howard Ehmke	3.69	1962	Bill Monbouquette	3.33
1926	Hal Witse	4.22	1963	Earl Wilson	3.75
1927	Slim Harriss	4.17	1964	Bill Monbouquette	4.04
1928	Ed Morris	3.52	1965	Bill Monbouquette	3.69
1929	Danny MacFayden	3.62	1966	Jose Santiago	3.66
1930	Milt Gaston	3.92	1967	Lee Stange	2.77
1931	Wilcy Moore	3.89	1968	Ray Culp	2.92
1932	Ivy Andrews	3.80	1969	Mike Nagy	3.11
1933	Bob Weiland	3.87	1970	Ray Culp	3.05
1934	Fritz Ostermueller	3.48	1971	Sonny Siebert	2.91
1935	Lefty Grove	*2.70	1972	Luis Tiant	*1.91
1936	Lefty Grove	*2.81	1973	Bill Lee	2.75
1937	Lefty Grove	3.02	1974	Luis Tiant	2.92

*Led league

YEAR	PITCHER	ERA	YEAR	PITCHER	ERA
1975	Bill Lee,		1989	Roger Clemens	3.13
	Rick Wise	3.95	1990	Roger Clemens	*1.93
1976	Luis Tiant	3.06	1991	Roger Clemens	*2.62
1977	Ferguson Jenkins	3.68	1992	Roger Clemens	*2.41
1978	Dennis Eckersley	2.99	1993	Frank Viola	3.14
1979	Dennis Eckersley	2.99	1994	Roger Clemens	2.85
1980	Bob Stanley	3.39	1995	Tim Wakefield	2.95
1981	Mike Torrez	3.69	1996	Roger Clemens	3.63
1982	Bob Stanley	3.10	1997	Tom Gordon	3.74
1983	Bob Ojeda	4.04	1998	Pedro Martinez	2.89
1984	Bruce Hurst	3.92	1999	Pedro Martinez	*2.07
1985	Oil Can Boyd	3.70	2000	Pedro Martinez	*1.74
1986	Roger Clemens	*2.48	2001	Tim Wakefield	3.90
1987	Roger Clemens	2.97	2002	Pedro Martinez	*2.26
1988	Roger Clemens	2.93	2003	Pedro Martinez	*2.22
			2004	Curt Schilling	3.26

*Led league

RED SOX SAVES LEADERS, YEAR BY YEAR

YEAR	PITCHER	SAVES	YEAR	PITCHER	SAVES
1901	Ted Lewis	1	1927	Danny MacFayden,	
1902	Nick Altrock	1		Red Ruffing	2
1903	Cy Young	2	1928	Ed Morris	5
1904	Cy Young	1	1929	Milt Gaston	2
1905	George Winter	3	1930	Milt Gaston,	
1906	Joe Harris,			Danny MacFayden,	2
	George Winter,		1931	Wilcy Moore	*10
	Cy Young	2	1932	Wilcy Moore	4
1907	Tex Pruiett,		1933	Bob Kline	4
	Cy Young	3	1934	Fritz Ostermueller	3
1908	Eddie Cicotte,		1935	Rube Walberg	3
	Cy Morgan,		1936	Jack Wilson	3
	Cy Young	2	1937	Jack Wilson	7
1909	Frank Arellanes	*8	1938	Archie McKain	6
1910	Charlie Hall	5	1939	Joe Heving	7
1911	Charlie Hall,		1940	Jack Wilson	5
	Smokey Joe Wood	5	1941	Mike Ryba	6
1912	Hugh Bedient	3	1942	Mace Brown	6
1913	Hugh Bedient,		1943	Mace Brown	9
	Charlie Hall	5	1944	Frank Barrett	8
1914	Dutch Leonard	*4	1945	Frank Barrett	3
1915	Carl Mays	*6	1946	Bob Klinger	*9
1916	Dutch Leonard	*5	1947	Earl Johnson	8
1917	Babe Ruth	2	1948	Earl Johnson	5
1918	Bullet Joe Bush	2	1949	Ellis Kinder,	
1919	Allen Russell	2*4		Walt Masterson	4
1920	Herb Pennock	2	1950	Ellis Kinder	9
1921	Allen Russell	3	1951	Ellis Kinder	*14
1922	Alex Ferguson,		1952	Al Benton	6
	Allen Russell	2	1953	Ellis Kinder	*27
1923	Jack Quinn	7	1954	Ellis Kinder	15
1924	Jack Quinn	7	1955	Ellis Kinder	18
1925	Ted Wingfield	2	1956	Ike Delock	9
1926	Ted Wingfield	3	1957	Ike Delock	11

*Led league
[2]2 more saves with New York

YEAR	PITCHER	SAVES	YEAR	PITCHER	SAVES
1958	Leo Kiely	12	1982	Mark Clear,	
1959	Mike Fornieles	11		Bob Stanley	14
1960	Mike Fornieles	*14	1983	Bob Stanley	33
1961	Mike Fornieles	15	1984	Bob Stanley	22
1962	Dick Radatz	*24	1985	Steve Crawford	12
1963	Dick Radatz	25	1986	Bob Stanley	16
1964	Dick Radatz	*29	1987	Wes Gardner	10
1965	Dick Radatz	22	1988	Lee Smith	29
1966	Don McMahon	9	1989	Lee Smith	25
1967	John Wyatt	20	1990	Jeff Reardon	21
1968	Lee Stange	12	1991	Jeff Reardon	40
1969	Sparky Lyle	17	1992	Jeff Reardon	[22]27
1970	Sparky Lyle	20	1993	Jeff Russell	33
1971	Sparky Lyle	16	1994	Ken Ryan	13
1972	Bob Bolin,		1995	Rick Aguilera	[222]20
	Bill Lee	5	1996	Heathcliff Slocumb	31
1973	Bob Bolin	15	1997	Heathcliff Slocumb	[2222]17
1974	Diego Segui	10	1998	Tom Gordon	*46
1975	Dick Drago	15	1999	Derek Lowe,	
1976	Jim Willoughby	10		Tim Wakefield	15
1977	Bill Campbell	*31	2000	Derek Lowe	**42
1978	Bob Stanley	10	2001	Derek Lowe	24
1979	Dick Drago	13	2002	Ugueth Urbina	40
1980	Tom Burgmeier	24	2003	Byung-Hyun Kim	16
1981	Bill Campbell	7	2004	Keith Foulke	32

*Led league
**Tied for league lead
[22]3 more saves with Atlanta (N.L.)
[222]12 more saves with Minnesota
[2222]10 more saves with Seattle

5
ALL-TIME RED SOX ROSTER

ALL-TIME RED SOX ROSTER—BATTERS

NAME	YEARS	POSITION	AB	R	H	HR	RBI	BB	SO	BA
Abad, Andy	2003	1B–OF	17	1	2	0	0	2	5	.118
Adair, Jerry	1967–68	SS–3B–2B	524	59	137	5	38	22	63	.261
Agbayani, Benny	2002	OF	37	5	11	0	8	6	5	.297
Agganis, Harry	1954–55	1B	517	65	135	11	67	57	67	.261
Agnew, Sam	1916–18	C	526	32	101	0	29	36	60	.192
Alcantara, Israel	2000–01	OF–1B–DH	83	12	23	4	10	6	20	.277
Alexander, Dale	1932–33	1B	689	98	228	13	96	80	41	.331
Alexander, Manny	2000	3B	194	30	41	4	19	13	41	.211
Alicea, Luis	1995	2B	419	64	113	6	44	63	61	.270
Allenson, Gary	1979–84	C	1027	112	231	19	128	130	182	.225
Almada, Mel	1933–37	OF	1171	160	319	6	102	111	66	.272
Alvarado, Luis	1968–70	SS–3B	234	22	47	1	11	10	43	.201
Anderson, Brady	1988	OF	148	14	34	0	12	15	35	.230
Andres, Ernie	1946	3B	41	0	4	0	1	3	5	.098
Andrew, Kim	1975	2B	2	0	1	0	0	0	0	.500
Andrews, Mike	1966–70	2B	2101	327	563	47	209	295	247	.268
Andrews, Shane	2002	3B–1B–OF	13	2	1	0	0	1	3	.077
Aparicio, Luis	1971–73	SS	1426	159	361	7	133	104	104	.253
Armas, Tony	1983–86	OF	2023	274	510	113	352	103	454	.252
Armbruster, Charlie	1905–07	C	352	24	53	0	12	51	0	.151
Asbjornson, Casper	1928–29	C	45	1	6	0	1	2	7	.133
Ashley, Billy	1998	DH	24	3	7	3	7	2	11	.292
Aspromonte, Ken	1957–58	2B	94	9	23	0	4	20	11	.245
Aulds, Doyle	1947	C	4	0	1	0	0	0	1	.250
Avila, Bobby	1959	2B	45	7	11	3	6	6	11	.244
Aviles, Ramon	1977	2B	0	0	0	0	0	0	0	—
Azcue, Joe	1969	C	51	7	11	0	3	4	5	.216
Baerga, Carlos	2002	DH–2B	182	17	52	2	19	7	20	.286
Bagby, Jim	1938–40, 46	OF	218	30	43	1	21	3	30	.197
Bailey, Bob	1977–78	DH	96	12	18	4	9	19	20	.187
Bailey, Gene	1920	OF	135	14	31	0	5	9	15	.230
Baker, Floyd	1953–54	3B	192	23	51	0	27	24	11	.266
Baker, Jack	1976–77	1B	26	1	3	1	2	1	6	.115
Baker, Tracy	1911	1B	0	0	0	0	0	0	0	—
Ball, Neal	1912–13	2B	103	19	19	0	10	12	13	.184
Barbare, Walter	1918	3B	29	2	5	0	2	0	1	.172
Barna, Babe	1943	OF	112	19	19	2	10	15	24	.170
Barrett, Bill	1929–30	OF	388	60	103	3	36	52	41	.265
Barrett, Bob	1929	3B	126	15	34	0	19	10	6	.270
Barrett, Jimmy	1907–08	OF	398	52	96	1	29	39	0	.241
Barrett, Marty	1982–90	2B	3362	417	935	17	311	304	206	.278
Barrett, Tom	1992	2B	3	1	0	0	0	2	0	.000

NAME	YEARS	POSITION	AB	R	H	HR	RBI	BB	SO	BA
Barry, Jack	1915–17, 19	2B	1074	116	241	2	78	93	67	.224
Batts, Matt	1947–51	C	558	67	152	9	96	60	53	.272
Baylor, Don	1986–87	DH	924	157	220	47	151	102	158	.238
Bell, Juan	1995	SS–2B	26	7	4	1	2	2	10	.154
Bellhorn, Mark	2004	2B–3B	523	93	138	17	82	88	177	.264
Beltre, Esteban	1996	3B–2B–SS	62	6	16	0	6	4	14	.258
Beniquez, Juan	1971–72, 74–75	OF	799	121	219	8	62	60	102	.274
Benjamin, Mike	1997–98	2B	465	58	122	4	46	19	100	.262
Benzinger, Todd	1987–88	OF–1B	628	83	165	21	113	44	121	.263
Berberet, Lou	1958	C	167	11	35	2	18	31	32	.210
Berg, Moe	1935–39	C	409	38	107	3	56	14	17	.262
Berger, Boze	1939	SS	30	4	9	0	2	1	10	.300
Berry, Charlie	1928–32	C	1029	109	277	14	130	84	110	.269
Berry, Sean	2000	3B	4	0	0	0	0	0	2	.000
Berryhill, Damon	1994	C	255	30	67	6	34	19	59	.263
Bevan, Hal	1952	3B	1	0	0	0	0	0	0	.000
Bichette, Dante	2000–01	DH–OF	505	58	145	19	63	28	98	.287
Bigelow, Elliot	1929	OF	211	23	60	1	26	23	18	.284
Bischoff, John	1925–26	C	260	19	70	1	35	21	27	.269
Bishop, Max	1934–35	2B	375	84	94	2	36	110	36	.251
Blackwell, Tim	1974–75	C	254	24	56	0	14	29	34	.220
Blosser, Greg	1993–94	OF	39	3	3	0	2	6	11	.077
Bluhm, Red	1918	PH	1	0	0	0	0	0	0	.000
Boggs, Wade	1982–92	3B	6213	1067	2098	85	687	1004	470	.338
Bolling, Milt	1952–57	SS	853	95	211	15	75	91	122	.247
Boone, Ike	1923–25	OF	978	152	325	22	168	115	51	.332
Boone, Ray	1960	1B	78	6	16	1	11	11	15	.205
Boudreau, Lou	1951–52	SS	275	38	73	5	49	30	12	.265
Bowen, Sam	1977–78, 80	OF	22	3	3	1	1	3	7	.136
Bradley, Hugh	1910–12	1B	261	33	53	2	30	22	0	.203
Brady, Cliff	1920	2B	180	16	41	0	12	13	12	.228
Bragg, Darren	1996–98	OF	1144	154	302	20	136	139	240	.264
Bratschi, Fred	1926–27	OF	168	12	46	0	19	14	15	.274
Bressoud, Eddie	1962–65	SS	1958	255	528	57	208	199	387	.270
Brett, Ken	1967, 69–71	P	61	9	18	3	6	3	10	.295
Brogna, Rico	2000	1B	56	8	11	1	8	3	13	.196
Brohamer, Jack	1978–80	3B–2B	493	64	126	3	42	44	31	.256
Brown, Adrian	2003	OF	15	2	3	0	1	1	4	.200
Brown, Kevin	2002	C	1	0	0	0	0	0	0	.000
Brumley, Mike	1991–92	SS–3B	119	16	25	0	5	10	22	.210
Brunansky, Tom	1990–92, 94	OF	1555	184	392	56	249	192	321	.252
Bucher, Jim	1944–45	3B	428	58	110	4	42	26	26	.257

NAME	YEARS	POSITION	AB	R	H	HR	RBI	BB	SO	BA
Buckner, Bill	1984–87, 90	1B	2070	240	577	48	324	110	120	.279
Buddin, Don	1956, 58–61	SS	2126	318	519	39	211	373	371	.244
Buford, Damon	1998–99	OF	513	76	133	16	80	43	117	.259
Burda, Bob	1972	1B	73	4	12	2	9	8	11	.164
Burkett, Jesse	1905	OF	573	78	147	4	47	67	0	.257
Burkhart, Morgan	2000–01	DH	106	19	27	5	22	18	36	.255
Burks, Ellis	1987–92, 2004	OF	2827	446	791	94	388	254	458	.280
Burleson, Rick	1974–80	SS	4064	514	1114	38	360	310	360	.274
Burns, George	1922–23	1B	1109	162	352	19	155	65	61	.317
Busby, Jim	1959–60	OF	102	16	23	1	5	5	18	.225
Bush, Joe	1918–21	P	325	42	93	0	40	18	41	.286
Byrd, Jim	1993	PR	0	0	0	0	0	0	0	—
Cabrera, Orlando	2004	SS	228	33	67	6	31	11	23	.294
Cady, Hick	1912–17	C	803	77	195	0	55	62	83	.243
Calderon, Ivan	1993	OF	213	25	47	1	19	21	28	.221
Camilli, Dolph	1945	1B	198	24	42	2	19	35	38	212
Campbell, Paul	1941–42, 46	1B–OF	41	7	4	0	0	3	12	.098
Canseco, Jose	1995–96	DH	756	132	225	52	163	105	175	.298
Carbo, Bernie	1974–78	OF	986	152	257	45	157	204	256	.261
Carey, Tom	1939–42, 46	2B–SS	250	28	65	0	28	5	11	.260
Carlisle, Walter	1908	OF	10	0	1	0	0	1	0	.100
Carlstrom, Swede	1911	SS	6	0	1	0	0	0	0	.167
Carlyle, Cleo	1927	OF	278	31	65	1	28	36	40	.234
Carlyle, Roy	1925–26	OF	441	58	137	9	65	20	46	.311
Carrigan, Bill	1906, 08–16	C	1970	194	506	6	235	206	59	.257
Cater, Danny	1972–74	1B	638	76	167	14	83	35	68	.262
Cepeda, Orlando	1973	DH	550	51	159	20	86	50	81	.289
Cerone, Rick	1988–89	C	560	59	143	7	75	54	72	.255
Chadbourne, Chet	1906–07	2B–OF	81	7	24	0	4	10	0	.296
Chamberlain, Wes	1994–95	OF	206	17	47	5	21	15	49	.228
Chaplin, Ed	1920–22	C	76	10	14	0	7	13	11	.184
Chapman, Ben	1937–38	OF	903	168	293	13	137	122	68	.324
Christopher, Joe	1966	OF	13	1	1	0	0	2	4	.077
Christopher, Lloyd	1945	OF	14	4	4	0	4	3	2	.286
Cicero, Joe	1929–30	OF	62	11	15	0	8	1	7	.242
Cissell, Bill	1934	2B	416	71	111	4	44	28	23	.267
Clark, Danny	1924	3B	325	36	90	2	54	51	19	.277
Clark, Jack	1991–92	DH	738	107	174	33	120	152	220	.236
Clark, Phil	1996	DH–1B–3B	3	0	0	0	0	0	1	.000
Clark, Tony	2002	1B	275	25	57	3	29	21	57	.207
Clinton, Lu	1960–64	OF	1427	190	359	49	198	114	306	.252
Cochran, George	1918	3B	60	7	7	0	3	10	6	.117

NAME	YEARS	POSITION	AB	R	H	HR	RBI	BB	SO	BA
Coffey, Jack	1918	3B	44	5	7	1	2	3	2	.159
Cole, Alex	1996	OF	72	13	16	0	7	8	11	.222
Coleman, Dave	1977	OF	12	1	0	0	0	1	3	.000
Coleman, Michael	1997, 99	OF	29	3	5	0	2	1	11	.172
Collier, Lou	2003	3B–OF	1	0	0	0	0	0	0	.000
Collins, Jimmy	1901–07	3B	2972	448	881	25	385	160	0	.296
Collins, Shano	1921–25	OF	1599	175	433	5	168	54	114	.271
Combs, Merrill	1947, 49–50	3B	92	13	20	1	7	19	9	.217
Congalton, Bunk	1907	OF	496	44	142	2	47	20	0	.286
Conigliaro, Billy	1969–71	OF	829	115	223	33	98	69	164	.269
Conigliaro, Tony	1964–67, 69–70, 75	OF	2955	441	790	162	501	264	577	.267
Connolly, Bud	1925	SS	107	12	28	0	21	23	9	.262
Connolly, Ed	1929–32	C	371	13	66	0	31	29	50	.178
Connolly, Joe	1924	OF	10	1	1	0	1	2	2	.100
Conroy, Bill	1942–44	C	386	41	76	5	30	69	75	.197
Consolo, Billy	1953–59	SS–2B	618	91	140	6	42	74	168	.227
Cooke, Dusty	1933–36	OF	1257	229	357	15	161	221	168	.284
Cooney, Jimmy	1917	2B	36	4	8	0	3	6	2	.222
Cooper, Cecil	1971–76	1B–DH	1330	191	377	40	181	81	190	.283
Cooper, Scott	1990–94	3B	1268	156	360	27	156	127	182	.284
Cordero, Wil	1996–97	OF	768	111	217	21	109	42	153	.283
Correll, Vic	1972	C	4	1	2	0	1	0	1	.500
Coughtry, Marlan	1960	2B	19	3	3	0	0	5	8	.158
Cox, Ted	1977	DH	58	11	21	1	6	3	6	.362
Cramer, Doc	1936–40	OF	3111	509	940	1	270	207	99	.302
Cravath, Gavvy	1908	OF	277	43	71	1	34	38	0	.256
Creeden, Pat	1931	2B	8	0	0	0	0	1	3	.000
Crespo, Cesar	2004	SS–OF–2B	79	6	13	0	2	0	20	.165
Criger, Lou	1901–08	C	1943	190	405	6	193	178	0	.208
Cronin, Joe	1935–45	SS	3892	645	1168	119	737	585	408	.300
Culberson, Leon	1943–47	OF	1188	147	319	14	129	99	121	.269
Cummings, Midre	1998, 2000	DH	145	21	41	5	17	23	22	.283
Cuyler, Milt	1996	OF	110	19	22	2	12	13	19	.200
Dahlgren, Babe	1935–36	1B	582	83	154	10	70	63	68	.265
Daley, Pete	1955–59	C	653	62	160	11	78	57	109	.245
Dallessandro, Dom	1937	OF	147	18	34	0	11	27	16	.231
Damon, Johnny	2002–04	OF	1852	344	533	46	224	209	215	.288
Danzig, Babe	1909	1B	13	0	2	0	0	2	0	.154
Darwin, Bobby	1976–77	OF–DH	115	10	21	3	14	2	39	.183
Daubach, Brian	1999–2002, 04	1B–OF–DH	1802	241	477	86	306	194	477	.265
Daughters, Bob	1937	PR	0	1	0	0	0	0	0	—

NAME	YEARS	POSITION	AB	R	H	HR	RBI	BB	SO	BA
Dawson, Andre	1993–94	DH	753	78	196	29	115	26	102	.260
Deer, Rob	1993	OF	143	18	28	7	16	20	49	.196
Delgado, Alex	1996	C	20	5	5	0	1	3	3	.250
Demeter, Don	1966–67	OF	269	38	78	10	33	8	53	.290
Dente, Sam	1947	3B	168	14	39	0	11	19	15	.232
Derrick, Mike	1970	OF	33	3	7	0	5	0	11	.212
Desautels, Gene	1937–40	C	1086	125	276	2	113	158	83	.254
Devine, Mickey	1920	C	12	1	2	0	0	1	2	.167
DeVormer, Al	1923	C	209	20	54	0	18	6	21	.258
Diaz, Bo	1977	C	1	0	0	0	0	0	1	.000
Diaz, Juan	2002	1B–DH	7	2	2	1	2	1	2	.286
Dickey, George	1935–36	C	34	1	1	0	1	3	6	.029
Didier, Bob	1974	C	14	0	1	0	1	2	1	.071
Dillard, Steve	1975–77	2B	313	46	82	2	28	24	33	.262
DiMaggio, Dom	1940–42, 46–53	OF	5640	1046	1680	87	618	750	571	.298
DiPietro, Bob	1951	OF	11	0	1	0	0	1	1	.091
Dodson, Pat	1986–88	1B	99	12	20	4	10	17	33	.202
Doerr, Bobby	1937–44, 46–51	2B	7093	1094	2042	223	1247	809	608	.288
Dominique, Andy	2004	1B	11	0	2	0	1	0	3	.182
Donahue, John	1923	OF	36	5	10	0	1	4	5	.278
Donahue, Pat	1908–10	C	266	22	59	3	31	26	0	.222
Donnels, Chris	1995	3B	91	13	23	2	11	9	18	.253
Doran, Tom	1904–06	C	38	2	4	0	0	4	0	.105
Dougherty, Patsy	1902–04	OF	1223	217	398	4	97	100	0	.268
Dowd, Tommy	1901	OF	594	104	159	3	52	38	0	.268
Doyle, Danny	1943	C	43	2	9	0	6	7	9	.209
Doyle, Denny	1975–77	2B	1197	155	313	6	111	65	100	.261
Dropo, Walt	1949–52	1B	1092	154	307	51	229	97	156	.281
Duffy, Frank	1978–79	3B–SS	107	12	27	0	4	6	12	.252
Dugan, Joe	1922	3B	341	45	98	3	38	9	28	.287
Durst, Cedric	1930	OF	302	29	74	1	24	17	24	.245
Dwyer, Jim	1979–80	OF	373	60	104	11	52	45	32	.279
Easler, Mike	1984–85	DH	1169	158	337	43	165	111	263	.288
Eggert, Elmer	1927	2B	3	0	0	0	0	1	1	.000
Eibel, Hack	1920	OF	43	4	8	0	6	3	6	.186
Engle, Clyde	1910–14	1B–3B	1680	238	445	6	163	177	52	.265
Esasky, Nick	1989–89	1B	564	79	156	30	108	66	117	.277
Evans, Al	1951	C	24	1	3	0	2	4	2	.125
Evans, Dwight	1972–90	OF–DH–1B	8726	1435	2373	379	1346	1337	1643	.272
Everett, Carl	2000–01	OF	905	143	254	48	166	79	217	.281
Evers, Hoot	1952–54	OF	709	93	177	25	90	52	98	.250
Ezzell, Homer	1924–25	3B	463	75	128	0	47	33	39	.276

NAME	YEARS	POSITION	AB	R	H	HR	RBI	BB	SO	BA
Fanzone, Carmen	1970	3B	15	0	3	0	3	2	2	.200
Farrell, Doc	1935	2B	7	1	2	0	1	1	0	.286
Farrell, Duke	1903–05	C	271	18	69	0	25	21	0	.255
Ferrell, Rick	1933–37	C	1791	221	541	16	240	269	75	.302
Ferrell, Wes	1934–37	P	396	64	122	17	82	49	44	.308
Ferris, Hobe	1901–07	2B	3689	383	876	34	418	135	0	.237
Ferriss, Dave	1945–50	P	372	44	93	1	52	37	46	.250
Fewster, Chick	1922–23	2B–SS	367	40	91	0	24	45	45	.248
Finney, Lou	1939–42, 44–45	OF–1B	1930	294	580	13	265	147	60	.301
Fiore, Mike	1970–71	1B	112	14	18	1	10	20	18	.161
Fisk, Carlton	1969, 71–80	C	3860	627	1097	162	568	389	588	.284
Fitzgerald, Howie	1926	OF	97	11	25	0	8	5	7	.258
Flagstead, Ira	1923–29	OF	2941	466	867	27	299	335	168	.295
Flaherty, John	1992–93	C	91	6	16	0	4	5	13	.176
Flair, Al	1941	1B	30	3	6	0	2	1	1	.200
Fletcher, Scott	1993–94	2B	665	112	179	8	56	53	49	.269
Floyd, Cliff	2002	OF–DH	171	30	54	7	18	15	28	.316
Fonville, Chad	1999	2B	2	1	0	0	0	2	0	.000
Foster, Eddie	1920–22	3B	907	110	240	0	79	108	42	.265
Fothergill, Bob	1933	OF	32	1	11	0	5	2	4	.344
Fowler, Boob	1926	3B	8	1	1	0	1	0	0	.125
Fox, Pete	1941–45	OF	1717	225	496	6	201	113	152	.289
Foxx, Jimmie	1936–42	1B	3288	721	1051	222	788	624	568	.320
Foy, Joe	1966–68	3B	1515	232	373	41	172	221	258	.246
Freeman, Buck	1901–07	OF–1B	3077	403	879	48	504	215	0	.286
Freeman, John	1927	OF	2	0	0	0	0	0	0	.000
French, Charlie	1909–10	2B	207	19	50	0	16	16	0	.242
Friberg, Bernie	1933	2B–3B	41	5	13	0	9	6	1	.317
Friend, Owen	1955	SS	42	3	11	0	2	4	11	.262
Frye, Jeff	1996–97, 1999–2000	2B	1176	179	347	9	117	123	150	.295
Fuller, Frank	1923	2B	21	3	5	0	0	1	1	.238
Gaetti, Gary	2000	DH	10	0	0	0	1	0	3	.000
Gaffke, Fabian	1936–39	OF	250	39	61	7	39	22	32	.244
Gagliano, Phil	1971–72	OF	150	20	43	0	23	21	18	.287
Gainer, Del	1914–17, 19	1B	716	92	196	8	92	67	105	.274
Gallagher, Bob	1972	PH	5	0	0	0	0	0	3	.000
Galvin, Jim	1930	PH	2	0	0	0	0	0	0	.000
Garbark, Bob	1945	C	199	21	52	0	17	18	10	.261
Garciaparra, Nomar	1996–2004	SS	3968	709	1281	178	690	279	406	.323
Gardner, Billy	1962–63	2B	283	26	70	0	13	14	58	.247
Gardner, Larry	1908–17	3B–2B	3919	495	1106	16	481	388	161	.282

NAME	YEARS	POSITION	AB	R	H	HR	RBI	BB	SO	BA
Garrison, Ford	1943–44	OF	178	18	48	1	13	11	18	.270
Gaston, Alex	1926, 29	C	417	51	93	2	30	27	36	.223
Gedman, Rich	1980–90	C	2856	315	741	83	356	206	448	.259
Geiger, Gary	1959–65	OF	2002	301	507	71	246	249	325	.253
Gelbert, Charlie	1940	3B	91	9	18	0	8	8	16	.198
Gerber, Wally	1928–29	SS	391	27	79	0	33	40	43	.202
Gernert, Dick	1952–59	1B	2255	337	568	101	377	336	420	.252
Gessler, Doc	1908–09	OF	831	112	249	3	109	82	0	.300
Geygan, Chappie	1924–26	SS	103	7	26	0	4	5	19	.252
Giambi, Jeremy	2003	DH–OF	127	15	25	5	15	26	42	.197
Giannini, Joe	1911	SS	2	0	1	0	0	0	0	.500
Gibson, Russ	1967–69	C	656	44	152	7	62	35	94	.232
Gilbert, Andy	1942, 46	OF	12	1	1	0	1	1	3	.083
Gile, Don	1959–62	1B	120	12	18	3	9	5	35	.150
Gilhooley, Frank	1919	OF	112	14	27	0	1	12	8	.241
Gilkey, Bernard	2000	OF	91	11	21	1	9	10	12	.231
Gillis, Grant	1929	2B	73	5	18	0	11	6	8	.247
Ginsberg, Joe	1961	C	24	1	6	0	5	0	2	.250
Gleason, Harry	1901–03	3B	254	33	57	2	27	10	0	.224
Glenn, Joe	1940	C	47	3	6	0	4	5	7	.128
Godwin, John	1905–06	3B	236	15	50	0	25	9	0	.212
Goggin, Chuck	1974	2B	1	0	0	0	0	0	1	.000
Gonzalez, Eusebio	1918	SS	5	2	2	0	0	1	1	.400
Gooch, Johnny	1933	C	77	6	14	0	2	11	7	.182
Goodman, Billy	1947–57	2B–1B–OF	4399	688	1344	14	464	561	245	.306
Gosger, Jim	1963, 65–66	OF	466	64	116	14	52	47	86	.249
Graham, Charlie	1906	C	90	10	21	1	12	10	0	.233
Graham, Lee	1983	OF	6	2	0	0	1	0	0	.000
Graham, Skinny	1934–35	OF	57	8	14	0	4	7	16	.246
Grebeck, Craig	2001	SS	41	1	2	0	2	2	9	.049
Green, Lenny	1965–66	OF	506	87	135	8	36	63	62	.267
Green, Pumpsie	1959–62	2B–SS	742	111	181	12	69	126	119	.244
Greenwell, Mike	1985–96	OF	4623	657	1400	130	726	460	364	.303
Griffin, Doug	1971–77	2B	2081	207	517	7	161	152	199	.248
Grimes, Ray	1920	1B	4	1	1	0	0	1	0	.250
Grimshaw, Myron	1905–07	1B	894	104	229	4	116	60	0	.256
Gross, Turkey	1925	SS	32	2	3	0	2	2	2	.094
Gubanich, Creighton	1999	C	47	4	13	1	11	3	13	.277
Guerra, Mike	1951	C	32	1	5	0	2	6	5	.156
Guerrero, Mario	1973–74	SS	503	37	121	0	34	23	43	.241
Guindon, Bobby	1964	1B–OF	8	0	1	0	0	1	4	.125
Gunning, Hy	1911	1B	9	0	1	0	2	2	0	.111

NAME	YEARS	POSITION	AB	R	H	HR	RBI	BB	SO	BA
Gutierrez, Jackie	1983–85	SS	734	90	181	4	50	28	87	.247
Gutierrez, Ricky	2004	2B–SS	40	6	11	0	3	2	6	.275
Gutteridge, Don	1946–47	2B–3B	178	28	33	3	11	19	20	.185
Hale, Odell	1941	3B	24	5	5	1	1	3	4	.208
Haley, Ray	1915–16	C	8	2	1	0	0	1	1	.125
Hancock, Garry	1978, 80–82	OF	254	26	58	4	26	7	28	.228
Haney, Fred	1926–27	3B	578	70	134	3	64	99	42	.232
Hardy, Carroll	1960–62	OF	788	124	186	13	87	97	161	.236
Harper, Tommy	1972–74	OF	1565	250	405	36	144	174	262	.259
Harrell, Billy	1961	SS	37	10	6	0	1	1	8	.162
Harrelson, Ken	1967–69	OF	661	94	173	41	131	78	108	.262
Harris, Joe	1922–25	OF–1B	1401	221	442	23	209	168	72	.315
Hartley, Grover	1927	C	244	23	67	1	31	22	14	.275
Haselman, Bill	1995–97, 03	C	604	77	152	19	83	51	127	.252
Hatcher, Billy	1992–94	OF	987	132	261	11	98	56	101	.264
Hatfield, Fred	1950–52	3B	200	32	39	3	19	29	30	.195
Hatteberg, Scott	1995–2001	C	1310	163	350	34	159	175	209	.267
Hatton, Grady	1954–56	3B	687	88	180	9	84	134	53	.262
Hayden, Jack	1906	OF	322	22	80	1	14	17	0	.248
Hayes, Frankie	1947	C	13	0	2	0	1	0	1	.154
Hearn, Ed	1910	SS	2	0	0	0	0	0	0	.000
Heep, Danny	1989–90	OF	389	39	108	5	57	36	40	.278
Heise, Bob	1975–76	3B	182	17	42	0	26	5	8	.231
Helms, Tommy	1977	DH	59	5	16	1	5	4	4	.271
Hemphill, Charlie	1901	OF	545	71	142	3	62	39	0	.261
Henderson, Dave	1986–87	OF	235	38	53	9	28	24	63	.226
Henderson, Rickey	2002	OF	179	40	40	5	16	38	47	.223
Hendryx, Tim	1920–21	OF	500	64	152	0	95	66	40	.304
Henriksen, Olaf	1911–17	OF	487	84	131	1	48	97	43	.269
Herrera, Mike	1925–26	2B	276	22	76	0	27	17	15	.275
Heving, Johnnie	1924–25, 28–30	C	794	81	213	0	68	52	45	.268
Hickman, Charlie	1902	OF	108	13	32	3	16	3	0	.296
Higgins, Pinky	1937–38, 46	3B	1294	183	386	16	240	171	130	.298
Hillenbrand, Shea	2001–03	3B–1B	1287	166	365	33	170	45	182	.284
Hiller, Hob	1920–21	3B–SS	30	4	5	0	2	2	5	.167
Hinkle, Gordie	1934	C	75	7	13	0	9	7	23	.173
Hinson, Paul	1928	PR	0	1	0	0	0	0	0	—
Hitchcock, Billy	1948–49	1B–2B	271	37	67	1	29	24	20	.247
Hoblitzell, Dick	1914–18	1B	1534	195	413	3	184	158	100	.289
Hobson, Butch	1975–80	3B	2230	285	561	94	358	147	495	.252
Hodapp, Johnny	1933	2B	413	55	129	3	54	33	14	.312
Hoderlein, Mel	1951	2B–3B	14	1	5	0	1	6	2	.357

NAME	YEARS	POSITION	AB	R	H	HR	RBI	BB	SO	BA
Hoey, Jack	1906–08	OF	500	39	116	0	35	15	0	.232
Hoffman, Glenn	1980–87	SS–3B	1927	228	473	22	197	126	273	.245
Hofmann, Fred	1927–28	C	416	34	104	0	40	32	51	.250
Hollins, Dave	1995	DH	13	2	2	0	1	4	7	.154
Holm, Billy	1945	C	135	12	25	0	9	23	17	.185
Hooper, Harry	1909–20	OF	6270	988	1707	30	497	826	289	.272
Horn, Sam	1987–89	DH	273	36	61	16	46	36	91	.223
Horton, Tony	1964–67	1B	350	34	91	8	42	21	66	.260
Hosey, Dwayne	1995–96	OF	146	33	40	4	10	15	33	.274
Housie, Wayne	1991	OF	8	2	2	0	0	1	3	.250
Howard, Elston	1967–68	C	319	31	66	6	29	31	69	.207
Howard, Paul	1909	OF	15	2	3	0	2	3	0	.200
Hughes, Terry	1974	3B	69	5	14	1	6	6	18	.203
Hughes, Tom	1902–03	P	123	21	37	1	16	5	0	.301
Hunter, Buddy	1971, 73, 75	2B	17	5	5	0	2	5	2	.294
Hunter, Herb	1920	OF	12	2	1	0	0	1	1	.083
Huskey, Butch	1999	DH	124	18	33	7	28	7	20	.266
Hyzdu, Adam	2004	OF	10	3	3	1	2	1	2	.300
Jackson, Damian	2003	2B–OF–SS–DH	161	34	42	1	13	8	28	.261
Jackson, Ron	1960	1B	31	1	7	0	0	1	6	.226
Jacobson, Baby Doll	1926–27	OF	549	55	158	6	93	27	34	.288
James, Chris	1995	OF	24	2	4	0	1	1	4	.167
Janvrin, Hal	1911, 13–17	SS–2B	1548	179	357	4	148	121	149	.231
Jefferson, Reggie	1995–99	DH	1398	207	442	50	215	96	300	.316
Jenkins, Tom	1925–26	OF	114	12	28	0	11	6	11	.246
Jensen, Jackie	1954–59, 61	OF	3857	597	1089	170	733	585	425	.282
Jensen, Marcus	2001	C	4	0	1	0	0	0	1	.250
Johns, Keith	1998	2B–DH	0	0	0	0	0	0	10	—
Johnson, Bob	1944–45	OF	1054	177	318	29	180	158	123	.302
Johnson, Deron	1974–76	3B	73	5	14	1	5	7	17	.192
Johnson, Roy	1932–35	OF	1954	313	611	31	327	227	147	.313
Jolley, Smead	1932–33	OF	942	104	280	27	164	51	49	.297
Jones, Charlie	1901	OF	41	6	6	0	6	1	0	.146
Jones, Dalton	1964–69	2B–1B	1842	210	447	26	186	139	222	.243
Jones, Jake	1947–48	1B	509	53	116	17	84	52	86	.228
Joost, Eddie	1955	2B	119	15	23	5	17	17	21	.193
Josephson, Duane	1971–72	C	388	49	97	11	46	26	46	.250
Judd, Oscar	1941–45	P	138	18	37	2	7	14	11	.268
Judge, Joe	1933–34	1B	123	23	37	0	24	15	5	.301
Jurak, Ed	1982–85	SS–1B–3B	259	32	70	1	32	33	44	.270
Kapler, Gabe	2003–04	OF	448	80	125	10	56	29	72	.279
Karow, Marty	1927	SS	10	0	2	0	0	0	2	.200

NAME	YEARS	POSITION	AB	R	H	HR	RBI	BB	SO	BA
Kasko, Eddie	1966	SS	136	11	29	1	12	15	19	.213
Kell, George	1952–54	3B	829	124	253	18	123	98	35	.305
Kellett, Red	1934	SS	9	0	0	0	0	1	5	.000
Keltner, Ken	1950	3B	28	2	9	0	2	3	6	.321
Kendall, Fred	1978	1B	41	3	8	0	4	1	2	.195
Kennedy, John	1970–74	2B–3B	783	98	190	13	78	51	147	.243
Keough, Marty	1956–60	OF	493	78	114	9	46	46	80	.231
Klaus, Billy	1955–58	SS–3B	1626	255	428	25	168	210	156	.263
Kleinow, Red	1910–11	C	161	9	25	1	8	22	0	.155
Knight, John	1907	3B	360	31	78	2	29	19	0	.217
Kosco, Andy	1972	OF	47	5	10	3	6	2	9	.213
Kroner, John	1935–36	2B–3B	302	41	88	4	62	27	25	.291
Krug, Marty	1912	SS	39	6	12	0	7	5	0	.308
Kutcher, Randy	1988–90	OF	246	48	55	3	23	24	66	.224
LaChance, Candy	1902–05	1B	1677	176	421	8	161	75	0	.251
LaForest, Ty	1945	3B	204	25	51	2	16	10	35	.250
LaFrancois, Roger	1982	C	10	1	4	0	1	0	0	.400
Lahoud, Joe	1968–71	OF	601	82	123	26	64	103	110	.205
Lake, Eddie	1943–45	SS	815	128	201	14	75	176	94	.247
Lamar, Bill	1919	OF	148	18	43	0	14	5	9	.291
Lancellotti, Rick	1990	1B	8	0	0	0	1	0	3	.000
Landis, Jim	1967	OF	7	1	1	1	1	1	3	.143
Lansford, Sam	1926	PH	1	1	0	0	0	0	0	.000
Lansford, Carney	1981–82	3B	881	126	279	15	115	80	76	.317
Lansing, Mike	2000–01	2B–SS	491	55	115	8	47	29	76	.234
LaPorte, Frank	1908	2B	156	14	37	0	15	12	0	.237
Lary, Lyn	1934	SS	419	58	101	2	54	66	51	.241
Lazor, Johnny	1943–46	OF	596	57	157	6	62	42	53	.263
Lee, Dud	1924–26	SS	550	60	131	0	48	74	36	.238
Legett, Lou	1933–35	C	43	6	12	0	2	2	4	.279
Lehner, Paul	1952	OF	3	0	2	0	2	2	0	.667
Leibold, Nemo	1921–23	OF	756	131	215	1	49	83	43	.284
Lemke, Mark	1998	2B	91	10	17	0	7	6	15	.187
Lenhardt, Don	1952, 54	OF	171	23	49	10	41	18	27	.287
Lepcio, Ted	1952–59	2B–3B	1622	181	401	53	200	166	350	.247
Lerchen, Dutch	1910	SS	15	1	0	0	0	1	0	.000
Lewis, Darren	1998–2001	OF	1489	220	381	13	132	145	205	.256
Lewis, Duffy	1910–17	OF	4325	500	1248	27	629	303	269	.289
Lewis, Jack	1911	2B	59	7	16	0	6	7	0	.271
Leyritz, Jim	1998	DH	129	17	37	8	24	21	34	.287
Lickert, John	1981	C	0	0	0	0	0	0	0	—
Lipon, Johnny	1952–53	SS	379	43	79	0	31	46	36	.208

NAME	YEARS	POSITION	AB	R	H	HR	RBI	BB	SO	BA
Litton, Greg	1994	2B–1B	21	2	2	0	1	0	5	.095
Lock, Don	1969	OF	58	8	13	1	2	11	21	.224
Loepp, George	1928	OF	51	6	9	0	3	5	12	.176
Lofton, James	2001	SS	26	1	5	0	1	1	4	.192
Lomasney, Steve	1999	C	2	0	0	0	0	0	2	.000
Lonergan, Walter	1911	2B	26	2	7	0	1	1	0	.269
Lord, Harry	1907–10	3B	1420	176	389	3	103	57	0	.274
Lucas, Johnny	1931–32	OF	3	0	0	0	0	0	1	.000
Lucey, Joe	1925	P	15	0	2	0	0	0	4	.133
Lupien, Tony	1940, 42–43	1B	1090	133	294	7	121	105	44	.270
Lynch, Walt	1922	C	2	1	1	0	0	0	0	.500
Lynn, Fred	1974–80	OF	3062	523	944	124	521	382	394	.308
Lyons, Steve	1985–86, 91–93	2B	758	94	190	10	63	59	128	.251
Macfarlane, Mike	1995	C	364	45	82	15	51	38	78	.225
Mack, Shane	1997	OF	130	13	41	3	17	9	24	.315
Madden, Tom	1909–11	C	67	6	20	0	7	5	0	.299
Mahay, Ron	1995, 97–98	P	20	3	4	1	3	1	6	.200
Mahoney, Chris	1910	P	7	1	1	0	0	0	0	.143
Mahoney, Jim	1959	SS	23	10	3	1	4	3	7	.130
Malave, Jose	1996–97	OF	106	12	24	4	17	2	27	.226
Mallett, Jerry	1959	OF	15	1	4	0	1	1	3	.267
Malzone, Frank	1955–65	3B	5273	641	1454	131	716	327	423	.276
Mantilla, Felix	1963–65	2B	1137	156	326	54	171	140	144	.287
Manto, Jeff	1996	3B	30	5	8	2	4	3	6	.267
Manush, Heinie	1936	OF	313	43	91	0	45	17	11	.291
Marquardt, Ollie	1931	2B	39	4	7	0	2	3	4	.179
Marshall, Bill	1931	PR	0	1	0	0	0	0	0	—
Marshall, Mike	1990–91	DH	174	14	50	5	19	4	45	.287
Martin, Babe	1948–49	C	6	0	2	0	0	0	1	.333
Martinez, Sandy	2004	C	4	0	0	0	0	0	2	.000
Marzano, John	1987–92	C	462	50	107	6	44	16	84	.232
Matchick, Tom	1970	3B	14	2	1	0	0	2	2	.071
Mauch, Gene	1956–57	2B	247	27	68	2	29	25	29	.275
Maxwell, Charlie	1950–52, 54	OF	207	18	42	3	17	25	53	.203
Mayer, Wally	1917–18	C	61	9	13	0	5	12	9	.213
Maynard, Chick	1922	SS	24	1	3	0	0	3	2	.125
McAuliffe, Dick	1974–75	2B–3B	287	32	59	5	25	40	42	.206
McBride, Tom	1943–47	OF	814	99	228	1	97	50	39	.280
McCann, Emmett	1926	SS–3B	3	0	0	0	0	0	11	.000
McCarty, Dave	2003–04	1B–OF	178	28	50	5	23	16	47	.281
McCarver, Tim	1974–75	C	49	4	15	0	4	5	4	.306
McConnell, Amby	1908–10	2B	990	144	254	2	80	77	0	.257

NAME	YEARS	POSITION	AB	R	H	HR	RBI	BB	SO	BA
McDermott, Mickey	1948–53	P	306	43	86	3	44	21	47	.281
McFarland, Ed	1908	C	48	5	10	0	4	1	0	.208
McGah, Eddie	1946–47	C	51	3	8	0	3	10	7	.157
McGee, Willie	1995	OF	200	32	57	2	15	9	41	.285
McGovern, Art	1905	C	44	1	5	0	1	4	0	.114
McGuire, Deacon	1907–08	PH	5	1	3	1	1	0	0	.600
McHale, Jim	1908	OF	67	9	15	0	7	4	0	.224
McInnis, Stuffy	1918–21	1B	2006	194	594	3	261	81	49	.296
McKeel, Walt	1996–97	C	3	0	0	0	0	0	1	.000
McLean, Larry	1901	1B	19	4	4	0	2	0	0	.211
McManus, Marty	1931–33	3B–2B	730	98	193	9	69	93	52	.264
McMillan, Norm	1923	3B	459	37	116	0	42	28	44	.253
McNair, Eric	1936–38	2B–SS	1045	137	289	16	157	60	73	.277
McNally, Mike	1915–17, 19–20	2B	592	96	137	0	40	51	55	.231
McNeely, Jeff	1993	OF	37	10	11	0	1	7	9	.297
McNeil, Norm	1919	C	9	0	3	0	1	1	0	.333
McWilliams, Bill	1931	PH	2	0	0	0	0	0	1	.000
Mejias, Roman	1963–64	OF	458	57	105	13	43	21	52	.229
Mele, Sam	1947–49, 54–55	OF	842	120	234	21	129	69	89	.278
Melillo, Ski	1935–37	2B	783	92	192	1	77	71	42	.245
Melvin, Bob	1993	C	176	10	39	3	23	7	44	.222
Menosky, Mike	1920–23	OF	1603	240	459	9	166	187	149	.286
Merced, Orlando	1998	OF–DH	9	0	0	0	2	2	3	.000
Merchant, Andy	1975–76	C	6	1	2	0	0	1	2	.333
Merloni, Lou	1998–2003	2B–SS–3B	720	91	194	9	78	49	132	.269
Merson, Jack	1953	2B	4	0	0	0	0	0	0	.000
Metkovich, Catfish	1943–46	OF–1B	1690	235	440	23	173	137	204	.260
Mientkiewicz, Doug	2004	1B	107	13	23	1	10	10	18	.215
Miles, Dee	1943	OF	121	9	26	0	10	3	3	.215
Millar, Kevin	2003–04	1B–OF–DH	1052	157	301	43	170	117	199	.286
Miller, Bing	1935–36	OF	185	27	56	4	32	15	13	.303
Miller, Elmer	1922	OF	147	16	28	4	16	5	10	.190
Miller, Hack	1918	OF	29	2	8	0	4	0	4	.276
Miller, Otto	1930–32	3B	761	87	212	0	83	41	41	.279
Miller, Rick	1971–77, 81–85	OF	2573	374	683	23	266	302	373	.265
Mills, Buster	1937	OF	505	85	149	7	58	46	41	.295
Mirabelli, Doug	2001–04	C	615	83	159	31	101	64	151	.259
Mitchell, Johnny	1922–23	SS	550	60	129	1	27	50	35	.235
Mitchell, Keith	1998	DH–OF	33	4	9	0	6	7	5	.273
Mitchell, Kevin	1996	OF	929	28	2	13	11	11	14	.304
Moncewicz, Freddie	1928	SS	1	0	0	0	0	0	1	.000
Montgomery, Bob	1970–79	C	1185	125	306	23	156	64	268	.258

NAME	YEARS	POSITION	AB	R	H	HR	RBI	BB	SO	BA
Moore, Bill	1926–27	C	87	9	18	0	4	13	10	.207
Morgan, Ed	1934	1B	528	95	141	3	79	81	46	.267
Morgan, Red	1906	3B	307	20	66	1	21	16	0	.215
Morton, Guy	1954	PH	1	0	0	0	0	0	1	.000
Moses, Jerry	1965, 68–70	C	472	42	131	13	57	27	74	.278
Moses, Wally	1946–48	OF	619	81	155	6	73	62	50	.250
Moskiman, Doc	1910	1B	9	1	1	0	1	2	0	.111
Moss, Les	1951	C	202	18	40	3	26	25	34	.198
Mueller, Bill	2003–04	3B–2B	923	160	284	31	142	110	133	.308
Mulleavy, Greg	1933	PR	0	1	0	0	0	0	0	—
Muller, Freddie	1933–34	2B	49	7	9	0	3	6	5	.184
Mundy, Bill	1913	1B	47	4	12	0	4	4	12	.255
Muser, Tony	1969	1B	9	0	1	0	1	1	1	.111
Myer, Buddy	1927–28	3B–SS	1005	137	303	3	91	101	43	.301
Myers, Hap	1910–11	1B	44	3	16	0	0	4	0	.364
Naehring, Tim	1990–97	3B	1872	254	527	49	250	236	312	.282
Narleski, Bill	1929–30	SS	358	41	95	0	32	28	27	.265
Neitzke, Ernie	1921	OF	25	3	6	0	2	4	4	.240
Nelson, Bry	2002	2B–OF	34	6	9	0	2	4	1	.265
Newman, Jeff	1983–84	C	195	16	39	4	10	15	47	.200
Newsome, Skeeter	1941–45	SS–1B	1681	169	437	4	137	105	73	.260
Niarhos, Gus	1952–53	C	93	10	13	0	6	16	13	.140
Nichols, Reid	1980–85	OF	759	105	203	15	78	59	100	.267
Niemiec, Al	1934	2B	32	2	7	0	3	3	4	.219
Niles, Harry	1908–10	OF	635	74	154	3	44	49	0	.243
Nixon, Otis	1994	OF	398	60	109	0	25	55	65	.274
Nixon, Russ	1960–65, 68	C	1337	108	358	13	138	83	153	.268
Nixon, Trot	1996, 98–2004	OF	2496	424	698	112	404	341	506	.280
Nonnenkamp, Red	1938–40	OF	262	49	69	0	24	33	23	.263
Nunamaker, Les	1911–14	C	356	42	88	0	34	27	8	.247
Nunnally, Jon	1999	DH–OF	14	4	4	0	1	0	6	.286
O'Berry, Mike	1979	C	59	8	10	1	4	5	16	.169
O'Brien, Jack	1903	OF	338	44	71	3	38	21	0	.210
O'Brien, Syd	1969	3B	263	47	64	9	29	15	37	.243
O'Brien, Tommy	1949–50	OF	156	24	32	3	13	24	17	.205
Offerman, Jose	1999–2002	2B–1B–DH	1798	295	482	30	186	260	275	.268
Oglivie, Ben	1971–73	OF	438	45	103	10	43	27	98	.235
Okrie, Len	1952	C	1	0	0	0	0	0	1	.000
O'Leary, Troy	1995–2001	OF	3456	490	954	117	516	276	562	.276
Oliver, Gene	1968	C	35	2	5	0	1	4	12	.143
Oliver, Joe	2001	C	12	1	3	0	1	1	3	.250
Oliver, Tom	1930–33	OF	1931	202	534	0	176	105	61	.277

NAME	YEARS	POSITION	AB	R	H	HR	RBI	BB	SO	BA
Olson, Karl	1951, 1953–55	OF	342	37	79	2	27	14	45	.231
Olson, Marv	1931–33	2B	457	67	110	0	30	70	30	.241
O'Neill, Bill	1904	OF	51	7	10	0	5	2	0	.196
O'Neill, Steve	1924	C	307	29	73	0	38	63	23	.238
Orme, George	1920	OF	6	4	2	0	1	3	0	.333
O'Rourke, Frank	1922	SS	216	28	57	1	17	20	28	.264
Ortiz, David	2003–04	DH–1B	1030	173	304	72	240	133	216	.295
Ortiz, Luis	1993–94	DH	30	3	6	0	7	1	7	.200
Ostdiek, Harry	1908	C	3	0	0	0	0	0	0	.000
Ostrowski, Johnny	1948–48	PH	1	0	0	0	0	0	1	.000
Owen, Marv	1940	3B–1B	57	4	12	0	6	8	4	.211
Owen, Mickey	1954	C	68	6	16	1	11	9	6	.235
Owen, Spike	1986–88	SS	820	111	200	8	76	97	79	.244
Owens, Frank	1905	C	2	0	0	0	0	0	0	.000
Pagliaroni, Jim	1955, 60–62	C	698	96	177	29	105	104	140	.254
Pankovits, Jim	1990	2B	0	0	0	0	0	0	0	—
Papi, Stan	1979–80	2B–SS	117	9	22	1	6	5	20	.188
Parent, Freddy	1901–07	SS	3846	519	1051	19	386	206	0	.273
Parrish, Larry	1988	1B	158	10	41	7	26	8	32	.259
Partee, Roy	1943–44, 46–47	C	859	75	226	2	97	107	99	.263
Paschal, Ben	1920	OF	28	5	10	0	5	5	2	.357
Patterson, Hank	1932	C	1	0	0	0	0	0	0	.000
Pavletich, Don	1970–71	C–1B	92	9	16	1	9	15	20	.174
Peacock, Johnny	1937–44	C	1297	137	355	1	153	122	48	.274
Pellagrini, Eddie	1946–47	3B	302	36	62	6	23	26	53	.205
Pemberton, Rudy	1996–97	OF	104	19	36	3	20	6	17	.346
Pena, Tony	1990–93	C	1669	166	390	17	161	129	231	.234
Perez, Tony	1980–82	1B	1087	126	289	40	175	87	207	.266
Perrin, Jack	1921	OF	13	3	3	0	1	0	3	.231
Pesky, Johnny	1942, 46–52	SS–3B	4085	776	1277	13	361	581	189	.313
Peters, Gary	1970–72	P	208	21	52	4	31	12	38	.250
Peterson, Bob	1906–07	C	131	11	25	1	9	11	0	.191
Petrocelli, Rico	1963, 65–76	SS–3B	5390	653	1352	210	773	661	926	.251
Philley, Dave	1962	OF	42	3	6	0	4	5	3	.143
Picinich, Val	1923–25	C	680	89	182	4	80	108	72	.268
Pickering, Calvin	2001	1B	50	4	14	3	7	8	13	.280
Pickering, Urbane	1931–32	3B	798	95	205	11	92	72	124	.257
Piersall, Jimmy	1950, 52–58	OF	3369	502	919	66	366	338	317	.273
Pirkl, Greg	1996	PH	2	0	0	0	0	0	1	.000
Pittinger, Pinky	1921–23	2B–SS–3B	454	37	104	0	27	18	33	.229
Plantier, Phil	1990–92	OF	512	74	137	18	68	71	127	.268
Plews, Herb	1959	2B	12	0	1	0	0	0	4	.083

NAME	YEARS	POSITION	AB	R	H	HR	RBI	BB	SO	BA
Polly, Nick	1945	3B	7	0	1	0	1	0	0	.143
Pond, Ralph	1910	OF	4	0	1	0	0	0	0	.250
Poquette, Tom	1979, 81	OF	156	14	51	2	23	8	7	.327
Porter, Dick	1934	OF	265	30	80	0	56	21	15	.302
Poulsen, Ken	1967	3B–SS	5	0	1	0	0	0	2	.200
Pozo, Arquimedez	1996–97	3B–2B	73	4	14	1	14	2	15	.192
Pratt, Del	1921–22	2B	1128	153	352	11	188	97	30	.312
Pratt, Larry	1914	C	4	0	0	0	0	0	4	.000
Pride, Curtis	1997, 2000	OF	22	5	6	1	1	1	8	.273
Prothro, Doc	1925	3B	415	44	130	0	51	52	21	.313
Purtell, Billy	1910–11	3B	250	20	58	1	22	19	0	.232
Pytlak, Frankie	1941, 45–46	C	367	38	95	2	40	31	19	.259
Quinones, Rey	1986	SS	190	26	45	2	15	19	26	.237
Quintana, Carlos	1988–91, 93	1B	1376	163	380	19	165	153	207	.276
Rader, Dave	1980	C	137	14	45	3	17	14	12	.328
Ramirez, Manny	2001–04	OF–DH	2102	402	674	154	466	333	450	.321
Reder, Johnny	1932	1B	37	4	5	0	3	6	6	.135
Reed, Jody	1987–92	2B–SS	2658	361	743	17	227	319	227	.280
Reese, Pokey	2004	SS–2B	244	32	54	3	29	17	60	.221
Reeves, Bobby	1929–31	3B	816	118	187	4	47	124	109	.229
Regan, Bill	1926–30	2B	2260	228	611	17	282	117	226	.270
Rehg, Wally	1913–15	OF	257	29	62	0	20	20	19	.241
Reichle, Dick	1922–23	OF	385	43	99	1	39	22	36	.257
Remy, Jerry	1978–84	2B	2809	385	802	2	211	214	247	.286
Renna, Bill	1958–59	OF	78	7	17	4	20	11	23	.218
Repulski, Rip	1960–61	OF	161	16	40	3	21	11	30	.248
Reynolds, Carl	1934–35	OF	657	94	191	10	121	51	48	.291
Rhodes, Karl	1995	OF	25	2	2	0	1	3	4	.080
Rhyne, Hal	1929–32	SS	1414	176	348	0	126	130	88	.246
Rice, Jim	1974–89	OF–DH	8225	1249	2452	382	1451	670	1423	.298
Richardson, Jeff	1993	2B–SS	24	3	5	0	2	1	3	.208
Richter, Al	1951, 53	SS	11	1	1	0	0	3	0	.091
Riggert, Joe	1911	OF	146	19	31	2	13	12	0	.212
Rigney, Topper	1926–27	SS	543	71	144	4	53	109	33	.265
Riles, Ernest	1993	2B–DH–3B	143	15	27	5	20	20	40	.189
Rising, Pop	1905	OF	29	2	3	0	2	2	0	.103
Rivera, Luis	1989–93	SS	1501	167	357	21	150	117	296	.238
Roberts, Dave	2004	OF	86	19	22	2	14	10	17	.256
Robidoux, Billy Jo	1990	1B	44	3	8	1	4	6	14	.182
Robinson, Aaron	1951	C	74	9	15	2	7	17	10	.203
Robinson, Floyd	1968	OF	24	1	2	3	0	3	4	.125
Rodgers, Bill	1915	2B	6	2	0	0	0	3	2	.000

NAME	YEARS	POSITION	AB	R	H	HR	RBI	BB	SO	BA
Rodriguez, Carlos	1994–95	SS–2B	204	20	60	1	18	13	15	.294
Rodriguez, Steve	1995	SS–DH	8	1	1	0	0	1	1	.125
Rodriguez, Tony	1996	SS	67	7	16	1	9	4	8	.239
Rogell, Billy	1925, 27–28	2B–SS–3B	672	80	157	2	74	57	92	.234
Rollings, Red	1927–28	3B	232	26	60	0	18	18	18	.259
Romero, Ed	1986–89	SS–3B–2B	656	81	155	2	48	46	53	.236
Romero, Mandy	1998	C–DH	13	2	3	0	1	3	3	.231
Romine, Kevin	1985–91	OF	630	89	158	5	55	49	124	.251
Rosar, Buddy	1950–51	C	254	24	64	2	25	26	18	.252
Rosenthal, Si	1925–26	OF	357	40	95	4	42	26	21	.266
Roth, Braggo	1919	OF	227	32	58	0	23	24	32	.256
Rothrock, Jack	1925–32	OF	1905	280	529	14	172	160	203	.278
Rowland, Rich	1994–95	C	147	15	32	9	21	11	46	.218
Royer, Stan	1994	3B	9	0	1	0	1	0	3	.111
Rudi, Joe	1981	DH	122	14	22	6	24	8	29	.180
Ruel, Muddy	1921–22, 31	C	802	81	216	1	79	91	47	.269
Ruffing, Red	1924–30	P	438	42	118	5	57	8	67	.269
Runnels, Pete	1958–62	1B–02B	2578	407	825	29	249	378	237	.320
Russell, Rip	1946–47	2B	326	30	65	7	38	21	37	.199
Ruth, Babe	1914–19	OF–P	1110	202	342	49	230	190	184	.308
Ryan, Jack	1929	OF	3	0	0	0	0	0	0	.000
Ryan, Mike	1964–67	C	705	55	142	7	70	61	129	.201
Rye, Gene	1931	OF	39	3	7	0	1	2	5	.179
Sadler, Donnie	1998–2000	2B	330	53	80	4	29	16	66	.242
Sadowski, Ed	1960	C	93	10	20	3	8	8	13	.215
Sanchez, Freddy	2002–03	SS–2B–3B	50	9	11	0	4	2	11	.220
Sanchez, Rey	2002	2B	357	46	102	1	38	17	31	.286
Santos, Angel	2001	2B	16	2	2	0	1	2	7	.125
Satriano, Tom	1969–70	C	292	30	63	3	24	43	35	.216
Sax, Dave	1985–87	C	50	3	16	1	7	3	5	.320
Scarritt, Russ	1929–31	OF	1026	119	294	3	120	48	89	.287
Schang, Wally	1918–20	C	C 942	137	274	126	181	114		.291
Scherbarth, Bob	1950	C	0	0	0	0	0	0	0	—
Schilling, Chuck	1961–65	2B	1969	230	470	23	146	176	236	.239
Schlesinger, Rudy	1965	PH	1	0	0	0	0	0	0	.000
Schmees, George	1952	OF	64	8	13	0	3	10	11	.203
Schmidt, Dave	1981	C	42	6	10	2	3	7	17	.238
Schofield, Dick	1969–70	2B	365	46	84	3	34	50	70	.230
Schreckengost, Ossee	1901	C	280	37	85	0	38	19	0	.304
Scott, Everett	1914–21	SS	3887	355	956	7	346	171	212	.246
Scott, George	1966–71, 77–79	1B–3B	4234	527	1088	154	562	418	850	.257

NAME	YEARS	POSITION	AB	R	H	HR	RBI	BB	SO	BA
Seeds, Bob	1933–34	1B–OF	236	26	57	0	24	21	21	.242
Selbach, Kip	1904–06	OF	1022	119	248	4	100	133	0	.243
Selby, Bill	1996	2B–3B	95	12	26	3	6	9	11	.274
Shaner, Wally	1926–27	OF	597	74	165	3	70	38	48	.276
Shanks, Howie	1923–24	3B	657	60	168	3	82	40	49	.256
Shannon, Red	1919	2B	290	36	75	0	17	17	42	.259
Shaw, Al	1907	C	198	10	38	0	18	0	.	192
Shea, Merv	1933	C	56	1	8	0	8	4	7	.143
Sheaffer, Danny	1987	C	66	5	8	1	5	0	14	.121
Shean, Dave	1918–19	2B	525	62	126	0	42	45	32	.240
Sheets, Andy	2000	SS	21	1	2	0	1	0	3	.095
Sheridan, Neill	1948	PH	1	0	0	0	0	0	1	.000
Shofner, Strick	1947	3B	13	1	2	0	0	0	3	.154
Shorten, Chick	1915–17	OF	294	27	66	0	27	20	20	.224
Shumpert, Terry	1995	2B	47	6	11	0	3	4	13	.234
Siebern, Norm	1967–68	1B	74	2	11	0	7	6	13	.149
Simmons, Al	1943	OF	133	9	27	1	12	8	21	.203
Sizemore, Ted	1979–80	2B	111	13	28	1	6	4	5	.252
Skinner, Camp	1923	OF	13	1	3	0	1	0	0	.231
Slattery, Jack	1901	C	3	1	1	0	1	1	0	.333
Small, Charlie	1930	OF	18	1	3	0	0	2	5	.167
Smith, Al	1964	3B–OF	51	10	11	2	7	13	10	.216
Smith, Broadway Aleck	1903	C	33	4	10	0	4	0	0	.303
Smith, Elmer	1922	OF	231	43	66	6	32	25	21	.286
Smith, George	1966	2B	403	41	86	8	37	37	86	.213
Smith, John	1931	1B	15	2	2	0	1	2	1	.133
Smith, Paddy	1920	C	2	0	0	0	0	0	1	.000
Smith, Reggie	1966–73	OF	3780	592	1064	149	536	425	498	.281
Snell, Wally	1913	C	12	1	3	0	0	0	1	.250
Snopek, Chris	1998	2B–3B	12	2	2	0	2	2	5	.167
Snyder, Earl	2004	3B	4	0	1	0	0	0	1	.250
Solters, Moose	1934–35	OF	444	76	128	7	66	20	57	.288
Speaker, Tris	1907–15	OF	3935	704	1327	39	542	459	61	.337
Spence, Stan	1940–41, 48–49	OF	682	101	161	16	103	110	57	.236
Spencer, Tubby	1909	C	74	6	12	0	9	6	0	.162
Spognardi, Andy	1932	2B	34	9	10	0	1	6	6	.294
Sprague, Ed	2000	3B	111	11	24	2	9	12	18	.216
Stahl, Chick	1901–06	OF	3004	464	871	17	339	280	0	.290
Stahl, Jake	1903, 08–10, 12–13	1B	1648	213	456	21	228	140	1	.277

NAME	YEARS	POSITION	AB	R	H	HR	RBI	BB	SO	BA
Stairs, Matt	1995	OF	88	8	23	1	17	4	14	.261
Standaert, Jerry	1929	1B	18	1	3	0	4	3	2	.167
Stanley, Mike	1996–2000	1B–DH–C	1425	224	391	73	254	234	293	.274
Stansbury, Jack	1918	3B	47	3	6	0	2	6	3	.128
Stapleton, Dave	1980–86	1B–2B	2028	238	550	41	224	114	162	.271
Statz, Jigger	1920	OF	3	0	0	0	0	0	0	.000
Steiner, Ben	1945–46	2B	308	40	79	3	20	31	29	.256
Steiner, Red	1945	C	59	6	12	0	4	14	2	.203
Stenhouse, Mike	1986	OF–1B	21	1	2	0	1	12	5	.095
Stephens, Gene	1952–53, 55–60	OF	1316	193	325	24	149	155	231	.247
Stephens, Vern	1948–52	SS–3B	2545	449	721	122	562	320	236	.283
Stokes, Al	1925–26	C	138	14	25	0	7	12	36	.181
Stone, George	1903	PH	2	0	0	0	0	0	0	.000
Stone, Jeff	1989–90	OF	17	4	4	0	2	1	3	.235
Storie, Howie	1931–32	C	25	2	5	0	0	3	2	.200
Stringer, Lou	1948–50	2B	69	18	17	2	9	5	17	.246
Strunk, Amos	1918–19	OF	597	77	156	0	52	49	26	.261
Stuart, Dick	1963–64	1B	1215	154	328	75	232	81	274	.270
Stumpf, George	1931–33	OF	238	28	55	1	27	23	25	.231
Stynes, Chris	2001	3B–2B	361	52	101	8	33	20	56	.280
Sullivan, Denny	1907–08	OF	906	106	220	1	51	58	0	.243
Sullivan, Haywood	1955, 57, 59–60	C	133	10	20	3	10	17	26	.150
Sullivan, Marc	1982, 84–87	C	360	37	67	5	28	18	92	.186
Sumner, Carl	1928	OF	29	6	8	0	3	5	6	.276
Swanson, Bill	1914	2B	20	0	4	0	0	3	4	.200
Sweeney, Bill	1930–31	1B	741	80	222	5	88	29	45	.300
Tabor, Jim	1938–44	3B	3074	393	838	90	517	230	305	.273
Taitt, Doug	1928–29	OF	547	57	162	3	67	44	37	.296
Tarbert, Arlie	1927–28	OF	86	6	16	0	7	4	13	.186
Tartabull, Jose	1966–68	OF	581	88	148	0	27	35	42	.255
Tarver, LaSchelle	1986	OF	25	3	3	0	1	1	4	.120
Tasby, Willie	1960	OF	385	68	108	7	37	51	54	.281
Tate, Bennie	1932	C	273	21	67	2	26	20	6	.245
Tatum, Jim	1996	3B	8	1	1	0	0	0	2	.125
Tavarez, Jesus	1997	OF	69	12	12	0	9	4	9	.174
Tebbetts, Birdie	1947–50	C	1408	151	404	19	189	174	110	.287
Thomas, Fred	1918	3B	144	19	37	1	11	15	20	.257
Thomas, George	1966–71	OF	435	60	115	9	49	42	86	.264
Thomas, Lee	1964–65	1B–OF	922	118	244	35	117	106	71	.265
Thomas, Pinch	1912–17	C	872	81	210	2	91	95	70	.241
Thomson, Bobby	1960	OF	114	12	30	5	20	11	15	.263
Thoney, Jack	1908–09, 11	OF	476	64	116	2	35	15	0	.244

NAME	YEARS	POSITION	AB	R	H	HR	RBI	BB	SO	BA
Throneberry, Faye	1952, 55–57	OF	505	64	128	12	53	50	115	.253
Tillman, Bob	1962–67	C	1617	131	382	49	194	167	325	.236
Tinsley, Lee	1994–96	OF	677	116	176	12	69	71	166	.260
Tobin, Jack	1926–27	OF	583	78	173	3	54	52	12	.297
Tobin, Jack	1945	3B	278	25	70	0	21	26	24	.252
Todt, Phil	1924–30	1B	3218	349	832	52	409	199	207	.259
Tomberlin, Andy	1994	OF	36	1	7	1	1	6	12	.194
Tonneman, Tony	1911	C	5	0	1	0	3	1	0	.200
Truesdale, Frank	1918	2B	36	6	10	0	2	4	5	.278
Umphlett, Tommy	1953	OF	495	53	140	3	59	34	30	.283
Unglaub, Bob	1904–05, 07–08	1B	944	91	237	2	100	37	0	.251
Vache, Tex	1925	OF	252	41	79	3	48	21	33	.313
Valdez, Julio	1980–83	SS–3B	87	11	18	1	8	1	18	.207
Valentin, John	1992–2001	SS–3B	3709	596	1043	121	528	441	487	.281
Valle, Dave	1994	C	76	6	12	1	5	9	18	.158
Van Camp, Al	1931–32	OF–1B	427	44	112	0	39	24	41	.262
Varitek, Jason	1997–2004	C	2708	963	733	97	418	298	576	.271
Vaughn, Mo	1991–98	1B	3828	628	1165	230	752	519	954	.304
Veach, Bobby	1924–25	OF	524	77	154	5	101	48	19	.294
Veras, Wilton	1999–2000	3B	282	35	74	2	27	12	34	.262
Vernon, Mickey	1956–57	1B	673	103	190	22	122	98	75	.282
Vick, Sammy	1921	OF	77	5	20	0	9	1	10	.260
Vitt, Ossie	1919–21	3B	997	143	223	1	81	132	34	.224
Vollmer, Clyde	1950–53	OF	805	136	211	40	172	116	148	.262
Vosmik, Joe	1938–39	OF	1175	210	354	16	170	125	59	.301
Wagner, Hal	1944, 46–47	C	658	65	174	7	96	107	51	.264
Wagner, Heinie	1906–13, 15–16, 18	SS–2B	3277	398	822	10	341	310	63	.251
Walker, Chico	1980–81, 83–84	2B	81	8	20	1	9	7	13	.247
Walker, Todd	2003	2B	587	92	166	13	85	48	54	.283
Walker, Tilly	1916–17	OF	804	109	207	5	83	48	83	.257
Walsh, Jimmy	1916–17	OF	202	30	52	0	14	29	16	.257
Walters, Bucky	1933–34	3B	283	37	69	8	46	22	36	.244
Walters, Fred	1945	C	93	2	16	0	5	10	9	.172
Walters, Roxy	1919–23	C	764	62	156	0	62	55	61	.204
Wambsganss, Bill	1924–25	2B	992	143	257	1	90	106	54	.259
Wanninger, Pee-Wee	1927	SS	60	4	12	0	1	6	2	.200
Warner, John	1902	C	222	19	52	0	12	13	0	.234
Warstler, Rabbit	1930–33	SS	1053	106	226	2	74	99	127	.215
Watson, Bob	1979	1B	312	48	105	13	53	29	33	.337
Watwood, Johnny	1932–33	OF	296	28	70	0	32	23	14	.236
Webb, Earl	1930–32	OF	1230	180	395	35	196	139	122	.321

Name	Years	Pos								
Webster, Lenny	1999	C	14	0	0	0	1	2	2	.000
Webster, Ray	1960	2B	3	1	0	0	1	1	0	.000
Wedge, Eric	1991–92, 94	DH	75	11	18	5	11	14	21	.240
Welch, Frank	1927	OF	28	2	5	0	4	5	1	.179
Welch, Herb	1925	SS	38	2	11	0	2	0	6	.289
Werber, Billy	1933–36	3B	2045	366	575	38	234	268	154	.281
Wertz, Vic	1959–61	1B	1007	116	276	37	212	97	129	.274
White, Sammy	1951–59	C	3342	316	881	63	404	214	356	.264
Whiteman, George	1907, 18	OF	226	24	59	1	29	20	9	.261
Whiten, Mark	1995	OF	108	13	20	1	10	8	23	.185
Whitt, Ernie	1976	C	18	4	4	1	3	2	2	.222
Wilber, Del	1952–54	C	308	25	71	11	59	17	47	.231
Wilhoit, Joe	1919	OF	18	7	6	0	2	5	2	.333
Williams, Dana	1989	DH–OF	5	1	1	0	0	0	1	.200
Williams, Denny	1924–25, 28	OF	321	46	85	0	18	28	17	.265
Williams, Dib	1935	3B–2B	251	26	63	3	25	24	23	.251
Williams, Dick	1963–64	1B–3B	205	25	46	7	23	22	35	.224
Williams, Ken	1928–29	OF	601	80	188	11	88	52	22	.313
Williams, Rip	1911	1B–C	284	36	68	0	31	24	0	.239
Williams, Ted	1939–42, 46–60	OF	7706	1798	2654	521	1839	2019	709	.344
Wilson, Archie	1952	OF	38	1	10	0	2	2	3	.263
Wilson, Earl	1959–60, 62–66	P	356	55	72	17	51	39	107	.202
Wilson, Gary	1902	2B	8	0	1	0	1	0	0	.125
Wilson, Les	1911	OF	7	0	0	0	0	2	0	.000
Wilson, Squanto	1914	1B	0	0	0	0	0	0	0	—
Winningham, Herm	1992	OF	234	27	55	1	14	10	53	.235
Winsett, Tom	1930–31, 33	OF	89	7	16	1	7	5	28	.180
Wolfe, Larry	1979–80	2B–3B	101	15	22	4	19	17	26	.218
Wolter, Harry	1909	1B–P–OF	121	14	29	2	10	9	0	.240
Wood, Smokey Joe	1908–15	P	496	63	121	5	50	40	31	.244
Wood, Ken	1952	OF	20	0	2	0	0	3	4	.100
Wright, Tom	1948–51	OF	176	27	50	1	30	18	27	.284
Yastrzemski, Carl	1961–83	OF–1B–DH	11988	1816	3419	452	1844	1845	1393	.285
Yerkes, Steve	1909, 11–14	2B–SS	1808	233	467	3	170	157	55	.258
York, Rudy	1946–47	1B	763	94	199	23	146	108	125	.261
Youkilis, Kevin	2004	3B	208	38	54	7	35	33	45	.260
Young, Cy	1901–08	P	1050	108	230	6	81	23	0	.219
Zarilla, Al	1949–50, 52–53	OF	1072	180	310	20	157	145	119	.289
Zauchin, Norm	1951, 55–57	1B	664	88	158	32	118	92	144	.238
Zupcic, Bob	1991–94	OF	707	89	181	6	72	53	121	.256

ALL-TIME RED SOX ROSTER—PITCHERS

NAME	YEARS	W	L	SV	ERA	IP	H	BB	SO
Aase, Don	1977	6	2	0	3.12	92	85	19	49
Adams, Bob	1925	0	0	0	7.89	6	10	3	1
Adams, Terry	2004	2	0	0	6.00	27	35	6	21
Adkins, Doc	1902	1	1	0	4.05	20	30	7	3
Aguilera, Rick	1995	2	2	20	2.67	30	26	7	23
Almonte, Hector	2003	0	1	0	8.22	8	9	7	6
Altrock, Nick	1902–03	0	3	1	4.15	26	32	11	8
Alvarez, Abe	2004	0	1	0	9.00	5	8	5	2
Andersen, Larry	1990	0	0	1	1.23	22	18	3	25
Anderson, Fred	1909, 13	0	6	0	5.38	65	87	22	37
Anderson, Jimmy	2004	0	0	0	6.00	6	10	3	3
Andrews, Ivy	1932–33	15	19	1	4.38	282	301	114	67
Aponte, Luis	1980–83	8	6	7	3.02	170	169	53	88
Appleton, Pete	1932	0	3	0	4.11	46	49	26	15
Arellanes, Frank	1908–10	24	22	8	2.28	410	358	85	148
Arrojo, Rolando	2000–02	14	9	6	4.39	256	238	84	173
Arroyo, Bronson	2003–04	10	9	1	3.86	196	181	51	156
Astacio, Pedro	2004	0	0	0	10.38	9	13	5	6
Atkins, Jim	1950, 52	0	1	0	3.60	15	15	11	2
Auker, Elden	1939	9	10	0	5.36	151	183	61	43
Avery, Steve	1997–98	16	14	0	5.64	220	255	113	108
Bader, Lore	1917–18	3	3	1	2.76	65	74	30	24
Bagby, Jim	1938–40, 46	37	38	4	4.69	568	671	258	181
Bailey, Cory	1993–94	0	2	0	5.40	20	22	15	15
Baker, Al	1938	0	0	0	9.35	8	13	2	2
Bankhead, Scott	1993–94	5	3	0	3.88	102	93	41	72
Banks, Willie	2001–02	2	1	1	2.68	50	37	18	36
Barberich, Frank	1910	0	0	0	7.20	5	7	2	0
Bark, Brian	1995	0	0	0	0.00	2	2	1	0
Barkley, Brian	1998	0	0	0	9.82	11	16	9	2
Barr, Steve	1974–75	1	1	0	3.38	16	18	13	5
Barrett, Frank	1944–45	12	10	11	3.17	176	170	71	75
Barry, Ed	1905–07	1	6	0	3.53	79	74	25	34
Baumann, Frank	1955–59	13	8	1	4.32	219	225	116	131
Bayne, Bill	1929–30	5	5	0	6.63	88	116	30	27
Beck, Rod	1999–2001	9	5	9	3.46	135	120	45	110
Bedient, Hugh	1912–14	43	35	9	3.05	667	648	167	314
Belinda, Stan	1995–96	10	2	12	4.12	98	82	48	75
Bell, Gary	1967–68	23	19	4	3.13	365	320	115	218
Benjamin, Mike	1997	0	0	0	0.00	1	0	0	0

NAME	YEARS	W	L	SV	ERA	IP	H	BB	SO
Bennett, Dennis	1965–67	12	13	0	3.96	286	299	98	166
Bennett, Frank	1927–28	0	1	0	2.71	13	16	6	1
Benton, Al	1952	4	3	6	2.39	38	37	17	20
Beville, Ben	1901	0	2	0	4.00	9	8	9	1
Billingham, Jack	1980	1	3	0	11.11	24	45	12	4
Bird, Doug	1983	1	4	1	6.65	68	91	16	33
Black, Dave	1923	0	0	0	0.00	1	2	0	0
Blethen, Clarence	1923	0	0	0	7.12	18	29	7	2
Boddicker, Mike	1988–90	39	22	0	3.49	529	527	166	344
Boerner, Larry	1932	0	4	0	5.02	61	71	37	19
Bolin, Bobby	1970–73	10	8	28	3.28	162	145	53	117
Bolton, Tom	1987–92	21	23	1	4.45	368	420	163	231
Borland, Toby	1997	0	0	0	13.64	3	6	7	1
Borland, Tom	1960–61	0	4	3	6.75	52	70	23	32
Bowers, Stew	1935–36	2	1	0	4.59	29	36	19	5
Bowman, Joe	1944–45	12	10	0	5.10	180	193	73	53
Bowsfield, Ted	1958–60	5	5	2	5.17	96	94	58	60
Boyd, Oil Can	1982–89	60	56	0	4.15	1017	1067	259	571
Bradley, Herb	1927–29	1	4	0	5.94	74	87	25	20
Brady, King	1908	1	0	0	0.00	9	8	0	3
Brandenburg, Mark	1996–97	4	4	0	4.81	69	77	24	63
Brandon, Bucky	1966–68	13	19	5	3.84	328	295	138	207
Brett, Ken	1967, 69–71	10	15	3	4.58	240	219	136	237
Brewer, Tom	1954–61	91	82	3	4.00	1509	1478	669	733
Brickner, Ralph	1952	3	1	1	2.18	33	32	11	9
Brillheart, Jim	1931	0	0	0	5.48	20	27	15	7
Brodowski, Dick	1952, 55	6	5	0	4.66	147	147	75	52
Brown, Hal	1953–55	13	14	0	4.40	288	305	100	130
Brown, Jamie	2004	0	0	0	5.87	8	15	4	6
Brown, Lloyd	1933	8	11	1	4.02	163	180	64	37
Brown, Mace	1942–43, 46	18	10	16	2.55	180	153	95	70
Brown, Mike	1982–86	12	18	0	5.57	238	302	91	106
Bullinger, Kirk	1999	0	0	0	4.50	2	2	2	0
Burchell, Fred	1907–09	13	12	0	2.94	242	220	78	112
Burgmeier, Tom	1978–82	21	12	40	2.72	411	409	98	217
Burkett, John	2002–03	25	17	0	4.85	355	401	97	231
Burton, Jim	1975, 77	1	2	1	2.75	56	60	20	42
Bush, Joe	1918–21	46	39	4	3.27	780	783	282	312
Bushelman, Jack	1911–12	1	1	0	3.65	20	17	15	10
Bushey, Frank	1927, 30	0	1	0	6.33	31	36	17	4
Butland, Bill	1940, 42, 46–47	9	3	1	3.88	151	138	56	62
Byerly, Bud	1958	1	2	0	1.78	30	31	7	16

NAME	YEARS	W	L	SV	ERA	IP	H	BB	SO
Caldwell, Earl	1948	1	1	0	13.00	9	11	11	5
Caldwell, Ray	1919	7	4	0	3.96	86	92	31	23
Campbell, Bill	1977–81	28	19	51	3.57	335	318	142	240
Carrasco, Hector	2000	1	1	0	9.40	7	15	5	7
Carroll, Ed	1929	1	0	0	5.62	67	77	20	13
Casale, Jerry	1958–60	15	17	0	4.90	279	276	158	150
Cascarella, Joe	1935–36	0	5	0	6.92	38	52	20	16
Castillo, Carlos	2001	0	0	0	6.00	3	3	0	0
Castillo, Frank	2001–02, 04	16	24	1	4.66	301	313	94	201
Cecil, Rex	1944–45	6	10	0	5.18	106	118	60	63
Chakales, Bob	1957	0	2	3	8.16	32	53	11	16
Chaney, Esty	1913	0	0	0	9.00	1	1	2	0
Charton, Pete	1964	0	2	0	5.26	65	67	24	37
Chase, Ken	1942–43	5	5	0	4.60	108	118	71	43
Chech, Charlie	1909	7	5	0	2.95	107	107	27	40
Checo, Robinson	1997–98	1	3	0	5.57	21	23	8	19
Chen, Bruce	2003	0	1	0	5.11	12	12	2	12
Chesbro, Jack	1909	0	1	0	4.50	6	7	4	3
Chittum, Nelson	1959–60	3	0	0	1.87	39	37	17	17
Cho, Jin Ho	1998–99	2	6	0	6.52	58	73	11	31
Cicotte, Eddie	1908–12	52	46	3	2.70	886	822	289	407
Cisco, Galen	1961–62, 67	6	12	1	6.28	158	183	86	77
Clark, Otie	1945	4	4	0	3.07	82	86	19	20
Clear, Mark	1981–85	35	23	38	4.27	400	354	300	403
Clemens, Roger	1984–96	192	111	0	3.06	2776	2359	856	2590
Clemons, Lance	1974	1	0	0	10.00	6	8	4	1
Cleveland, Reggie	1974–78	46	41	4	4.04	753	778	225	342
Clevenger, Tex	1954	2	4	0	4.79	68	67	29	43
Clowers, Bill	1926	0	0	0	0.00	2	2	0	0
Collins, Ray	1909–15	84	62	4	2.51	1336	1246	269	511
Collins, Rip	1922	14	11	0	3.76	211	219	103	69
Comstock, Ralph	1915	1	0	0	2.00	9	10	2	1
Cone, David	2001	9	7	0	4.31	136	148	57	115
Conley, Gene	1961–63	29	32	2	4.57	482	518	154	261
Connolly, Ed	1964	4	11	0	4.91	81	80	64	73
Cooper, Guy	1914–15	1	1	0	4.88	24	23	11	5
Cormier, Rheal	1995, 99–2000	12	8	0	4.12	247	266	66	151
Corsi, Jim	1997–99	9	7	2	3.35	148	139	63	103
Coumbe, Fritz	1914	1	2	1	1.44	62	49	16	17
Cramer, Doc	1938	0	0	0	4.50	4	3	3	1
Crawford, Paxton	2000–01	5	1	0	4.15	65	65	26	42
Crawford, Steve	1980–82, 84–87	19	16	17	4.15	382	456	126	195

NAME	YEARS	W	L	SV	ERA	IP	H	BB	SO
Cremins, Bob	1927	0	0	0	5.09	5	5	3	0
Crouch, Zach	1988	0	0	0	6.92	1	4	2	0
Croushore, Rich	2000	0	1	0	5.74	5	4	5	3
Culp, Ray	1968–73	71	58	0	3.50	1092	958	404	794
Cuppy, Nig	1901	4	6	0	4.15	93	111	14	22
Curry, Steve	1988	0	1	0	8.18	11	15	14	4
Curtis, John	1970–73	26	23	0	3.65	404	420	140	227
Darwin, Danny	1991–94	34	31	3	4.14	534	527	141	350
Deal, Cot	1947–48	1	1	0	7.01	17	23	10	8
Deininger, Pep	1902	0	0	0	9.75	12	19	9	2
Delock, Ike	1952–53, 55–63	83	72	31	4.01	1208	1211	514	661
Denman, Brian	1982	3	4	0	4.78	49	55	9	9
Deutsch, Mel	1946	0	0	0	5.71	6	7	3	2
Deviney, Hal	1920	0	0	0	15.00	3	7	2	0
Dickman, Emerson	1936, 38–41	22	15	8	5.33	350	403	153	126
DiNardo, Lenny	2004	0	0	0	4.23	28	34	12	21
Dinneen, Bill	1902–07	85	85	3	2.81	1501	1372	338	602
Dobens, Ray	1929	0	0	0	3.82	28	32	9	4
Dobson, Joe	1941–43, 46–50, 54	106	72	9	3.57	1544	1464	604	690
Dodge, Sam	1921–22	0	0	0	5.14	7	12	4	3
Doherty, John	1996	0	0	0	5.71	6	8	4	3
Donohue, Pete	1932	0	1	0	7.80	13	18	6	1
Dopson, John	1989–93	26	30	0	4.29	485	510	176	248
Dorish, Harry	1947–49, 56	7	11	2	4.53	181	197	71	71
Dorsey, Jim	1984–85	0	1	0	16.88	8	18	12	6
Drago, Dick	1974–75, 78–80	30	29	41	3.55	547	517	184	305
Dreisewerd, Clem	1944–46	6	6	0	4.17	106	115	26	31
Dubuc, Jean	1918	0	1	0	4.21	11	11	5	1
Duliba, Bob	1965	4	2	1	3.78	64	60	22	27
Dumont, George	1919	0	4	0	4.33	35	45	19	12
Durham, Ed	1929–32	19	38	1	4.44	503	540	156	139
Earley, Arnold	1960–65	10	19	14	4.45	362	381	174	297
Eckersley, Dennis	1978–84, 98	88	71	1	3.92	1372	1408	312	771
Ehmke, Howard	1923–26	51	64	8	3.83	990	1042	330	373
Eibel, Hack	1920	0	0	0	3.50	10	10	3	5
Ellsworth, Dick	1968–69	16	7	0	3.07	208	212	41	110
Ellsworth, Steve	1988	1	6	0	6.75	36	47	16	16
Embree, Alan	2002–04	7	5	3	3.90	141	122	38	125
Erdos, Todd	2001	0	0	0	4.96	16	15	8	7
Eshelman, Vaughn	1995–97	15	9	0	6.07	212	256	111	118

NAME	YEARS	W	L	SV	ERA	IP	H	BB	SO
Evans, Bill	1951	0	0	0	4.12	15	15	8	3
Farr, Steve	1994	1	0	0	6.23	13	24	3	8
Fassero, Jeff	2000	8	8	0	4.78	130	153	50	97
Ferguson, Alex	1922–25	32	48	5	4.20	650	711	242	199
Ferrell, Wes	1934–37	62	40	1	4.11	878	982	310	314
Ferriss, Boo	1945–50	65	30	8	3.64	880	914	314	296
Finch, Joel	1979	0	3	0	4.87	57	65	25	25
Fine, Tommy	1947	1	2	0	5.50	36	41	19	10
Finnvold, Gar	1994	0	4	0	5.95	36	45	15	17
Fischer, Hank	1966–67	3	5	1	2.65	58	59	19	44
Fleming, Bill	1940–41	2	3	1	4.42	88	85	44	44
Florie, Bryce	1999–2001	2	5	1	5.32	88	102	41	66
Flowers, Ben	1951, 53	1	4	3	3.72	82	89	25	38
Foreman, Frank	1901	0	1	0	9.00	8	8	2	1
Foreman, Happy	1926	0	0	0	3.70	7	3	5	3
Fornieles, Mike	1957–63	39	35	48	4.08	643	655	245	342
Fortune, Gary	1920	0	2	0	5.83	42	46	23	10
Fossas, Tony	1991–94	7	5	4	3.98	161	153	72	118
Fossum, Casey	2001–03	14	11	2	4.42	230	239	84	190
Foster, Rube	1913–17	58	34	3	2.36	842	726	305	294
Foulke, Keith	2004	5	3	32	2.17	83	63	15	79
Fox, Chad	2003	1	2	3	4.50	18	19	17	19
Foxx, Jimmie	1939	0	0	0	0.00	1	0	0	1
Francis, Ray	1925	0	2	0	7.71	28	44	13	4
Freeman, Hersh	1952–53, 55	2	4	0	4.80	54	64	23	21
Frohwirth, Todd	1994	0	3	1	10.79	27	40	17	13
Fuhr, Oscar	1924–25	3	12	0	6.29	172	238	69	57
Fullerton, Curt	1921–25, 33	10	37	3	5.11	423	483	211	104
Gale, Rich	1984	2	3	0	5.56	44	57	18	28
Galehouse, Denny	1939–40, 47–49	34	31	3	4.25	555	621	176	197
Gallagher, Ed	1932	0	3	0	12.53	24	30	28	6
Garces, Rich	1996–2002	23	8	5	3.78	307	257	147	270
Gardiner, Mike	1991–92	13	20	0	4.80	261	266	105	170
Gardner, Wes	1986–90	17	26	12	4.73	403	392	188	316
Garman, Mike	1969, 71–73	2	2	0	4.96	56	64	36	26
Garrison, Cliff	1928	0	0	0	7.88	16	22	6	0
Gaston, Milt	1929–31	27	52	4	3.95	636	674	220	215
Gibson, Norwood	1903–06	34	32	0	2.93	609	525	208	258
Gillespie, Bob	1950	0	0	0	20.77	1	2	4	0
Glaze, Ralph	1906–08	15	21	0	2.89	340	303	85	137
Gomes, Wayne	2002	1	2	1	4.64	21	20	12	15

NAME	YEARS	W	L	SV	ERA	IP	H	BB	SO
Gonzales, Joe	1937	1	2	0	4.35	31	37	11	11
Gordon, Tom	1996–99	25	25	68	4.45	495	476	220	432
Gray, Dave	1964	0	0	0	9.00	13	18	20	17
Gray, Jeff	1990–91	4	7	10	3.28	112	92	25	91
Gregg, Vean	1914–16	9	11	3	3.42	221	213	99	108
Griffin, Marty	1928	0	3	0	5.01	38	42	17	9
Grilli, Guido	1966	0	1	0	7.66	5	5	9	4
Grissom, Marv	1953	2	6	0	4.70	59	61	30	31
Gross, Kip	1999	0	2	0	7.80	13	15	8	9
Grove, Lefty	1934–41	105	62	4	3.34	1540	1587	447	743
Grundt, Ken	1996–97	0	0	0	10.91	3	6	0	0
Gumpert, Randy	1952	1	0	1	4.11	20	15	5	6
Gunderson, Eric	1995–96	2	2	0	6.99	30	34	17	16
Guthrie, Mark	1999	1	1	2	5.83	46	50	20	36
Hageman, Casey	1911–12	0	2	0	3.93	18	21	8	9
Hall, Charley	1909–13	46	32	10	2.89	691	625	278	336
Hammond, Chris	1997	3	4	1	5.93	65	81	27	48
Hancock, Josh	2002	0	1	0	3.68	7	5	2	6
Haney, Chris	2002	0	0	1	4.20	30	32	10	15
Hanson, Erik	1995	15	5	0	4.24	187	187	59	139
Harikkala, Tim	1999	1	1	0	6.23	13	15	6	7
Harper, Harry	1920	5	14	0	3.04	163	163	66	71
Harris, Bill	1938	5	5	1	4.03	80	83	21	26
Harris, Greg	1989–94	39	43	16	3.91	651	601	304	489
Harris, Joe	1905–07	3	30	2	3.35	317	284	88	137
Harris, Mickey	1940–41, 46–49	43	42	1	3.92	688	723	290	369
Harris, Reggie	1996	0	0	0	12.56	4	7	5	4
Harriss, Slim	1926–28	28	42	2	4.37	459	529	132	148
Harshman, Jack	1959	2	3	0	6.56	25	29	10	14
Hartenstein, Chuck	1970	0	3	1	8.05	19	21	12	12
Hartley, Mike	1995	0	0	0	9.00	7	8	2	2
Hartman, Charlie	1908	0	0	0	4.50	2	1	2	1
Hash, Herb	1940–41	8	7	4	4.98	128	130	91	39
Hassler, Andy	1978–79	3	3	1	4.97	45	61	20	30
Hausmann, Clem	1944–45	9	14	4	4.19	262	270	129	73
Heep, Danny	1990	0	0	0	9.00	1	4	0	0
Heffner, Bob	1963–65	11	20	6	4.60	332	342	98	231
Heflin, Randy	1945–46	4	11	0	3.86	117	118	73	45
Heimach, Fred	1926	2	9	0	5.65	102	119	42	17
Henry, Bill	1952–55	15	20	1	3.79	318	321	139	140
Henry, Butch	1997–98	7	3	6	3.57	93	97	22	57

NAME	YEARS	W	L	SV	ERA	IP	H	BB	SO
Henry, Jim	1936–37	6	1	0	4.72	92	90	51	44
Hermanson, Dustin	2002	1	1	0	7.77	22	35	7	13
Hernandez, Ramon	1977	0	1	1	5.67	13	14	7	8
Herrin, Tom	1954	1	2	0	7.31	28	34	22	8
Hesketh, Joe	1990–94	31	26	2	4.04	495	520	197	351
Hetzel, Eric	1989–90	3	7	0	6.12	85	100	49	53
Heving, Joe	1938–40	31	11	12	3.83	308	347	98	132
Hillman, Dave	1960–61	3	5	0	3.69	115	111	35	53
Hinrichs, Paul	1951	0	0	0	21.82	3	7	4	1
Hisner, Harley	1951	0	1	0	4.50	6	7	4	3
Hockette, George	1934–35	4	4	0	4.08	88	105	18	25
Hoeft, Billy	1959	0	3	0	5.59	18	22	8	8
Holcombe, Ken	1953	1	0	1	6.00	6	9	3	1
Hooper, Harry	1913	0	0	0	0.00	2	2	1	0
House, Tom	1976–77	2	3	4	5.60	51	54	25	33
Howard, Chris	1994	1	0	1	3.63	40	35	12	22
Howe, Les	1923–24	2	0	0	3.38	37	34	9	10
Howry, Bob	2002–03	1	3	0	6.45	22	33	7	18
Hoy, Peter	1992	0	0	0	7.30	4	8	2	2
Hoyt, Waite	1919–20	10	12	1	3.85	227	222	69	73
Hudson, Joe	1995–97	6	7	2	4.40	127	149	69	62
Hudson, Sid	1952–54	16	22	7	3.73	362	392	115	137
Hughes, Ed	1905–06	3	2	0	4.78	43	53	12	11
Hughes, Tom	1902–03	23	10	0	2.69	294	283	84	127
Hughson, Tex	1941–44, 46–49	96	54	17	2.94	1376	1270	372	693
Humphrey, Bill	1938	0	0	0	9.00	2	5	1	0
Hunt, Ben	1910	2	3	0	4.05	47	45	20	19
Hurd, Tom	1954–56	13	10	11	3.96	186	177	97	96
Hurst, Bruce	1980–88	88	73	0	4.23	1459	1569	479	1043
Husting, Bert	1902	0	1	0	9.00	8	15	8	4
Irvine, Daryl	1990–92	4	5	0	5.69	63	71	33	27
Jacobson, Beany	1907	0	0	0	9.00	2	2	3	1
Jamerson, Lefty	1924	0	0	0	18.00	1	1	3	0
James, Bill	1919	3	5	0	4.09	73	74	39	12
Jarvis, Ray	1969–70	5	7	1	4.64	116	122	57	44
Jenkins, Ferguson	1976–77	22	21	0	3.47	402	391	79	247
Johnson, Earl	1940–41, 46–50	40	32	16	4.28	541	547	270	248
Johnson, Hank	1933–35	16	15	3	4.72	311	359	141	145
Johnson, John Henry	1983–84	4	4	2	3.62	117	122	47	108

NAME	YEARS	W	L	SV	ERA	IP	H	BB	SO
Johnson, Rankin	1914	4	9	0	3.08	99	92	34	24
Johnson, Vic	1944–45	6	7	2	4.56	113	132	61	28
Johnston, Joel	1995	0	1	0	11.25	4	2	3	4
Jones, Bobby	2004	0	1	0	5.40	3	3	8	3
Jones, Rick	1976	5	3	0	3.37	104	133	26	45
Jones, Sad Sam	1916–21	64	59	4	3.39	1045	1069	338	307
Jones, Todd	2003	2	1	0	5.52	29	32	13	31
Judd, Oscar	1941–45	20	18	3	3.68	354	321	187	142
Kallio, Rudy	1925	1	4	0	7.70	19	28	9	2
Karger, Ed	1909–11	21	17	1	3.25	382	367	117	155
Karl, Andy	1943	1	1	1	3.46	26	31	13	6
Karr, Benn	1920–22	16	27	2	4.31	393	444	107	99
Kellett, Al	1924	0	0	0	0.00	0	0	2	0
Kellum, Win	1901	2	3	0	6.38	48	61	7	8
Kelly, Ed	1914	0	0	0	0.00	2	1	1	4
Kemmerer, Russ	1954–55, 57	6	4	0	4.47	97	94	58	51
Kennedy, Bill	1953	0	0	2	3.70	24	24	17	14
Kiecker, Dana	1990–91	10	12	0	4.68	192	201	77	114
Kiefer, Joe	1925–26	0	4	0	5.20	45	49	25	8
Kiely, Leo	1951, 54–56, 58–59	25	25	28	3.44	502	541	184	206
Killilay, Jack	1911	4	2	0	3.54	61	65	36	28
Kim, Byung-Hyun	2003–04	10	6	16	3.72	97	87	25	75
Kim, Sun-Woo	2001–02	2	2	0	6.50	71	84	28	45
Kinder, Ellis	1948–55	86	52	91	3.28	1142	1086	403	557
Kinney, Walt	1918	0	0	0	1.80	15	5	8	4
Kison, Bruce	1985	5	3	1	4.11	92	98	32	56
Kline, Bob	1930–33	23	26	6	4.82	398	441	178	72
Kline, Ron	1969	0	1	1	4.76	17	24	17	7
Klinger, Bob	1946–47	4	3	14	3.00	99	91	49	28
Knackert, Brent	1996	0	1	0	9.00	10	16	7	5
Kolstad, Hal	1962–63	0	4	2	6.60	72	81	41	42
Koonce, Cal	1970–71	3	5	2	3.98	97	86	40	46
Kramer, Jack	1948–49	24	13	1	4.63	317	359	113	96
Krausse, Lew	1972	1	3	1	6.38	61	74	28	35
Kreuger, Rick	1975–77	2	2	0	4.11	35	36	17	13
Kroh, Rube	1906–07	2	4	0	2.08	43	35	12	13
Lacy, Kerry	1996–97	3	1	3	5.59	56	75	30	27
Lake, Eddie	1944	0	0	0	4.20	19	20	11	7
Lamabe, Jack	1963–65	16	20	7	4.88	354	408	117	219
Lamp, Dennis	1988–91	20	16	2	3.76	393	402	107	216
Landis, Bill	1967–69	9	8	4	4.50	168	154	90	132

NAME	YEARS	W	L	SV	ERA	IP	H	BB	SO
Larose, John	1978	0	0	0	22.50	2	3	3	0
Lee, Bill	1969–78	94	68	13	3.64	1503	1627	448	578
Lee, Sang-Hoon	2000	0	0	0	3.08	12	11	5	6
LeFebvre, Bill	1938–39	1	1	0	6.83	30	43	14	8
Leheny, Regis	1932	0	0	0	16.67	3	5	3	1
Leister, John	1987, 90	0	2	0	8.50	36	56	16	19
Leonard, Dutch	1913–18	90	63	11	2.13	1361	1134	412	771
Leroy, Louis	1910	0	0	0	11.25	4	7	2	3
Leskanic, Curtis	2004	3	2	2	3.58	28	24	16	22
Lewis, Duffy	1913	0	0	0	18.00	1	3	0	1
Lewis, Ted	1901	16	17	1	3.53	316	299	91	103
Lilliquist, Derek	1995	2	1	0	6.26	23	27	9	9
Lisenbee, Hod	1929–32	15	33	0	4.87	484	541	164	104
Littlefield, Dick	1950	2	2	1	9.27	23	27	24	13
Lockwood, Skip	1980	3	1	2	5.32	46	61	17	11
Lollar, Tim	1985–86	7	5	1	5.48	110	108	74	72
Lonborg, Jim	1965–71	68	65	2	3.94	1099	1031	403	784
Looney, Brian	1995	0	1	0	17.23	5	12	4	2
Lowe, Derek	1997–2004	70	55	85	3.72	1037	1024	312	673
Lucey, Joe	1925	0	1	0	9.00	11	18	14	2
Lucier, Lou	1943–44	3	4	0	3.97	79	101	40	25
Lundgren, Del	1926–27	5	14	0	6.51	167	195	115	50
Lyle, Sparky	1967–71	22	17	69	2.85	331	294	133	275
Lyon, Brandon	2003	4	6	9	4.12	59	73	19	50
Lyons, Steve	1991	0	0	0	0.00	1	2	0	1
MacFayden, Danny	1926–32	52	78	4	4.23	1167	1273	430	344
MacLeod, Bill	1962	0	1	0	5.29	2	4	1	2
MacWhorter, Keith	1980	0	3	0	5.53	42	46	18	21
Maddux, Mike	1995–96	7	3	1	3.97	154	162	42	97
Magrini, Pete	1966	0	1	0	9.86	7	8	8	3
Mahay, Ron	1997–98	4	1	1	3.00	51	45	26	36
Mahomes, Pat	1996–97	3	0	2	6.86	22	24	16	11
Mahoney, Chris	1910	0	1	1	3.27	11	16	5	6
Malaska, Mark	2004	1	1	0	4.50	20	21	12	12
Maloy, Paul	1913	0	0	0	9.00	2	2	1	0
Manzanillo, Josias	1991	0	0	0	18.00	1	2	3	1
Marchildon, Phil	1950	0	0	0	6.92	1	1	2	0
Marcum, Johnny	1936–38	26	30	4	4.68	450	537	124	141
Marichal, Juan	1974	5	1	0	4.87	57	61	14	21
Martinez, Anastacio	2004	2	1	0	8.44	11	13	6	5
Martinez, Pedro	1998–2004	117	37	0	2.52	1384	1044	309	1683

NAME	YEARS	W	L	SV	ERA	IP	H	BB	SO
Martinez, Ramon	1999–2000	12	9	0	5.70	148	157	75	104
Masterson, Walt	1949–52	15	11	7	5.02	253	274	160	121
Matthews, William	1909	0	0	0	3.23	17	16	10	6
Mays, Carl	1915–19	72	51	12	2.21	1105	918	290	399
McCabe, Dick	1918	0	1	0	2.78	10	13	2	3
McCall, Windy	1948–49	0	1	0	12.74	11	19	11	8
McCarthy, Tom	1985	0	0	0	10.80	5	7	4	2
McCarty, Dave	2004	0	0	0	2.45	4	2	1	4
McDermott, Mickey	1948–53	48	34	8	3.80	774	647	504	499
McDill, Allen	2001	0	0	0	5.52	15	13	7	16
McDonald, Jim	1950	1	0	0	3.79	19	23	10	5
McGlothen, Lynn	1972–73	9	9	0	4.07	168	174	67	128
McGraw, Bob	1919	0	2	0	6.74	27	33	17	6
McHale, Marty	1910–11, 16	0	3	0	5.90	29	41	13	18
McKain, Archie	1937–38	13	12	8	4.60	237	271	108	93
McLaughlin, Jud	1931–33	0	0	0	10.25	24	42	17	4
McMahon, Doc	1908	1	0	0	3.00	9	14	0	3
McMahon, Don	1966–67	9	9	11	2.82	96	79	51	67
McNaughton, Gordon	1932	0	1	0	6.43	21	21	22	6
Melendez, Jose	1993–94	2	2	0	4.18	32	30	13	23
Mendoza, Ramiro	2003–04	5	6	0	5.73	97	123	27	49
Meola, Mike	1933, 36	0	2	1	7.25	24	34	12	9
Mercker, Kent	1999	2	0	0	3.50	26	23	13	17
Merena, Spike	1934	1	2	0	2.91	25	20	16	7
Meyer, Russ	1957	0	0	0	5.40	5	10	3	1
Michaels, John	1932	1	6	0	5.13	81	101	27	16
Midkiff, Dick	1938	1	1	0	5.10	35	43	21	10
Mills, Dick	1970	0	0	0	2.43	4	6	3	3
Minarcin, Rudy	1956–57	1	0	2	4.14	54	53	38	25
Minchey, Nate	1993–94, 96	3	7	0	6.53	62	95	27	37
Mitchell, Charlie	1984–85	0	0	0	4.00	18	19	6	9
Mitchell, Fred	1901–02	6	7	0	4.07	113	123	56	36
Moford, Herb	1959	0	2	0	11.38	9	10	6	7
Molyneaux, Vince	1918	1	0	0	3.36	11	3	8	1
Monbouquette, Bill	1958–65	96	91	1	3.69	1622	1649	408	969
Moore, Wilcy	1931–32	15	23	14	4.31	270	293	97	65
Morehead, Dave	1963–68	35	56	0	4.17	665	581	373	526
Moret, Roger	1970–75	41	18	6	3.43	559	490	272	334
Morgan, Cy	1907–09	22	25	2	2.30	384	295	155	179
Morris, Ed	1928–31	42	45	6	4.12	662	680	287	251

NAME	YEARS	W	L	SV	ERA	IP	H	BB	SO
Morrissey, Frank	1901	0	0	0	2.09	4	5	2	1
Morton, Kevin	1991	6	5	0	4.59	86	93	40	45
Moseley, Earl	1913	9	5	0	3.13	121	105	49	62
Moser, Walter	1911	0	1	0	4.01	25	37	11	11
Moyer, Jamie	1996	7	1	0	4.50	90	111	27	50
Mueller, Gordie	1950	0	0	0	10.29	7	11	13	1
Muffett, Billy	1960–62	9	15	2	4.47	242	254	74	123
Mulligan, Joe	1934	1	0	0	3.62	45	46	27	13
Mulroney, Frank	1930	0	1	0	3.00	3	3	0	2
Murphy, Johnny	1947	0	0	3	2.80	55	41	28	9
Murphy, Rob	1989–90	5	13	16	4.00	162	182	73	161
Murphy, Tom	1976–77	4	6	8	4.35	112	135	37	45
Murphy, Walter	1931	0	0	0	9.00	2	4	1	0
Murray, George	1923–24	9	20	0	5.48	258	287	119	67
Murray, Matt	1995	0	1	0	19.09	3	11	3	1
Musser, Paul	1919	0	2	0	4.11	20	26	8	14
Mustaikis, Alex	1940	0	1	0	9.00	15	15	15	6
Myers, Elmer	1920–22	17	14	0	4.16	275	317	80	75
Myers, Mike	2004	1	0	0	4.20	15	16	6	9
Nabholz, Chris	1994	3	4	0	6.64	42	44	29	23
Nagle, Judge	1911	1	1	0	3.33	27	27	6	12
Nagy, Mike	1969–72	19	10	0	3.99	365	370	190	151
Neitzke, Ernie	1921	0	0	0	6.16	7	8	4	1
Nelson, Joe	2004	0	0	0	16.87	3	4	3	5
Neubauer, Hal	1925	1	0	0	12.23	10	17	11	4
Newhauser, Don	1972–74	4	3	5	2.39	53	44	42	37
Newsom, Bobo	1937	13	10	0	4.46	208	193	119	127
Newsome, Dick	1941–43	35	33	0	4.50	526	575	214	138
Nichols, Chet	1960–63	5	8	6	3.36	174	174	76	91
Nipper, Al	1983–87	42	43	0	4.62	694	739	250	342
Nippert, Merlin	1962	0	0	0	4.50	6	4	4	3
Nixon, Willard	1950–58	69	72	3	4.39	1234	1277	530	616
Nomo, Hideo	2001	13	10	0	4.50	198	171	96	220
Nourse, Chet	1909	0	0	0	7.20	5	5	5	3
Oberlin, Frank	1906–07	2	8	0	3.82	80	86	37	31
O'Brien, Buck	1911–13	29	23	0	2.57	414	370	146	200
O'Doul, Lefty	1923	1	1	0	5.43	53	69	31	10
Ohka, Tomokazu	1999–2001	6	13	0	4.61	135	160	51	85
Ojeda, Bob	1980–85	44	39	1	4.21	719	734	285	425
Oliver, Darren	2002	4	5	0	4.66	58	70	27	32
Olmsted, Hank	1905	1	2	0	3.24	25	18	12	6
Olson, Ted	1936–38	1	1	0	7.19	58	75	25	18

NAME	YEARS	W	L	SV	ERA	IP	H	BB	SO
O'Neill, Emmett	1943–45	15	26	0	4.82	351	344	252	143
Ontiveros, Steve	2000	1	1	0	10.19	5	9	4	1
Osinski, Dan	1966–67	7	4	4	3.09	131	129	42	82
Ostermueller, Fritz	1934–40	59	65	13	4.38	1083	1184	491	422
Palm, Mike	1948	0	0	0	6.00	3	6	5	1
Papai, Al	1950	4	2	2	6.75	51	61	28	19
Pape, Larry	1909, 11–12	13	9	3	2.80	283	287	91	84
Parnell, Mel	1947–56	123	75	10	3.50	1753	1715	758	732
Partenheimer, Stan	1944	0	0	0	18.00	1	3	2	0
Patten, Case	1908	0	1	0	15.00	3	8	1	0
Pattin, Marty	1972–73	32	28	1	3.73	472	470	134	287
Paxton, Mike	1977	10	5	0	3.83	108	134	25	58
Pena, Alejandro	1995	1	1	0	7.41	24	33	12	25
Pena, Jesus	2000	0	0	0	3.00	3	3	3	1
Pena, Juan	1999	2	0	0	0.69	13	9	3	15
Pennington, Brad	1996	0	2	0	2.77	13	6	15	13
Pennock, Herb	1915–17, 19–22, 34	61	59	6	3.67	1089	1169	299	358
Person, Robert	2003	0	0	1	7.71	12	11	8	10
Pertica, Bill	1918	0	0	0	3.00	3	3	0	1
Peters, Gary	1970–72	33	25	2	4.23	521	553	191	322
Petry, Dan	1991	0	0	1	4.44	22	21	12	12
Phillips, Ed	1970	0	2	0	5.32	24	29	10	23
Pichardo, Hipolito	2000–01	8	4	1	3.97	100	105	36	54
Pierce, Jeff	1995	0	3	0	6.60	15	16	14	12
Piercy, Bill	1922–24	16	33	0	4.48	430	489	201	95
Pipgras, George	1933–35	9	9	1	4.55	137	153	53	58
Pizarro, Juan	1968–69	6	9	4	3.78	117	111	50	88
Plympton, Jeff	1991	0	0	0	0.00	5	5	4	2
Poindexter, Jennings	1936	0	2	0	6.73	11	13	16	2
Pole, Dick	1973–76	14	14	1	4.56	310	358	111	147
Porterfield, Bob	1956–58	7	16	1	4.65	232	237	94	82
Portugal, Mark	1999	7	12	0	5.51	150	179	41	79
Potter, Nels	1941	2	0	0	4.50	20	21	16	6
Prentiss, George	1901–02	3	2	0	4.59	51	62	16	9
Price, Joe	1989	2	5	0	4.35	70	71	30	52
Pruiett, Tex	1907–08	4	18	5	2.83	232	221	80	82
Pulsipher, Bill	2001	0	0	0	5.32	22	25	14	16
Quantrill, Paul	1992–94	9	16	2	3.47	210	231	64	105
Quinn, Frank	1949–50	0	0	0	3.38	24	20	10	4
Quinn, Jack	1922–25	45	54	14	3.65	833	946	190	226

NAME	YEARS	W	L	SV	ERA	IP	H	BB	SO
Radatz, Dick	1962–66	49	34	104	2.65	557	420	213	627
Rainey, Chuck	1979–82	23	14	1	4.38	360	374	158	161
Rapp, Pat	1999	6	7	0	4.12	146	147	69	90
Reardon, Jeff	1990–92	8	9	88	3.41	153	146	42	109
Reed, Jerry	1990	2	1	2	4.80	45	55	16	17
Reeves, Bobby	1931	0	0	0	3.70	7	6	1	0
Remmerswaal, Win	1979–80	3	1	0	5.50	56	65	21	36
Renko, Steve	1979–80	20	18	0	4.15	336	354	109	189
Reyes, Carlos	1998	1	1	0	3.52	38	35	14	23
Rhodes, Gordon	1932–35	27	45	4	4.63	677	763	282	230
Rich, Woody	1939–41	5	3	1	4.87	92	95	38	36
Ripley, Allen	1978–79	5	6	1	5.36	138	169	47	60
Ripley, Walt	1935	0	0	0	9.00	4	7	3	0
Ritchie, Jay	1964–65	2	3	2	3.00	117	126	40	90
Robinson, Jack	1949	0	0	0	2.25	4	4	1	1
Rochford, Mike	1988–90	0	1	0	9.61	10	18	9	2
Rodriguez, Frank	1995	0	2	0	10.59	15	21	10	14
Rogers, Lee	1938	1	1	0	6.50	28	32	18	7
Roggenburk, Garry	1966, 68–69	0	1	0	5.41	18	23	9	12
Rohr, Billy	1967	2	3	0	5.11	42	43	22	16
Romo, Vicente	1969–70	14	12	17	3.60	235	231	93	160
Rose, Brian	1997–2000	11	15	0	5.73	192	218	66	96
Ross, Buster	1924–26	7	12	1	5.01	190	233	74	31
Rothrock, Jack	1928	0	0	0	0.00	1	0	0	0
Ruffing, Red	1924–30	39	96	8	4.61	1122	1226	459	450
Rupe, Ryan	2003	1	1	0	6.30	10	13	1	7
Russell, Allan	1919–22	28	28	10	3.74	528	561	211	210
Russell, Jack	1926–32, 36	41	94	0	4.58	1215	1480	294	202
Russell, Jeff	1993–94	1	9	45	3.61	75	69	27	63
Ruth, Babe	1914–19	89	46	4	2.19	1190	934	425	483
Ryan, Jack	1909	3	3	0	3.34	59	65	20	24
Ryan, Ken	1992–95	9	9	22	3.66	138	127	75	120
Ryba, Mike	1941–46	36	25	16	3.41	583	587	189	219
Saberhagen, Bret	1997–99, 2001	26	17	0	3.90	335	352	50	205
Sadowski, Bob	1966	1	1	0	5.41	33	41	9	11
Sambito, Joe	1986–87	4	6	12	5.79	82	100	32	65
Sanders, Ken	1966	3	6	2	3.81	47	36	28	33
Santana, Marino	1999	0	0	0	15.75	4	8	3	4
Santiago, Jose	1966–70	33	23	8	3.42	460	418	159	326
Sauerbeck, Scott	2003	0	1	0	6.48	17	17	18	18
Sayles, Bill	1939	0	0	0	7.07	14	14	13	9
Scarborough, Ray	1951–52	13	14	4	5.01	261	280	96	100

NAME	YEARS	W	L	SV	ERA	IP	H	BB	SO
Schanz, Charley	1950	3	2	0	8.33	23	25	24	14
Schilling, Curt	2004	21	6	0	3.26	227	206	35	203
Schiraldi, Calvin	1986–87	12	7	15	3.27	135	111	55	148
Schlitzer, Biff	1909	4	4	1	3.49	70	68	17	23
Schmees, George	1952	0	0	0	3.00	6	9	2	2
Schmitz, Johnny	1956	0	0	0	0.00	4	5	4	0
Schourek, Pete	1998, 2000–01	5	18	0	4.81	182	196	67	119
Schroll, Al	1958–59	1	4	0	4.66	56	53	26	33
Schwall, Don	1961–62	24	22	0	4.09	361	347	231	180
Seanez, Rudy	2003	0	1	0	6.23	9	11	6	9
Seaver, Tom	1986	5	7	0	3.80	104	114	29	72
Segui, Diego	1974–75	8	13	16	4.32	179	177	92	121
Seibel, Phil	2004	0	0	0	0.00	4	0	5	1
Sele, Aaron	1993–97	38	33	0	4.41	622	660	269	478
Sellers, Jeff	1985–88	13	22	0	4.97	330	364	164	226
Settlemire, Merle	1928	0	6	0	5.47	82	116	34	12
Shea, John	1928	0	0	0	18.00	1	1	1	0
Sheldon, Rollie	1966	1	6	0	4.97	80	106	23	38
Shepherd, Keith	1995	0	0	0	36.00	1	4	2	0
Shields, Ben	1930	0	0	0	9.00	10	16	6	1
Shiell, Jason	2003	2	0	1	4.63	23	23	17	23
Shore, Ernie	1914–17	58	32	3	2.12	839	732	204	272
Short, Bill	1966	0	0	0	4.34	8	10	2	2
Shouse, Brian	1998	0	1	0	5.62	8	9	4	5
Siebert, Sonny	1969–73	57	41	5	3.46	820	787	248	528
Simmons, Pat	1928–29	0	2	2	3.67	76	75	41	18
Sisler, Dave	1956–59	24	25	4	4.79	421	421	213	222
Skok, Craig	1973	0	1	1	6.27	29	35	11	22
Slayton, Steve	1928	0	0	0	3.86	7	6	3	2
Slocumb, Heathcliff	1996–97	5	10	48	4.02	130	126	89	124
Smith, Bob	1955	0	0	0	0.00	2	1	1	1
Smith, Charlie	1909–11	14	6	1	2.36	183	166	38	64
Smith, Dan	2000	0	0	0	8.18	3	2	3	1
Smith, Doug	1912	0	0	0	3.00	3	4	0	1
Smith, Eddie	1947	1	3	0	7.41	17	18	18	15
Smith, Frank	1910–11	1	2	0	5.64	30	28	14	9
Smith, George	1930	1	2	0	6.59	74	92	49	21
Smith, Lee	1988–90	12	7	58	3.04	169	138	79	209
Smith, Pete	1962–63	0	1	0	6.74	19	18	8	7
Smith, Riverboat	1958	4	3	0	3.78	67	61	45	43
Smith, Zane	1995	8	8	0	5.61	111	144	23	47
Smithson, Mike	1988–89	16	20	2	5.43	270	319	72	134

NAME	YEARS	W	L	SV	ERA	IP	H	BB	SO
Sommers, Rudy	1926–27	0	0	0	9.00	16	21	17	2
Sothoron, Allen	1921	0	2	0	13.50	6	15	5	2
Spanswick, Bill	1964	2	3	0	6.89	65	75	44	55
Sparks, Tully	1902	7	9	0	3.47	143	151	40	37
Speaker, Tris	1914	0	0	0	9.00	1	2	0	0
Spring, Jack	1957	0	0	0	0.00	1	0	0	2
Sprowl, Bobby	1978	0	2	0	6.38	13	12	10	10
Stallard, Tracy	1960–62	2	7	2	4.71	138	110	98	115
Stange, Lee	1966–70	28	35	18	3.45	602	571	168	304
Stanifer, Rob	2000	0	0	0	7.62	13	22	4	3
Stanley, Bob	1977–89	115	97	132	3.64	1707	1858	471	693
Stanton, Mike	1995–96	5	3	1	3.61	77	75	31	56
Steele, Elmer	1907–09	9	12	1	2.20	205	171	29	79
Stephenson, Jerry	1963, 65–68	8	19	1	5.54	229	248	137	177
Stewart, Sammy	1986	4	1	0	4.38	64	64	48	47
Stigman, Dick	1966	2	1	0	5.44	81	85	46	65
Stimson, Carl	1923	0	0	0	22.50	4	12	5	1
Stobbs, Chuck	1947–51	33	23	1	4.70	507	502	254	232
Stone, Dean	1957	1	3	1	5.09	51	56	35	32
Sturdivant, Tom	1960	3	3	1	4.98	101	106	45	67
Suchecki, Jim	1950	0	0	0	4.50	4	3	4	3
Sullivan, Frank	1953–60	90	80	6	3.47	1505	1455	475	821
Suppan, Jeff	1995–97, 2003	12	10	0	5.88	220	268	74	131
Susce, George	1955–58	18	14	2	4.23	304	293	135	126
Swindell, Greg	1998	2	3	0	3.38	24	25	13	18
Swormstedt, Len	1906	1	1	0	1.29	21	17	0	6
Taitt, Doug	1928	0	0	0	27.00	1	2	2	1
Tanana, Frank	1981	4	10	0	4.01	141	142	43	78
Tannehill, Jesse	1904–08	62	38	1	2.50	886	836	154	342
Tatum, Ken	1971–73	2	6	13	4.03	87	88	43	36
Taylor, Harry	1950–52	7	9	2	4.65	110	119	56	31
Taylor, Scott	1992–93	1	2	0	6.30	26	27	16	15
Terry, Yank	1940, 42–45	20	28	2	4.09	457	463	196	167
Thielman, Jake	1908	0	0	0	38.57	1	3	0	0
Thomas, Blaine	1911	0	0	0	0.00	5	3	7	0
Thomas, Tommy	1937	0	2	0	4.09	11	16	4	4
Thormahlen, Hank	1921	1	7	0	4.49	96	101	34	17
Tiant, Luis	1971–78	122	81	3	3.36	1775	1630	501	1075
Timlin, Mike	2003–04	11	8	3	3.83	160	152	28	121
Tolar, Kevin	2003	0	0	0	9.00	4	5	2	3
Tomberlin, Andy	1994	0	0	0	0.00	2	1	1	1
Torrez, Mike	1978–82	60	54	0	4.51	1013	1108	420	480

NAME	YEARS	W	L	SV	ERA	IP	H	BB	SO
Trautwein, John	1988	0	1	0	9.00	16	26	9	8
Trimble, Joe	1955	0	0	0	0.00	2	0	3	1
Trlicek, Ricky	1994, 97	4	5	0	6.32	46	58	34	17
Trout, Dizzy	1952	9	8	1	3.64	134	133	68	57
Trujillo, Mike	1985–86	4	4	1	5.12	90	119	29	23
Tudor, John	1979–83	39	32	1	3.96	637	645	208	382
Turley, Bob	1963	1	4	0	6.10	41	42	28	35
Urbina, Ugueth	2001–02	1	7	49	2.81	80	60	23	103
Valdez, Carlos	1998	1	0	0	0.00	3	1	5	4
Valdez, Sergio	1994	0	1	0	8.18	14	25	8	4
Vandenberg, Hy	1935	0	0	0	20.38	5	15	4	2
Van Dyke, Ben	1912	0	0	0	3.15	14	13	7	8
VanEgmond, Tim	1994–95	2	4	0	6.80	45	47	27	27
Veale, Bob	1972–74	4	4	15	3.46	57	54	19	51
Veras, Dario	1998	0	1	0	10.12	8	12	7	2
Viola, Frank	1992–94	25	21	0	3.40	453	428	178	221
Volz, Jake	1901	1	0	0	9.00	7	6	9	5
Wade, Jake	1939	1	4	0	6.23	48	68	37	21
Wagner, Charlie	1938–42, 46	32	23	0	3.91	528	532	245	157
Wagner, Gary	1969–70	4	4	7	4.13	57	54	34	29
Wakefield, Tim	1995–2004	114	99	22	4.31	1846	1788	719	1329
Walberg, Rube	1934–37	21	27	5	4.44	452	511	177	177
Wall, Murray	1957–59	13	14	14	4.09	188	187	61	80
Wasdin, John	1997–2000	19	16	3	4.66	340	346	98	236
Waslewski, Gary	1967–68	6	9	2	3.54	147	142	60	79
Weaver, Monte	1939	1	0	1	6.65	20	26	13	6
Weiland, Bob	1932–34	15	35	4	4.33	468	491	224	189
Welch, Johnny	1932–36	33	40	5	4.66	583	656	242	242
Welzer, Tony	1926–27	10	14	1	4.78	311	381	124	85
Wenz, Fred	1968–69	1	0	0	5.25	12	9	12	14
Werle, Bill	1953–54	0	2	0	3.46	36	48	11	18
West, David	1998	0	0	0	27.00	2	7	7	4
White, Matt	2003	0	1	0	27.00	4	10	3	0
Widmar, Al	1947	0	0	0	13.85	1	1	2	1
Wight, Bill	1951–52	9	8	0	4.73	143	142	77	43
Williams, Dave	1902	0	0	0	5.29	19	22	11	7
Williams, Stan	1972	0	0	0	6.28	4	5	1	3
Williams, Ted	1940	0	0	0	4.50	2	3	0	1
Williamson, Scott	2003–04	0	2	1	3.31	49	31	27	49
Willoughby, Jim	1975–77	14	16	20	3.56	202	194	65	99
Wills, Ted	1959–62	6	9	1	6.01	106	132	60	63
Wilson, Duane	1958	0	0	0	5.71	6	10	7	3

NAME	YEARS	W	L	SV	ERA	IP	H	BB	SO
Wilson, Earl	1959–60, 62–66	56	58	0	4.10	1024	951	481	714
Wilson, Jack	1935–41	67	67	20	4.44	1068	1141	564	563
Wilson, Jim	1945–46	6	8	0	3.41	145	123	88	50
Wilson, John	1927–28	0	2	0	4.46	30	37	19	9
Wiltse, Hal	1926–28	18	35	1	4.80	427	493	176	111
Wingfield, Ted	1924–27	24	44	5	4.21	545	615	177	65
Winn, George	1919	0	0	0	7.66	5	6	1	0
Winter, George	1901–08	82	97	3	2.91	1600	1503	370	543
Winters, Clarence	1924	0	1	0	20.57	7	22	4	3
Wise, Rick	1974–77	47	32	0	3.96	657	678	164	344
Wittig, Johnnie	1949	0	0	0	9.00	2	2	2	0
Wolcott, Bob	1999	0	0	0	8.06	7	8	3	2
Wolter, Harry	1909	4	4	0	3.51	59	66	30	21
Wood, Joe	1944	0	1	0	6.49	10	13	3	5
Wood, Smokey Joe	1908–15	117	56	8	1.99	1416	1117	412	986
Wood, Wilbur	1961–64	0	5	0	4.84	91	100	26	43
Woodard, Steve	2003	1	0	0	5.09	18	23	5	12
Woods, John	1924	0	0	0	0.00	1	0	3	0
Woods, Pinky	1943–45	13	21	3	3.97	379	388	206	124
Woodward, Bob	1985–88	4	4	0	5.03	100	118	36	45
Workman, Hoge	1924	0	0	0	8.50	18	25	11	7
Worthington, Al	1960	0	1	0	7.69	12	17	11	7
Wright, Jim	1978–79	9	4	0	3.82	139	141	31	71
Wyatt, John	1966–68	14	13	28	2.92	176	139	72	142
Wyckoff, Weldon	1916–18	0	0	1	3.94	30	27	23	21
Young, Cy	1901–08	192	112	9	2.00	2728	2347	299	1341
Young, Matt	1991–92	3	11	0	4.91	159	161	95	126
Young, Tim	2000	0	0	0	6.43	7	7	2	6
Zahniser, Paul	1925–26	11	30	1	5.06	349	445	158	65
Zeiser, Matt	1914	0	0	0	1.80	10	9	8	0
Zuber, Bill	1946–47	6	1	0	3.85	107	97	70	52